GCSE English
A Complete Course

Susan Davies

with contributions by
Ken Elliott and Roy Hopwood

Heinemann Educational Publishers
Halley Court, Jordan Hill, Oxford OX2 8EJ
A division of Reed Educational and Professional Publishing Ltd

OXFORD   MELBOURNE   AUCKLAND
JOHANNESBURG   BLANTYRE   GABORONE
IBADAN   PORTSMOUTH (NH) USA   CHICAGO

First published 1997

2001 2000
10 9 8 7 6 5

ISBN 0 435 10194 3

Designed and typeset by Moondisks Ltd, Cambridge
Cover design by Aricot Vert Design
Cover photo by Allsport/Sylvain Cazenave/Vandystadt
Photo research by Valerie Mulcahy
Printed and bound in the UK by Bath Press

INTRODUCTION

GCSE English: A Complete Course is designed to help you get the best possible grade you can in your GCSE English examination. It contains the essential reading material you need to complete your coursework assignments and to practise reading and response for the final examination. It also develops your skills in writing and in speaking and listening. **GCSE English: A Complete Course** is particularly appropriate for students on one-year courses. However, as it meets the requirements of all new GCSE English syllabuses it is an ideal coursebook for *all* students preparing for GCSE English.

How to use this book

The units in this book cover the skills and content you need for GCSE English. Each unit focuses on a specific area so that you can see exactly which skills you are practising, which coursework assignments you are covering and which parts of the examination you are preparing for.

This book is not designed for you to start at the beginning and work all the way through to the end. For example, you may complete your Shakespeare coursework (Unit 8) before you complete all of the reading and response to non-fiction (Unit 4). Your tutor or teacher may decide on the order in which you will complete this book. However, as a general guide you may wish to follow the outline below.

◆ **Unit 1** focuses on **speaking and listening** skills and provides an introduction to other oral activities throughout the book. You should complete this unit at the beginning of your course.

◆ **Units 2 and 3** focus on **personal writing** skills and **writing for audience and purpose**. They provide coursework assignments for writing and preparation for writing practice throughout the book. They should be completed close to the beginning of your course.

◆ **Units 4 and 5** focus on practising **reading and responding** to the sorts of non-fiction and fiction texts you will find on your examination papers. You should complete the first section in each unit during the first term of your course. Then, throughout your course, make sure you complete *at least three* sections from each unit. Do at least one section from each unit just before your examination.

◆ **Units 6, 7 and 8** provide **literature coursework** assignments. We suggest you complete one of these (poetry and short stories, for example) in the second part of the first term of your course and one (Shakespeare, for example) in the second term.

◆ **Unit 9** provides practice in **writing skills**. You should refer to this unit throughout your course. Cross-references throughout the book will help you to do this.

CONTENTS

UNITS

	1 Approaching oral coursework	**2** Personal writing and description	**3** Writing for audience and purpose	**4** Non-fiction and media
SEG — Coursework				
Oral	✓	✓	✓	✓
1 Personal writing: fiction		✓		
2 Personal writing: non-fiction		✓		✓
3 Shakespeare				
4 Pre-1900 author				
5 Post-1900 author				
SEG — Exam Paper 1				
1 Reading: non-fiction and media				✓
2 Writing to argue			✓	✓
SEG — Exam Paper 2				
1 Reading texts from other cultures				
2 Persuasive and analytical writing			✓	✓
NEAB Post-16 Syllabus — Coursework				
Oral	✓	✓	✓	✓
1 Shakespeare				
2 Texts from other cultures				
3 Media				✓
4 Original writing		✓		
Exam Paper 1				
1 Reading: non-fiction				✓
2 Writing to argue, persuade, instruct			✓	✓
Exam Paper 2				
1 Response to pre-1900 prose and post-1900 poets				
2 Writing to inform, explain, describe			✓	✓
NEAB Standard				
This syllabus is as NEAB post-16 except that pre-1900 literature is a coursework unit while texts from other cultures are in the *Anthology*.				

5 Fiction and texts from many cultures	6 Short stories for coursework	7 Poetry	8 Shakespeare coursework: Macbeth	9 Get it right
✓			✓	
✓				✓
✓				✓
			✓	
	✓	✓		
	✓	✓		
✓				✓
✓				
✓				✓
✓			✓	
			✓	
✓		✓		
✓				✓
✓				✓
				✓

UNITS

UNITS		1 Approaching oral coursework	2 Personal writing and description	3 Writing for audience and purpose	4 Non-fiction and media
WJEC Coursework	Oral	✓	✓	✓	✓
	1 Shakespeare				
	2 Texts from other cultures				
	3 Pre-1900 poetry and further reading				
	4 Best writing		✓	✓	✓
WJEC Exam Paper 1	1 Reading post-1900 prose				
	2 Imaginative writing		✓		✓
WJEC Exam Paper 2	1 Reading non-fiction and media				✓
	2 Writing to inform and persuade			✓	✓
MEG Coursework	Oral	✓	✓	✓	✓
	1 Shakespeare				
	2 Writing to inform, explain and describe			✓	✓
	3 Pre-1900 prose				
	4 Post-1900 prose				
	5 Imaginative writing		✓		✓
MEG Exam Papers 1 & 3	1 Reading non-fiction and media				✓
	2 Writing to discuss, argue and persuade			✓	✓
MEG Exam Papers 2 & 4	1 Reading texts from other cultures				
	2 Imaginative writing		✓		✓

5 Fiction and texts from many cultures	6 Short stories for coursework	7 Poetry	8 Shakespeare coursework: Macbeth	9 Get it right
✓			✓	
			✓	
✓		✓		
	✓	✓		
				✓
✓				
✓				✓
✓				✓
✓			✓	
			✓	
				✓
	✓			
	✓			
✓				✓
✓				✓
✓		✓		
✓				✓

UNITS

		1 Approaching oral coursework	2 Personal writing and description	3 Writing for audience and purpose	4 Non-fiction and media
London — Coursework	Oral	✓	✓	✓	✓
	1 Shakespeare				
	2 Texts from other cultures				
	3 Pre-1900 prose				
	4 Imaginative writing		✓		✓
Exam Papers 2 & 4	1 Reading non-fiction and poetry				✓
	2 Writing to inform, explain and describe			✓	✓
Exam Papers 3 & 5	1 Media				✓
	2 Writing to argue, persuade and instruct			✓	✓
	3 Writing to analyse, review and comment				✓
NICCEA — Coursework	Oral	✓	✓	✓	✓
	1 Shakespeare				
	2 Poetry: pre-1900 and other cultures				
	3 Writing to argue, persuade, instruct			✓	✓
	4 Imaginative writing		✓		✓
Exam Paper 1	1 Reading prose texts				
	2 Writing to analyse, review and comment				✓
Exam Paper 2	1 Writing to inform, explain and describe				✓
	2 Reading non-fiction				✓

5 Fiction and texts from many cultures	6 Short stories for coursework	7 Poetry	8 Shakespeare coursework: Macbeth	9 Get it right
✓			✓	
			✓	
✓		✓		
	✓			
✓				✓
		✓		
				✓
✓				✓
				✓
✓			✓	
			✓	
✓		✓		
✓				✓
✓				✓
✓				
				✓
				✓

APPROACHING ORAL COURSEWORK

Introduction

Speaking and Listening in GCSE English is worth 20% of the final assessment grade. It will form part of your overall grade in English, and will also be recorded separately on your results certificate.

During the course you may be expected to undertake various activities, including discussions, role play, giving an account of an event both actual and imaginary, dialogues, arguments and debates. These may take place in pairs, groups or in a whole class situation.

You will find speaking and listening activities in most of the units in this book. This unit helps you to focus on the skills you need to improve. You may wish to refer back to it as you work through the rest of the book.

You will need to show your assessor that you can communicate clearly and confidently with others, structuring your ideas logically. You will need to use Standard English where and when appropriate and also show that you can listen to others sympathetically and respond appropriately.

Any person who dominates the group will not necessarily get the best mark for speaking and listening. Your assessor is looking for people who help others to put across their points, not people who want to hear their own voice.

facilitating

inhibiting

Talking and reporting

Assignment 1

Breaking the ice

Work in pairs. If you have never worked with your partner, find out a little about each other. Do this by asking each other questions. You could start by discussing what courses you are taking and why, or where your home is and so on.

If you already know each other well, you could talk about something that has happened to you recently such as a holiday or trip. Find out as much about each other as you can. When you are satisfied you have enough information, join with two other pairs to make a group of six and each report your findings to the group.

FOCUS

Questions and reporting back

♦ Try to avoid asking questions that simply require a yes/no answer. Ask questions that require detailed responses from your partner. For example, *What did you most enjoy about the holiday?* is a better question than the simpler *Did you enjoy the holiday?*

♦ When you are being asked questions, listen carefully. Work with your partner as a team — both of you will benefit from doing well.

♦ Try not to interrupt when your partner is talking.

♦ When reporting back, you should have some notes to help you, but try not to read them word for word — use them as prompts only.

♦ Organise your reporting back so that it has a logical structure and is easily understood by an audience unfamiliar with the information.

Assignment 2

Guess the famous person

Work in groups. In this activity you each choose a famous person you admire but do not tell anyone who it is. Each person describes his or her famous person, and the group asks questions. You must answer honestly! When asked, describe your person physically and explain why you admire him or her.

Once the group has guessed the identity of your person you have to justify *why* you think this person is the *Most interesting famous person*. This may involve you in discussion with group members who disagree with your point of view.

One person from your group should be appointed as an assessor of the person describing his or her person. Use the Observer's checklist on page 16 and give feedback to the speaker. Choose a new assessor each time a new person describes his or her famous person. When each person's case has been presented, consider your own performance. Did you describe your famous person well? Did you listen carefully to others? Did you ask useful questions? How could you improve your performance?

Group work

The types of things you can be asked to do in a group can vary immensely, so it is difficult to give advice that will suit every situation perfectly. However, here are some tips worth thinking about:

♦ Groups often have to report their findings to the class. First, elect the person who will report back, so that they can prepare for this and make the notes (so they can read them!). However, the rest of the group should not just sit back. It is likely that your group discussion is being assessed and people who are silent do not score highly on speaking and listening exercises. The group will also need to appoint a chairperson who ensures that the task is undertaken quickly and efficiently; this also relieves some of the pressure on the reporter.

♦ Do not elect the same person as the reporter every time. It is important that you all develop your speaking and listening skills.

♦ If you are the chairperson, you must ensure that everyone participates in the discussion.

♦ If anyone in your group already knows something about the activity, perhaps they could lead the discussion – expertise can be useful.

♦ Look at the assignment and make sure you know exactly what you are being asked to do. Read the task aloud in the group so that everyone is clear about it.

♦ Focus on the task carefully; if there is a time limit, be sure that you cover the activity fully in the time allowed.

♦ Remember that different assignments will need different approaches. The way you work on one assignment will not necessarily work for another. Be flexible in your approach.

♦ In an oral exercise you are being assessed on your ability to communicate with each other. It is a big mistake to spend your time writing your own small pieces for the final presentation. You need to be seen discussing ideas and interacting together, then spending a small amount of time putting the visual presentation together as a group.

♦ Never lose your temper. It will not help you to win an argument and can often damage your case with fellow listeners. Remain calm and rational and rely on good debating skills and forceful, well thought-out arguments to win your case.

You will find this chart useful for speaking and listening activities throughout the book.

Observer's checklist

Date . . . . Speaker's name . . . . Observer's name . . . .

Tick appropriate descriptions.

Volume	Just right ☐	Too loud ☐	Too soft ☐
Speed/Pacing	Just right ☐	Too fast ☐	Too slow ☐

	Never	Once/Twice	Frequently	Comments
Puts ideas persuasively				
Expresses ideas clearly				
Listens to others				
Responds appropriately				
Asks questions/Asks for clarification				
Draws others into the conversation				
Sums up				
Breaks silences by starting conversation in a constructive way				
Introduces a new aspect of the topic				
Uses too many 'fillers', e.g. 'You know' 'Right'				
Interrupts a speaker before he/she has completed a point				
Shouts				
Uses aggressive gestures, e.g. pointing finger, banging fist				
Hogs the conversation				
Doesn't participate				
Uses disruptive behaviour, e.g. completely changes the subject, yawns loudly				

Positive points (rows 1–9)

Negative points (rows 10–16)

Giving a talk

On some courses you may be expected to prepare a short talk for a small group or your class.

Prepare a mini-talk that you can give to the group. This can be about a hobby, an interest, a job or your family. As an alternative to this you could choose to talk about something you feel strongly about. Remember that this will be assessed. You should be able to answer questions from the group and should not rely on reading a 'speech' from a sheet of paper. You could use notes to help you and you may wish to bring in equipment if you are talking about a hobby.

Remember that when you are speaking individually to a small group, or reporting back to the class you should:

♦ Speak in a clear, loud voice. It is not just what you say, but how you say it that is important. If your content is good but the way you put it across to the audience is dull, or if you are simply too quiet for your audience to hear, they will quickly lose interest.

♦ Use your eyes as well as your voice. Good speakers look at the audience and hold their attention with eye contact.

♦ Try to vary the way you speak. Politicians realise how important it is to have an interesting voice and many have had training to modify their voice tone. You must try to avoid speaking in a monotone.

♦ Use the correct vocabulary and language structures for the occasion. This is called using the correct register. For instance, you cannot use slang in an interview for a job – if you did you would be using an inappropriate register.

♦ Prepare it well. Practise what you are going to say in your head so that you are clear about it. Good presentation is important and is a skill that is useful in everyday life. If you are using visual aids, make sure that they are numbered and in the correct order.

Key Points

You will find opportunities for oral work on pages 24, 27, 42, 66, 74 and 114.

UNIT 2

PERSONAL WRITING AND DESCRIPTION

Introduction

For GCSE English you will produce pieces of writing for coursework and also in timed conditions in your exam. The best way to improve your writing is to give yourself many opportunities to practise. Remember that writing is a skill and, like learning a new sport or learning to drive, the more you practise the better your writing will become.

♦ This book gives you many opportunities to practise writing and to reflect on the writing you do.

♦ This unit and the next look at examples of writing and help you to think about what is good or could be improved in your own writing.

♦ At the end of the unit, a GCSE examiner gives comments and guidance on how to write well in the examination, using examples.

♦ You will find writing assignments in all the units so you can practise writing or produce pieces for coursework at the same time as covering your GCSE reading.

♦ On page 192 you will find 'Get it right', a writing skills section. This section provides essential practice in the basic skills of spelling, grammar and punctuation. It also reminds you how to set out your work in a variety of formats. This has been placed at the end of the book so you can look up key points easily. However, **you must not leave this section until the end**! The basic skills of spelling, grammar and punctuation are very important and can cost you marks in the exam if you make mistakes.

Personal writing

Many students find writing about something that has happened to them easier than making up a story. This is not surprising as the storyline or plot is already there and all you have to do is carefully re-tell the story. But what makes a piece of personal writing alive and interesting to the reader?

Look at this piece of personal writing by Roald Dahl. It is taken from his autobiography, *Going Solo*. In it he tells about a character he met on board his ship …

My Cabin Companion

Everyone on the ship was completely dotty, but none, as it turned out, was quite as dotty as my cabin companion, U.N. Savory.

The first sign of *his* dottiness was revealed to me one evening as our ship was running between Malta and Port Said. It had been a stifling
5 afternoon and I was having a brief rest on my upper berth before dressing for dinner …

I lay still on my bunk with my eyes half open. Below me, U.N. Savory was getting dressed. There wasn't room in the cabin for two of us to change our clothes simultaneously, so we took it in turns to go first. It was
10 his turn to dress first tonight. He had tied his bow-tie and now he was putting on his black dinner-jacket. I was watching him rather dreamily through half-closed eyes, and I saw him reach into his sponge-bag and take out a small carton. He stationed himself in front of the washbasin mirror, took the lid off the carton and dipped his fingers into it. The
15 fingers came out with a pinch of white powder or crystals, and this stuff he proceeded to sprinkle very carefully over the shoulders of his dinner-jacket.

Suddenly I was fully alert. What on earth was the man up to? I didn't want him to know that I had seen, so I closed my eyes and pretended to
20 be asleep. Really I was trying to figure out why U.N. Savory should be going around and trying to kid everyone he had dandruff. Three days later I had the answer.

As usual I seated myself at the bar and began sipping a beer. By gosh, it was hot. I decided to go on deck and smoke a pipe before dinner. It
25 would be cooler there. I stood up and felt for my pipe. I realised that I had left it in our cabin. I stood up and made my way downstairs to the cabin and opened the door. There was a strange man sitting in shirtsleeves on U.N. Savory's bunk and as I stepped inside, the man gave a queer little

yelp and jumped to his feet as though a cracker had gone off in the seat
30 of his pants.

The stranger was totally bald and that is why it took me a second or two
to realise that he was in fact none other than U.N. Savory himself. It is
extraordinary how hair on the head or the lack of it will completely
change a person's appearance. U.N. Savory looked like a different man.
35 To start with, he looked fifteen years older, and in some subtle way he
seemed also to have diminished, grown much shorter and smaller. As I
said, he was almost totally bald, and the dome of his head was as pink
and shiny as a ripe peach. He was standing up now and holding in his two
hands the wig he had been about to put on as I walked in. 'You had no
40 right to come back,' he shouted. 'You said you'd finished.' Little sparks
of fury were flashing in his eyes.

'I'm … I'm most awfully sorry,' I stammered. 'I forgot my pipe.'

He stood there glaring at me with that dark, malevolent glint in his eye
and I could see little droplets of perspiration oozing out of his pores on
45 his bald head. I felt very bad. I didn't know what to say next. 'Just let me
get my pipe and I'll clear out,' I mumbled.

'Oh no you don't!' he shouted. 'You've seen it now and you're not
leaving this room until you've made me a promise! Promise me you
won't tell a soul! Promise me that!'

50 'I won't tell anyone,' I said. 'I give you my word.'

'I suppose you think I'm crazy,' he said.

I said nothing. I could think of nothing to say.

'You do, don't you?' he said. 'You think I'm crazy.'

'Not at all,' I answered. 'A man can do as he likes.'

55 'It's business,' he said. 'I do it purely for business reasons. I work in
Amritsar, in the Punjab. That is the homeland of the Sikhs. To a Sikh, hair
is a sort of religion. A Sikh never cuts his hair. He either rolls it up on the
top of his head or in a turban. A Sikh doesn't respect a bald man.'

'In that case I think it's very clever of you to wear a wig.' I had to live
60 in the cabin with U.N. Savory for several days yet and I didn't want a row.
'It's quite brilliant,' I added.

'Do you honestly think so?' he said, melting.

'It's a stroke of pure genius.'

'I go to a lot of trouble to convince all those Sikh wallahs it's my own
65 hair,' he went on.

'You mean the dandruff bit?'

'You saw it then?'

'Of course I saw it. It was brilliant.'

The man was as potty as a pilchard.

Adapted from *Going Solo* by Roald Dahl

Reading

♦ What do you learn about U.N. Savory?
♦ What do you like or dislike about the description?
♦ Roald Dahl could simply have told us that he shared his cabin with a man who wore a wig and put powder on his shoulders to look like dandruff. How has he made the information much more interesting than this? Think about:
  – the way he tells the story, focusing on two specific incidents
  – his use of description and conversation.

Key Points

♦ In his writing, Roald Dahl uses **adjectives** to help make his descriptions interesting.
♦ **Adjectives** work with **nouns**. They help to make the meaning of the noun clearer or fuller. For example, in *My Cabin Companion* we learn that:
'It had been a *stifling* afternoon'
and later, that the man has
'...a *dark*, *malevolent* glint in his eye'.
♦ Using adjectives in your own writing will help to bring your descriptions to life. Be careful not to use too many adjectives – use them in places where they will really help to make an impact!

Your own personal writing

When asked for a piece of personal writing, most people draw on events from their own lives. Our lives are packed full of events from major happenings such as first days at school, birthdays, weddings, funerals, family quarrels and births, to tiny details about our everday lives and the people we knew and know. So how do you choose what to write about? Most good writers are extremely selective. Interesting personal writing is usually about people and events that had a great impact upon us. Read this description written by a student about her grandmother.

My Grandmother

My grandmother was probably one of the most important people in my life. She was made more special by the fact that she was my only living grandparent. She was my gran on my mum's side. My father's family were all Polish Jews and had all been killed in the holocaust.

5   My gran lived in Weymouth which was a long way away from where we lived. Every summer I would be wrapped up like Paddington Bear, a label stuck on my jacket and off I would go on my holidays. The guard, there were such things then, was responsible for me and would pass over the duly delivered parcel to my gran at the other end.

10   My gran lived in a red brick council house: 200 Abbotsbury Road. I loved that house and even now I am dying to knock the door and state proudly: 'My gran lived here!' Daft, isn't it? Maybe when I am old I will do it. My gran used to say you can get away with a lot when you're old!

The house, like my gran, was old and everything in it spoke out of
15   another age. She had been born in 1896. She had long hair which she wore coiled into a bun and she always wore the same style frocks with a little trim of lace around the V-neck and a cameo brooch. All her dresses were hand-made on an old sewing machine that for many years after her death remained in the garage gathering dust. I remember her most striking piece
20   of furniture was a huge table that filled her back parlour. At night we would sit at the table and listen to the Archers on the radio. We would eat Edam cheese and home-made bread with lashings of her home-made raspberry jam, just the two of us. I was all of seven and I don't think I had a clue what or who the Archers were but it felt good to sit there like a grown-up. Gran
25   was a fine cook and had once worked in a country house. My job every

night was to go to the pantry to get the jam. I can still smell her pantry now, full of all sorts of jams, chutneys and preserves.

Her bathroom was Victorian almost and the window was quite low down. I would brush my teeth and look down from it to the back garden 30 where my gran was often pottering or sitting on a garden swing chair she had. Sometimes she would look up instinctively and wave. I can see her now bending over a small spade and brushing a strand of her long coiled hair that had escaped away from her face.

I can't remember it raining when I was a child in Weymouth and when 35 it did rain it would happen late at night so that in the morning you would wake to smell sweet, damp grass. At night though, the pervading smell rose from gran's garden fire, a rich, evocative scent that still haunts me to this day, along with the picture I have of her tending it and adding twigs.

It is hard to say what it was about my gran that made her so special. We 40 spent days together on my uncle's farm where she helped out, we went to the beach, we ate ice-cream, we played slot machines, we fed the swans. When I went home she came too, but only for a while. Once a month a huge parcel would arrive with a letter inside for me and home-made goodies for all the family. In it was the scent of her home-baking, her 45 home and of course her. When she died at the age of 79 a chapter of my life came to an end. She used to say to me, what will remain of us is love, and I have to say she spoke true.

Reading

♦ What do you learn about the writer's grandmother?
♦ How does the writer bring her grandmother to life in this extract?

Writing

Write a few paragraphs describing someone you know. You may choose to:
♦ Write a general description of the character. Focus on specific details and things the character does or did, as well as their physical appearance.
♦ Describe a specific incident. Focus on particular details and bring the character to life through the incident you are describing.

Review your writing

♦ Have you shown why and how the character is interesting to you?
♦ Have you brought your character to life by focusing on a specific incident or on the details which make your character special?

Picturing people

Group oral work

1 Look at the photographs, and give each of the characters an identity.

♦ Decide on their full names and their ages. What do they do?
  What qualifications do they have? Where do they come from?

♦ What are they doing at this point in time? What do the photographs
  represent?

♦ What clues have you used in each photograph to help you?

♦ Imagine a memory, an event from the past, for each of these characters.

Making words work

2 Sometimes people cannot think of interesting words to describe simple things. Try to do this activity very quickly:

♦ In your group make a list of thirty words that you could use to describe a character's eyes, nose, mouth, hair.

♦ Think of ten words to describe the way someone walks.

♦ Think of ten words that would describe someone's personality.

3 Before you do this activity, make sure you have read the Focus box, below. Look back at the character profiles you have just created. Think of five images to describe each character. Your images might be phrases making use of adjectives, similes or metaphors.

FOCUS

Description

The following descriptions are taken from Roald Dahl's *Going Solo* on pages 19–21.

'…jumped to his feet as though a cracker had gone off in the seat of his pants.'

'…the dome of his head was as pink and shiny as a ripe peach.'

'Little sparks of fury were flashing in his eyes.'

'The man was as potty as a pilchard.'

In all of them Roald Dahl brings the character to life by using words or images we're not quite expecting. To say that something *is like* something else is a **simile**. For example, '*the dome of his head was as pink and shiny as a ripe peach*'.

To say that something *is* something else is a **metaphor**. For example, Roald Dahl describes the anger in the man's eyes as '*little sparks of fury*'.

Similes and metaphors help to make your writing lively. Another way to make your descriptions interesting is to use **adjectives** (see Key Points, page 21). Instead of just saying 'the man has a moustache' you might say '*the man has a **black**, **drooping** moustache*'.

Writing

Imagine that you had met one of the characters you created on page 24. Your meeting is similar to the way in which Roald Dahl met U.N. Savory in *My Cabin Companion* (page 19). Read the Focus box above, then write a description of the character, making it as detailed as you can.

Sometimes the most interesting things to write about are the incidents we remember years after they happened – often because they are just impossible to forget! Look at this extract about an event that a student found embarrassing.

How's your dad?

I realised as I got older and I suppose wiser that my parents were different to other children's. How different becomes apparent the older I get.

As time moves on meeting old school friends can be hazardous. You always have to ask tentatively about their parents, as they do about yours.
5 After all no-one lives forever and eventually you're bound to put your foot in it. Along the lines of 'How's your dad? I remember when …' and they reply 'We buried him last year.'

Well I was having that type of conversation, except they were asking me. And it was that question said as it was, 'How's your dad, he always
10 was a bit nuts?' that has prompted me to write this!

Well, first of all, he's still very much alive and to this day he can still embarrass me like no-one else can. This episode occurred when I was eighteen and he was at least sixty. We used to travel all around the country going to dog shows. We showed beagles and used to do really
15 well. Nearly every Saturday in the summer meant a trip far away to a dog show. Dad would wake me with a cuppa at about four o'clock which was roughly half an hour before we needed to leave. Anyway, I was really looking forward to this show. The judge was a good one, that meant he/she judged the dog and not the other end of the lead. The show was
20 always well attended and all my friends would be there. Anyway, I washed and dressed quickly and headed for a quick bowl of cereal and that was when it happened. I saw him – my dad that is – and the outfit he intended to wear. We lived on a smallholding, all of seven acres, and my dad had always fancied himself as 'Lord of the Manor'. My father loves
25 clothes and dressing up and there he was twirling around and asking me 'What do you think?!'

Well, what I thought is still unprintable!

My dad had bought himself a new outfit. Deerstalker hat, tweed jacket, check shirt, knickerbocker trousers, long socks and brogues. I didn't trust
30 myself to speak – I merely turned and retraced my foosteps up the stairs to my mum, who didn't accompany us to the shows as she stayed home to mind the family business.

Once in her room I informed her of the outfit and said I wasn't going to the show. I begged her to make him change, I cajoled, I shouted.
35 Nothing worked! Her attitude was that, a) he was a grown man and he could wear what he wanted, AND b) she smiled when she said this – she wasn't going to the show so it wouldn't affect her.

Well, the day was ruined. I spent it avoiding my father and watching my friends laugh. And I suppose you think my friends were all adolescent
40 eighteen year olds, but I had been showing dogs for a long time and these were people who I had grown up with and none was less than forty!

And here the story would have ended if only my father had not visited my 'rock and roll' older brother in London.

Roll the clock forward one month after the London trip and
45 approximately the same time of morning. I rose assured that my dad's deerstalking days were over. The sun was shining, dawn had broken on a glorious new era. Because if I thought I had a bad day at the Show my dad's was worse – all his friends laughed every time he walked by; and though my dad loves cracking jokes, he doesn't like being the butt of
50 them. Ah, another mid-life crisis over, I innocently thought.

As I walked in the kitchen the immortal words hit me 'What do you think?' I looked and this time I did speak. 'Are you doing this for a bet? Or are you trying to ruin what is left of my childhood?'

'What do you mean?' my dad said innocently as he stood there in his
55 new London purchases: white jeans, a white bomber jacket with fur around the collar, a navy shirt open half way down his chest revealing greying chest hair and a gold medallion.

There was only one thing to do and even then I wasn't holding my breath.

'MUM!' I shouted desperately. And to this day I can still hear that faintly
60 muffled, hysterical giggle floating down the stairs as if in mocking reply.

Group oral work

The piece you have just read recalls an episode in this student's life. Most people can recall a time when they were embarrassed by something or someone. Sometimes it is possible to tell the story so that it sounds like a totally made up story – a fiction.

1 What did you think of the story above? What did you like or dislike about it? Does the writer keep you entertained?

2 Do you remember a time when your family or friends embarrassed you? Share your memory with your group if you wish. If you can't think of an embarrassing episode, think of one that was humorous or memorable.

Memories into writing

It is not enough to recall a memory for personal writing. You must also make it memorable. Read the outline of an incident recalled from childhood and discuss in your group how you would turn it into a longer piece of writing.

> It was a normal Saturday morning and my older brother was playing music loudly in his room. My mum warned him that if he didn't tidy his room as she'd asked him a thousand times that morning then he would be in trouble. She said that the next time she visited his room if it wasn't cleaned she would throw everything out of the window to teach him a lesson. My brother usually had his window wide open to hide the smell of his cigarette smoke from my mum, should she happen to walk in.
>
> Later that morning she returned to my brother's room. Finding it still untidy she casually threw his stuff out of the window as she had threatened to do. Unfortunately, this was the one morning Geoff had not opened the window! There was the most enormous smash and …

Can you imagine the rest?

Writing

You are now ready to write a longer piece of personal writing. Decide what you would like to write about. Did you relate a funny or embarrassing memory to your group? Are there people or events in your life that you would like to focus on? Any of the following subjects is suitable for using in a coursework folder, but you should discuss your choice of topic with your teacher or lecturer first.

♦ A person you remember – it could be a friend or a relative. Why have you chosen them?
♦ An embarrassing or funny memory you have.
♦ A holiday that you enjoyed or did not enjoy.
♦ A happy or sad occasion that you can recall.
♦ Your first job and pay packet.
♦ Memories of school days – possibly your first day at school.

If you are finding this task really difficult, you could look at some old family photographs. Choose one or two that you could write about, explaining when they were taken and what was so special about them.

Personal writing

♦ To write well you need to think carefully about planning and drafting your work (see page 238).

♦ Remember that what makes writing memorable, especially in autobiography, is the detail. You have to paint a picture in words for the reader.

♦ If you are writing about a character, you must make that character come alive to the reader, so that they can visualise them. If necessary re-read some of the extracts in this unit to help you.

♦ If you are writing about an episode in your life – a holiday for instance – describe in detail the journey and the setting. Where did you go? Who did you go with? What can you remember about the place?

♦ When you think that you know what you are going to write about, try writing the first two paragraphs. Read them carefully and think about how you could improve them. Then ask a fellow student to read your work and you read theirs. Offer advice to each other if it is needed.

♦ Check your work carefully when you have finished your final draft. Are your tenses consistent? Check with Key Points, below. Is your spelling correct?

Key Points

When you are writing, make sure that you use the correct **tenses**. A common error in personal writing is changing from one tense to another in the wrong places. Look at the paragraph below.

> I was feeling incredibly anxious on my way to visit my sister in hospital. I crossed the road, walk through the hospital gates and I see a row of ambulances, reminding me of the ambulance which brought her here the week before.

Is this incident being written about as if it is in the present or past? Which words make it confusing to work out the answer?

♦ A verb in the **past tense** describes an action which has happened *before now*:

I *was* feeling incredibly anxious...

I *crossed* the road...

♦ A verb in the **present tense** describes an incident as if it is happening now:

I ... *walk* through the hospital gates...

I *see* a row of ambulances...

You will find more about tenses in 'Get it right' on page 197.

In a good piece of personal writing you will interest your readers by relating a story in a way which holds their attention throughout. Make sure you concentrate on significant points – do not feel you have to include *everything*.

Take a look at these two pieces of writing. They are both the beginning of pieces of personal writing. The first was prompted by the title, **'Describe an occasion when you felt ashamed of yourself'**.

As I waited at the bus stop, I felt very excited to see the film 'Seven' at the local cinema. I had been looking forward to see the film all week. As I waited patiently for Gemma, who was always late for everything, I inspected my new blouse for any creases.

When she finaly arrived I got my bus fare money out of my new leather purse. When the bus arrived, I got on and noticed it was nearly full, there was only a seat by an old deaf man or a weird punk rocker, I decided to sit by the old fogey and let Gemma have the pleasure to sit by the punk rocker.

I sat down, Gemma sat in front, the journey was about five minutes and I was really glad to get off.

There was a gigantic que in the cinema, and I was weary that we'd ever get in. As we finaly got in, I saw Claire the biggest blabbermouch of the whole school, I tried to avoid her, but it was useless she'd spotted me and of course came to talk with me. I stood for a quarter of an hour listening to her latest gossips which didn't appeal to me in the slighest way. I tried my very best not to scream the place down or squash my coke carton, so I politely made an excuse that I desperatly needed the toilet. I waited in the toilet with Gemma for at least ten minutes, waiting for Claire to get bored of waiting, and to go in. We decided to make a dash for it. By the time we got in, the first twenty minutes of the film had been lost, and I completly lost the whole storyline. I chewed angrily at my pop corn. I resented Claire.

Response

Does this piece of writing hold your attention? Are you eager to find out what might happen next? How do you think this writing might be improved?

Examiner's comment

This story is almost certainly based on personal experience, although it is quite likely there is some exaggeration, or even fiction, to make the story more interesting. The basic situation is quite promising but it is a long time before the story takes shape.

It is quite easy to follow the story, but there are too many errors.

♦ The use of 'to see' in paragraph 1 is clumsy.

♦ Twice in paragraph 2 the candidate uses commas where there should be full stops. This is a common error we find in many scripts, so do watch out for it!

♦ There are quite a lot of spelling mistakes such as 'finaly' and 'que'.

The content of the story, its style and overall structure would probably push it towards a Grade C. However, the errors in the writing such as spelling and sentence construction would probably make it a Grade D.

The second piece of writing we are going to look at was prompted by the title, **'My greatest regret'**.

> The room they were keeping him in was dark and silent, as the nurse had shut the door and drawn the dingy brown curtains, shutting out the bright sunshine of a warm summer afternoon. I stood by the door for some moments, not looking at the figure which lay helpless in the bed. I didn't want to look at Dad. I didn't know what to expect. I didn't want to see signs of death.
>
> It seemed as if hours had passed before I finally edged forward. The sheets covering the bed were pale green; the blanket white. I looked at his hands first. They were paler than usual, almost white. Slowly, my eyes moved their way up to his face, where they rested.
>
> It was not an alarming picture – he was the same old Dad with the same old receding hair line, the same wrinkles and the same distinctive features. But I was shocked, even so. This was my Dad. My Dad who was lying on a hospital bed, so helpless, so pale, dependent on a machine that was breathing for him through tubes down his nose. It was only last night that I'd left home. It seemed like years ago now, a different time. I'd been so angry...

Response

Does this piece of writing hold your attention? Are you eager to find out what might happen next? How do you think this writing might be improved?

Examiner's comment

This writer really knows how to tell a story, even when it is a 'true' story. The opening catches our attention immediately and creates a setting which is familiar in some ways but also mysterious. We notice the effective use of words such as 'dark' and 'silent', and the 'dingy brown curtains' which create a contrast with the bright sunshine of the normal world outside. The spelling and punctuation are flawless. This is a clear Grade A*.

WRITING FOR AUDIENCE AND PURPOSE

Introduction

Before you begin to plan most pieces of writing it is important to ask:

♦ *Who* is this piece of writing for? *Who* is the audience?

♦ *What* is this piece of writing for? Is it to provide information? Is it to persuade the audience to adopt a particular viewpoint? Is it to explain how something is done? Is it to describe someone or something?

In this unit you will be given the opportunity to write for several different audiences and purposes. At the end of the unit a GCSE examiner gives useful advice, using examples.

Read the following extracts, then look at the activity on the next page.

MEDICINE AND WAR

THROUGHOUT **HISTORY**, men who have fought in wars have had little in the way of medical care. Most armies included doctors but treatment was reserved for officers. Although 18th-century ships had surgeons, sailors often died from infection because conditions were unhygienic.

In the Crimean War (1853–1856), when many soldiers were dying in filthy conditions because of the lack of medical care, there was a public outcry. Florence Nightingale was asked to go to the Crimea to care for the wounded – the first time that women had been allowed to nurse in the British Army.

Timelines 'Medicine'

In place of war

For the first time I have started to hear the word 'war' lately, in connection with things European.

As a girl in the Twenties, I innocently wondered why there were men on the streets with sleeves or trouser legs pinned up where they should have had arms or legs, blind men selling matches and one man with no legs, on a pram-wheeled trolley.

Most tragic of all were the men destroyed in mind by the horrors of the Somme, Ypres and Passchendaele. These were the men who fought the Great War, the 'war to end all wars', and came back to unemployment and degradation.

In the Thirties, while we ordinary people knew starvation as men tried to feed their families and women slaved to make the money go round, Hitler was arming his youth and setting up the Gestapo.

We saw the air raid shelters dug in gardens and parks and were issued with gas masks, identity cards and ration books. On September 3, 1939, the people were called once more to fight and this time the conflict came to our shores.

Look on the war memorials, at the names and ages of those killed in action, a generation lost fighting for flag, King and country. This is why we joined the Common Market, so our children would never have to go to war. I embrace the chance to save our young ones from a lifetime of fear.

Mrs J. Bull, London E3

The Daily Mail

Leave your car at home!

In the last hundred years, cars have revolutionised the way we travel … but at what cost? If you're a driver, using your car less is one of the most important things you can do to help the environment – and help make it easier for everyone to get around. Here's why.

It's a choke!

Car fumes are the leading cause of smogs which are choking our towns and cities and a major contributor to poor air quality in rural areas threatening the health of as many as one in five people.
Pregnant women, young children and people who suffer from heart and lung disease are most at risk.

Going nowhere.

With 21 million cars already clogging up UK roads, travelling can be a slow and frustrating experience. If we don't do anything to cut car use, there could be more than 30 million cars competing for road space by the year 2025.
Road congestion already costs our economy some £15 billion every year.

Climate catastrophe?

Road traffic is the fastest growing cause of carbon dioxide, the main 'greenhouse gas'. Rising levels of greenhouse gases in our atmosphere threaten to make the Earth hotter, leading to disastrous changes in the world's climate.
Cars pump out 14% of all the UK's carbon dioxide pollution.

Carmaggeddon.

Making cars, producing fuel and building roads gobbles up precious natural resources, destroys and poisons huge areas of land, and wrecks communities and nature areas across the globe.
In the UK, road-building threatens to damage or destroy over 50 of our finest wildlife reserves.

What a waste!

When cars are scrapped, many materials end up being dumped in the ground or burnt in incinerators, poisoning our air, water and soil with harmful chemicals.
Each year 1,400,000 cars are scrapped worldwide.

Friends of the Earth

Campaign to curb spread of cocaine in clubland

Alex Bellos

Cocaine is approaching the popularity of ecstasy and amphetamines as a dance drug, drugs safety campaigners will claim today at the launch of the first government-funded campaign targeting cocaine use.

The London Dance Safety Campaign says clubbers in their mid-twenties are starting to take cocaine because it is less disorientating than ecstasy and so fits in better with professional lifestyles.

In the most high profile government-backed anti-drugs campaign since the Heroin Screws You Up series in the 1980s, posters spelling out the risks of cocaine use will be put in London Underground stations alongside similar warnings about ecstasy, speed and LSD.

Ciaran O'Hagan, of the national drugs agency, Release, said yesterday that cocaine was now a close third behind ecstasy and amphetamines.

The Guardian

Activity

♦ For each of the extracts above, decide *who* the writer was writing for.
♦ How did you reach your decision? What can you say about the format in which each piece is written and the language used?

★★★★★ **DELUXE**
REID'S HOTEL
FUNCHAL,
MADEIRA

Sun terraces with
views across the
Atlantic Sea

Ten acres of
exotic gardens

Swimming
pools

Tennis
courts

Assignment 1

Imagine that you work for the travel company which is going to include this
new hotel in its summer brochure. You have to visit the hotel to ensure that the
facilities are as described by the owners.

Look carefully at the picture above and the notes on the next page. Write a
factual report for your company about the hotel. You could use the headings
suggested on the report form. There is more about reports on page 234.

Before you begin writing, think about:
♦ Who is the intended audience?
♦ What is the purpose of the information – to inform or persuade?

Notes

Location
Just outside of Funchal in Madeira right by the Atlantic sea and ten minutes from the centre

About 40 minutes drive from the airport

Funchal is a busy little town. There is a lively market and shops including some clothes shops. It has a few lively bars and clubs

The southern cliffs of Madeira rise up behind the resort

Traffic can be very busy – sometimes difficult to walk along narrow pavements

Car is very useful for getting into mountains and to other places

Local language is Portuguese

Hotel
New purpose built hotel. Resembles a cosy country mansion. Built slightly up hillside. Views of beach

Hotel accommodation and facilities
167 rooms

Friendly service with all amenities

Three pools, tennis courts and games room

Children's pool

Formal and informal restaurants

Two bars and an additional one poolside

Sun terraces

10 acres of exotic gardens

Sauna, beauty parlour, hairdresser

Extensive range of activities for children and teenagers

Free bus into Funchal

Helicopter excursions to Porto Santo

2 golf courses nearby

Sunshine Holidays Report Form	
Hotel Name	
Place	
Researcher	
Date	
Location	
Hotel Site	
Accommodation	
Facilities	
Local Amenities	

Writing to persuade

Read these following descriptions, taken from travel brochures, of holiday resorts in the Algarve, Portugal.

Kaleidoscopic colours abound, from the shimmering turquoise ocean across golden sandy beaches, over
5 fantastic time-eroded sandstone cliffs to luscious green fairways and meadows.

The natural hospitality of the Algarveans is a legacy of the
10 500 year Moorish occupation of the region, along with, some say, that distinct lack of urgency in day to day life! The Moors came from North
15 Africa looking for fertile land to grow their oranges, grapes, figs and almonds and named the land 'Al Gharb' – and visitors can still
20 see their influence today.

The Algarve is a land of contrast where one moment you'll see a wizened, sun-wrinkled elder leading his
25 donkey and cart to the market, and the next you'll enter a beautiful leisure complex or majestic marina.

The beach lover will find over
30 60 easily accessible beaches plus dozens more which offer a more challenging point of entry! The nature lover will find over 300 different
35 species of bird, either resident or regular visitors, plus a veritable explosion of colour amidst flora and fauna as spring approaches.

40 The sports enthusiast will rejoice in a superb array of golf courses, tennis courts, clay pigeon shooting and several lawn bowling clubs
45 where you can take part in competitions.

Winter weather, as we know it, seldom appears in these parts; the pace of life from
50 Autumn to Spring time is even more leisurely than usual and it is easy to make lasting friendships.

A meandering stroll through
55 cobbled streets of picturesque towns and sleepy villages; a brisk, invigorating walk along the super coastline; peaceful
60 relaxation as you bask in the afternoon sun. The charm of the Algarve lies in its endearing blend of quaint simplicity and warm
65 sophistication.

Vale Sao Joao
Apartments

Vale Sao Joao, with its lovely landscaped gardens, is situated just 400 metres from the beach of Areias de Sao Joao, which is reached via a partially sloping road. The
5 popular Tres Palmeiras Restaurant is nearby, with one or two bars and restaurants in the locality. A quiet and peaceful winter haven, Vale Sao Joao is within one kilometre of the popular Montechoro area where you will
10 find a selection of bars and restaurants, plus Praia da Oura beach. In the other direction, a 1.5 kilometre stroll will find you overlooking Albufeira town, and the fisherman's beach.

Vale Sao Joao's beautiful grounds are
15 looked after with devotion by Fernando and Irmalinda, the resident caretakers. The accommodation is built on three floors and most of the apartments are similar in design. Attractive pine furnishings include a sofa,
20 armchairs and dining table in the living room, kitchen with two or four ring cookers, mini-oven and fridge. There is a full bathroom, and the beds are twins. There is also satellite T.V. in every apartment.

25 The gardens at the Vale Sao Joao are truly delightful. Between the apartment house and a large swimming pool is a picturesque gully with carob trees, pampas grass, shrubs and flowers, and a bridge in order to cross the
30 pool area and fabulous lawns.

The lovely setting is ideal for a quiet and peaceful winter break, with its wonderful location so close to the coastline. We should mention though that the immediate area is
35 tricky for those with walking difficulties.

Vale Sao Joao

Prices are in £'s per person   Code No: SW1016

Departures on or between	7 Nts	14 Nts	Child (7 or 14)	Extra Week
02 Nov–08 Nov	199	219	129	–
09 Nov–15 Nov	185	195	109	24
16 Nov–22 Nov	169	–	99	24
23 Nov–13 Dec	–	–	–	
14 Dec–18 Dec	–	–	–	
19 Dec–27 Dec	219	299	FREE	–
28 Dec–03 Jan	249	259	FREE	49
04 Jan–31 Jan	149	179	79	24
01 Feb–07 Feb	169	199	99	24
08 Feb–14 Feb	189	219	149	29
15 Feb–21 Feb	225	239	149	34
22 Feb–07 Mar	179	199	109	29
08 Mar–21 Mar	189	213	129	29
22 Mar–28 Mar	225	315	179	44
29 Mar–04 Apr	259	275	179	44
05 Apr–11 Apr	229	259	159	39
12 Apr–25 Apr	224	249	129	39
26 Apr–30 Apr	219	245	109	39

Prices are based on: Four full fare paying passengers sharing a one bedroom apartment.
Supplements per full fare paying passenger per week:
3 sharing 1 bedroom apartment £7
2 sharing 1 bedroom apartment £13
Single in 1 bedroom apartment £32
3 sharing studio apartment £6
2 sharing studio apartment £11
Single in studio apartment £27

For flight details and supplements see page 7.
Prices are per full fare paying passenger, inclusive of return flights, transfers, airport taxes, accommodation and security charges.
One child up to 15 years of age per two full fare paying passengers and sharing accommodation pays the child price and does not count towards occupancy.

Reading

If you are working as an individual, make brief notes in response to these questions. If you are working in a group, discuss the questions, then make notes to prepare for your own writing.

♦ How has the travel company tried to persuade people to come to the Algarve? Think about what they have written about the Algarve and how they have written it.
♦ Advertisements often use positive words that create a 'feel good' factor. Pick out any words like this.
♦ What might attract you to Portugal and the Algarve?
♦ What type of people might be attracted by this advertisement?

Assignment 2

Imagine that your factual report on the hotel on page 34 has met with your company's approval and they have decided to include it in their summer brochure. Now you have been asked to write the description of the resort and the hotel for the brochure.

♦ Decide who you are going to target. The hotel is obviously a family hotel but young people may also enjoy staying there. Your target audience will affect what you decide to say and how you choose to say it.
♦ You can use the details included in your report but you can also add any other details about facilities that are likely to be available. For example, you may wish to talk about water sports on offer at the beach or describe the night-life in more detail.
♦ You will need to use positive language to persuade your target audience that this is the place they really want to go for their next holiday.

Key Points

♦ Now is a good time to review your **basic writing skills**. Are there any specific grammar, punctuation or spelling errors which you tend to repeat? Your tutor or teacher may help you to identify these.
♦ You will find examples of common errors and hints about how to improve your writing in the Key Points sections throughout this book and in 'Get it right' starting on page 192.

Writing to explain, describe – and complain

Imagine that you are a holiday-maker who stays at a hotel similar to the Vale Sao Joao on page 37 – maybe on a family holiday or on your honeymoon. The holiday does not meet your expectations and you keep a diary of complaints about the resort and the accommodation.

The plane was delayed by eight hours

Arrived tired and hungry at 2 in the morning

No food available

Work on hotel not finished

Builders woke us every morning at 6.00 am except Sunday!

Food was awful and very little choice

Portions small – not that we wanted to eat more of it, even a
stray dog we tried to give it to outside didn't want it!

Further from the sea than we were told. The sea was miles
away in reality! At least a twenty minute walk – especially
when you had to walk back uphill at the end of the day!

Not enough patio furniture for the numbers of guests

No bar on the outside terrace

Plane delayed by 12 hours coming home and no food offered at
the airport

The hotel staff were rude; like something out of Fawlty Towers!

Assignment 3

Write a letter of complaint to the travel company. Refer to the section on letter writing on page 226 to remind yourself of the layout of a formal letter.

Before you start, remember that:

♦ Business letters tend to be short, though not necessarily sweet!

♦ In the first paragraph you should introduce your reason for writing.

♦ In the second and, if necessary, a third paragraph you should describe your grievances. Do not be abusive.

♦ The final paragraph should explain the action you want the company to take and what you will do if they do not comply.

♦ The company should be given a date after which you will contact them again if nothing is done.

♦ This is a formal letter – be polite at all times and avoid slang.

Assignment 4

Now you decide to write to a friend telling them about your holiday from hell. The layout of this letter will be different and with a friend you can use informal language and show a little more of your real feelings. However, it is wise to avoid bad language in an assignment.

Review your writing

Look back at the three pieces of writing you have completed in this unit. Is each piece clearly aimed at a different audience and for a different purpose? Have you used different vocabulary and a different tone in each piece? How could you improve your writing?

Key Points

♦ Remember to look out for **common errors** in your writing. A frequent common error is mixing up the usage of **have** and **of**. Many students write 'of' when they should write 'have'.

♦ For example:

　We should of gone on holiday to France instead. ✗
　We should _have_ gone on holiday to France instead. ✔

　He would of fixed the bike if you had asked him. ✗
　He would _have_ fixed the bike if you had asked him. ✔

　You might of warned me. ✗
　You might _have_ warned me. ✔

To argue a point of view clearly you first need to have the facts to support your ideas. Read the articles on this page and the next, each of which give the arguments for and against an issue.

TO BELIEVE OR NOT TO BELIEVE IN GHOSTS

Reasons for believing in Ghosts

1 People have believed in Ghosts for hundreds of years. They think the dead can come back to haunt them.

2 Ghosts have been seen all over the world. There are many different stories about Ghosts.

3 In the United Kingdom there are estimated to be about 10,000 reputedly haunted sites.

4 Animals can behave in strange ways. They can see or feel things which people cannot.

5 There are Ghost stories about modern houses as well as old and creepy ones.

6 One in seven people think that they have seen a Ghost.

Reasons for not believing in Ghosts

1 Most people have never seen a Ghost.

2 People who think they have seen a Ghost might be ill.

3 No one can really prove that there are Ghosts.

4 Since we have had electric lights there have not been so many Ghost stories.

5 Smugglers were good at telling Ghost stories. This helped to keep people away from the places where they brought in their boats and smuggled goods.

Ghost Hunters

Should they all be banned?

YES The horrendous killing of 16 school-children and their teacher in the quiet Scottish town of Dunblane yesterday proves yet again that the time is long overdue to introduce a total ban on all firearms. Manchester, too, has seen fatal shootings.

The simple fact is that there are far too many guns in this country, and it is therefore far too easy for them to get into the wrong hands. Yesterday's slaughter in Scotland may have been the work of a maniac, but the fact remains that if he had not been able to get his hands on guns, he would not have been able to cause such terrible slaughter of innocent little children.

There have been too many such incidents involving guns. The Home Secretary should announce today that he is banning everyone, except police and the armed forces, from owning firearms. If that upsets some sportsmen, then that's tough. He might at least save some lives.

NO Let us not be panicked into intro-ducing hurried and unworkable legislation. The horrific shootings in Scotland yesterday were truly tragic, but that doesn't mean we should ban all firearms instantly. Many people in Britain need shotguns.

Farmers have to control vermin on their land, and to defend their sheep against foxes and other marauders. Are we suggesting that their weapons should be taken off them?

There are the many, well-run gun clubs in Britain, whose members are respectable and responsible. They get their firearms only after satisfying strict police rules, and they have to keep them in secure conditions. Shooting is an established sport, and people should be allowed to practise it if they wish.

If you ban guns, the only people to have them will be criminals, and rest assured that they will still get hold of them. A ban is just not on.

How you voted on:

FIREARMS

In the wake of the horrific killings at the school in Dunblane on Wednesday, we asked you yesterday if you thought that all firearms should be banned in this country. The result was close, with just over half the callers saying all firearms should be banned.

YES   53%

NO   47%

Manchester Evening News

Group oral work

Choose either the debate on ghosts or firearms, and discuss how you feel about it. Use the evidence in the articles and any other ideas you have to add weight to your arguments.

Assignments

1 Read the debate on Firearms. Individually, decide whether or not you agree with the issue. Have the arguments in the article helped to persuade you? How?

2 Read the article on Ghosts, and decide whether or not you believe in them. Write a few paragraphs to convince other people of your point of view. Use the information in the article and your own ideas.

Writing an argument

Many examination boards expect you to write essays arguing your point of view about an issue. Read the following title.

'The law is an ass. You can vote at eighteen, drive a car at eighteen but marry with your parents' consent at sixteen and have a child. But you still cannot drink legally or go to an eighteen movie. I think something should be done about this ridiculous state of affairs. I vote that we reduce the age of voting, driving, drinking and viewing to sixteen.'

Discuss this view of the law and whether you agree with this writer's viewpoint.

Step 1

Before you start to write, you need to be clear about how you feel.

♦ You may feel that the law is correct as it is.

♦ You may want to alter some laws and leave others as they are.

To help you decide, explore the discussion from different viewpoints. How do you feel about the following questions?

1 The law is to be changed, and young people will have to be eighteen before they can learn to drive.
   ♦ Why might the law have been changed?
   ♦ Do you think it is a good idea?
   ♦ In some places in America you can drive at the age of fifteen. How do you feel about this?
2 Do you think people are old enough to get married at sixteen? If so, should they be able to vote and drink alcohol?
3 At one time only married women could vote. Could we introduce a law where married women under the age of eighteen could vote? Why? Why not?

Step 2

When you have decided on your point of view, you have to prove your argument. To do this you must **state your case**. Write down your reasons for holding your point of view. Imagine you are in a court of law and you have to provide evidence to support your case.

♦ Explain your point of view at the outset, and the decision-making process which led you to it.

♦ Prove your argument is a strong and valid one – make sure you have at least five or six points to support your opinion.

You should also **attack** the arguments of the opposition, so you need to consider which arguments the opposition are likely to use and how you will argue against them.

Step 3

The **good essay** will:

♦ make the writer's viewpoint very clear. This is the most important part of the essay – the rest of it supports why the writer holds that opinion

♦ be planned, and follow a logical structure

♦ ensure that the viewpoint does not change, unless you have clearly stated that there are reasons for being unsure and are trying to present both points of view.

Now write your argument.

Key Points

You will find further practice in writing an argument in 'Television is bad for the brain', on pages 76–81.

An examiner advises...

♦ To be a good writer you need to think about **what** you are saying and **how** you are saying it, to interest the reader. Never forget your audience.

♦ If you are expressing opinions or writing to persuade or inform, think about the viewpoint you are going to take.

♦ Take care with the planning and organization of your writing.

Look at the beginning of this letter to the editor of a National newspaper expressing a personal opinion on the subject of the Lottery.

> Dear Editor
> I feel that I have got mixed feelings about the National Lottery each time there is a roll over it creates more hype than what's need   it takes up valuable room, uneaconomiclly when other, more important subjects should be taking priority. The best part of the National Lottery is the live draw   this gives people great excitment which otherwise they may not have   I think that three roll overs is enough and if there were any more then this would take the prize money to rediculous amounts   if it did happen to roll over again then the money should go to where the rest of it goes eg sports and leisure facilities. I agree with you by not giving any of the money to charities because larger charities would get more prefferance over the smaller ones even though they may be of equal importance...

Examiner's comment

This kind of writing really needs a sense of purpose. In trying to put his 'mixed feelings' this writer does not establish a convincing viewpoint. We are left wondering what exactly he is trying to say and why he wanted to write the letter.

The format is recognisable as a letter but it is careless and there are many spelling and grammar errors.

To improve the letter would require careful planning. It is possible to explore both sides of an argument but the writer does need to sort out where he stands and to develop the ability to use words such as 'although'. The letter needs paragraphs. As it stands, this piece of writing would be a Grade E/F.

Now look at a second letter on the same subject.

> Dear Sir/Madam,
> Having seen the many letters printed in the last edition of your newspaper concerning the National Lottery, I felt compelled to write in order to point out the many problems which have arisen in our society due to this institution.
>
> I have suffered first-hand because of the National Lottery myself; I have had to watch my daughter and son-in-law separate because of it. They won the 'jackpot' several months ago, and ever since then have argued bitterly over how to share out the money and what to do with it. This case is now likely to go to court.
>
> This is just one of the many problems the National Lottery causes. It not only divides families, but the whole idea behind it is wrong. It is wrong to encourage gambling, and the National Lottery does just that...

Examiner's comment

This response takes a hostile stance on the issue and argues it through forcefully. The first paragraph establishes the reason for writing and the line of argument. The format is perfect and the writer has a good sense of audience. She knows that a letter to a newspaper demands some formality and has adopted an appropriate style and tone. The writing is accurate, too. This is a clear Grade A*.

Key Points

For help with paragraphing, see 'Get it right', page 213.

UNIT 4

NON-FICTION and MEDIA

Introduction

Non-fiction texts include autobiographies, biographies, journals, diaries, letters, travel writing and leaflets. Media texts include magazines, newspapers, radio, television and film.

When you are responding to written non-fiction and media texts you need to think about these points:

♦ **Who** is the author writing for?

♦ **What** is the author trying to do? Look at whether he or she is giving you information, trying to persuade you to adopt a particular viewpoint, or writing to entertain.

♦ What is **fact** and what is **opinion**? They are often interwoven and it may be difficult to distinguish one from the other. You may have to think hard about this.

♦ Why is the writing **laid out** in a particular way? Look at the headings, subheadings and use of illustrations or photographs.

♦ Why has the author chosen to write in a particular **style**? Think about why he or she has chosen particular words and phrases.

This unit gives you practice in responding to non-fiction and to written media texts using questions similar to those you will find on your exam papers. At the end of the unit, a GCSE examiner explains how you can improve your grade by thinking about how to approach the questions in the examination. This unit also offers writing questions which can be used for exam practice or coursework and assignments for oral coursework.

And when did you last see your father?

This extract is taken from the first chapter of Blake Morrison's autobiographical account of the life of his father, who was a doctor. The book is a very moving account of how Blake Morrison comes to terms with his father's life and death.

   This is a good passage to use for practice. In it we learn a great deal about the father and the reaction of his family to his behaviour. Read the passage carefully once, then answer the questions.

Oulton Park

A hot September Saturday in 1959, and we are stationary in Cheshire. Ahead of us, a queue of cars stretches out of sight around the corner. We haven't moved for ten minutes. Everyone has turned his engine off, and now my father does so too. In the sudden silence we can hear the distant
5 whinge of what must be the first race of the afternoon, a ten-lap event for saloon cars. It is quarter past one. In an hour the drivers will be warming up for the main event, the Gold Cup - Graham Hill, Jack Brabham, Roy Salvadori, Stirling Moss and Joakim Bonnier. My father has always loved fast cars, and motor-racing has a strong British following just now, which
10 is why we are stuck here in this country lane with hundreds of others cars.

   My father does not like waiting in queues. He is used to patients waiting in queues to see him, but he is not used to waiting in queues himself. A queue, to him, means a man being denied the right to be where he wants to be at a time of his own choosing, which is at the front, now.
15 Ten minutes have passed. What is happening up ahead? What fat-head has caused this snarl-up? Why are no cars coming the other way? Has there been an accident? Why are there no police to sort it out? Every two minutes or so my father gets out of the car, crosses to the opposite verge and tries to see if there is movement up ahead. There isn't. He gets back
20 in and steams some more. The roof of our Alvis is down, the sun beating on to the leather upholstery, the chrome, the picnic basket. The hood is folded and pleated into the mysterious crevice between the boot and the narrow back seat where my sister and I are scrunched together as usual. The roof is nearly always down, whatever the weather: my father loves
25 fresh air, and every car he has owned has been a convertible, so that he can have fresh air. But the air today is not fresh. There is a pall of high-rev exhaust, dust, petrol, boiling-over engines.

In the cars ahead and behind, people are laughing, eating sandwiches, drinking from beer bottles, enjoying the weather, settling into the familiar
30 indignity of waiting-to-get-to-the-front. But my father is not like them. There are only two things on his mind: the invisible head of the queue and, not unrelated, the other half of the country lane, tantalizingly empty.

'Just relax, Arthur,' my mother says. 'You're in and out of the car like a blue-tailed fly.'

35 But being told to relax only incenses him. 'What can it be?' he demands. 'Maybe there's been an accident. Maybe they're waiting for an ambulance.' We all know where this last speculation is leading, even before he says it. 'Maybe they need a doctor.'

'No, Arthur,' says my mother, as he opens the door again and stands on
40 the wheel-arch to crane ahead.

'It must be an accident,' he announces. 'I think I should drive up and see.'

'No, Arthur. It's just the numbers waiting to get in. And surely there must be doctors on the circuit.'

45 It is one-thirty and silent now. The saloon race has finished. It is still over an hour until the Gold Cup itself, but there's another race first, and the cars in the paddock to see, and besides…

'Well, I'm not going to bloody well wait here any longer,' he says. 'We'll never get in. We might as well turn round and give up.' He sits
50 there for another twenty seconds, then leans forward, opens the glove compartment and pulls out a stethoscope, which he hooks over the mirror on the windscreen. It hangs there like a skeleton, the membrane at the top, the metal and rubber leads dangling bow-legged, the two ivory earpieces clopping bonily against each other. He starts the engine,
55 releases the handbrake, reverses two feet, then pulls out into the opposite side of the road.

'No,' says my mother again, half-heartedly. It could be that he is about to do a three-point turn and go back. No it
60 couldn't…

My father does not drive particularly quickly past the marooned cars ahead. No more than twenty miles an hour. Even so, it *feels* fast,
65 and arrogant, and all the occupants turn and stare as they see us coming. Some appear to be angry. Some are shouting. 'Point to the stethoscope,

pet,' he tells my mother, but she has slid down sideways in her passenger
70 seat, out of sight, her bottom resting on the floor, from where she berates
him.

'God Almighty, Arthur, why do you have to do this? Why can't you
wait like everyone else? What if we meet something coming the other
way?' Now my sister and I do the same, hide ourselves below the seat.
75 Our father is on his own. He is not with us, this bullying, shaming
undemocratic cheat. Or rather, we are not with him.

My face pressed to the sweet-smelling upholstery, I imagine what is
happening ahead. I can't tell how far we have gone, how many blind
corners we have taken. If we meet something, on this narrow country lane,
80 we will have to reverse past all the cars we have just overtaken. That's if
we can stop in time. I wait for the squeal of brakes, the clash of metal.

After an eternity of – what? – two minutes, my mother sticks her head
up and says, 'Now you've had it,' and my father replies, 'No, there's
another gate beyond,' and my sister and I raise ourselves to look. We are
85 up level with the cars at the head of the queue, which are waiting to turn
left into the brown ticket holders' entrance, the plebs' entrance. A steward
steps out of the gateway towards us, but my father, pretending not to see
him, doesn't stop. He drives ahead, on to the clear piece of road where,
two hundred yards away, half a dozen cars from the opposite direction are
90 waiting to turn into another gateway. Unlike those we have left behind,
these cars appear to be moving. Magnanimous, my father waits until the
last of them has turned in, then drives through the stone gateposts and
over the bumpy grass to where an armbanded steward in a tweed jacket
is waiting by the roped entrance.

95 'Good afternoon, sir. Red ticket holder?' The question does not come
as a shock: we have all seen the signs, numerous and clamorous, saying
RED TICKET HOLDERS' ENTRANCE. But my father is undeterred.

'These, you mean,' he says, and hands over his brown tickets.

'No, sir, I'm afraid these are brown tickets.'

100 'But there must be some mistake. I applied for red tickets. To be honest,
I didn't even look.'

'I'm sorry, sir, but these are brown tickets, and brown's the next
entrance, two hundred yards along. If you just swing round here, and…'

'I'm happy to pay the difference.'

105 'No, you see the rules say…'

'I know where the brown entrance is, I've just spent the last hour
queuing for it by mistake. I drove up here because I thought I was red. I
can't go back there now. The queue stretches for miles. And these
children, you know, who'd been looking forward…'

110 By now half a dozen cars have gathered behind us. One of them parks. The steward is wavering.

'You say you applied for red.'

'Not only applied for, paid for. I'm a doctor, you see' – he points at the stethoscope – 'and I like being near the grand-stand.'

115 This double *non-sequitur* seems to clinch it.

'All right, sir, but next time please check the tickets. Ahead and to your right.'

And when did you last see your father? by Blake Morrison

Reading

1 What do you learn about the father from this passage? What do you think of him and what he does? Use these prompts to help you:
  ♦ What does he like? What does he dislike?
  ♦ What does he do to avoid the queue?
  ♦ Would you do this?
  ♦ How does he deal with his family's reaction?
  ♦ How does this make you feel?
  ♦ How does he deal with the man at the gate?
  ♦ What ideas do you have about the type of person he is?
  ♦ Would you like him?

2 What do we learn about the rest of his family? How do they react to the father's behaviour? Use these prompts to help you:
  ♦ How does the mother try to pacify him?
  ♦ Look at the way his son describes him, 'this bullying, shaming, undemocratic cheat'.
  ♦ What does the family do when he overtakes?

FOCUS

Questioning the text

When you read a passage you will not always be given prompts for your answers as you are in questions 1 and 2. If you are not given prompts, you must ask yourself similar questions as you read and try to read between the lines. When responding to a text you must search for evidence to support your ideas. It is like being in a court of law: you have to prove your case.

3 What do you learn about the boy's character from this passage?

- Look for evidence in the passage which tells you about the boy's character.
- Decide what the evidence tells you about his character.
- Before you begin to write, decide in which order you are going to make your points. What evidence from the passage will you use to support each point?

4 How successful is the writer in building up a picture of this family and this event in their life and how does he sustain our interest?

FOCUS

Thinking about language

Question 4 is more demanding than questions 1, 2 and 3. You need to do more than discuss **what** the passage is about. You need to consider **how** the author writes. You must discuss the words used to describe events and the way Morrison uses words to build up the atmosphere in the car as the family waits in the queue. Finally, you need to think about how Morrison makes us want to read on. You could follow this structure:

- Look at the description of the queue and the car in the first three paragraphs. Pick out any lines or questions that you think give a good sense of atmosphere and explain why they do so.
- Look at the description of the father. Explain how the writer brings out his personality through descriptions of his behaviour and through his speech.
- Look at the description of the stethoscope (lines 52–55). Why does the writer describe it?
- Explain how the author builds up tension towards the end of the passage.

Writing assignments

1 Write an account of a tense incident which highlighted the worst characteristics of your family or friends.

2 Imagine that you have had to wait for a very long time in a traffic jam as a result of roadworks that were supposed to have been finished. Write a letter to your local council to complain about these roadworks. Explain how frustrated you felt and why – maybe you were trying to get to an airport on time, or you were late for a meeting. Also tell them about the behaviour of other drivers and passengers in the queue – perhaps someone left their car to complain to the people working on the road.

♦ When you are writing **sentences**, a common error is to use a comma where there should be a full stop followed by a new sentence. Take a look at this piece of writing.

> I'm writing to complain about the plans for a new road to be built at the end of Stocklake in Ayslesbury, I think it is a disgrace that the council can even think about building on fields and cutting down trees.
>
> I understand there is a need for another road to take traffic away from the town centre, however I think you could choose a route which would do less harm to the environment. You will be destroying woodlands which are home to animals and birds, local people have seen foxes and even badgers there.

Where do you think the commas should be replaced by full stops in this extract?

♦ Another fault, although maybe not as common, is to write a sentence which does not make complete sense. For example:

> It's a good idea to go to college after school. As you may not get a job without good qualifications.

'As you may not get a good job without good qualifications' is not a sentence because it does not make complete sense on its own. It should be joined to the first sentence to make one long sentence:

> It's a good idea to go to college after school, as you may not get a job without good qualifications.

♦ Always read through your own work to make sure:
 – your sentences make sense
 – you have begun new sentences in sensible places.

♦ You will find more about sentences on page 193.
 – You will find help with writing letters on page 226.
 – You will find help with personal writing on pages 19–31.

Drugs and sport

Reading

Read the article **I quit athletics because I refuse to take drugs**, on the opposite page.

1 Why did Matt Simson decide not to take drugs?

2 What evidence does he give to suggest that drug taking in shot putting is a big problem?

Read the article **Fuelled by drugs and hypocrisy** on pages 56–57.

3 List the drugs that are taken by ordinary people which could get you banned if you were an athlete.

4 What does the writer think about athletes and drug taking? How does he put this viewpoint across to the reader?

FOCUS

Looking at technique

The second part of question 4 is more challenging. It asks you to look at the content of the passage *and* the way the writer organises his material and the tone/mood of the passage.

♦ Look at the headline to the article. What is the writer suggesting by choosing these words?

♦ Look at the structure of the article. Why has the writer chosen to present the information in this order?

♦ Look at the 'other' drugs that ordinary people use. Why does the writer mention these? What type of people does he suggest take drugs?

♦ How does the writer use language to put across his own point of view?

5 Compare the two articles. How do the writers' attitudes to drug-taking in athletics differ? Which writer do you agree with and why? You might ask yourself:
   ♦ Why did Matt Simson quit athletics?
   ♦ What does the writer of 'Fuelled by drugs and hypocrisy' think about drug taking in everyday life?
   ♦ What does this writer think of athletics and drug taking? Why does he believe we shouldn't scorn them?
   Look at the last paragraph of each extract to help you.

'I quit athletics because I refuse to take drugs'

In the summer of 1994 I won the gold medal for England in the shot putt at the Commonwealth Games in Canada. This summer, at the age of 25, I turned my back on the sport I love.

It was something I did with reluctance but earlier this year I had to make a difficult choice. I knew that if I wanted to be the best in the world, to win a medal at next year's Olympic Games in America, I had to start taking anabolic steroids.

I discussed this with my wife Tonya, and to be truthful I was sorely tempted. Obtaining steroids would not have been a problem. I could have got them from a gym, from fellow athletes, even from a doctor.

Tonya was adamant that drug taking was wrong and she was worried about the long-term effects it might have on my health. For a time, I wavered but in the end I decided that I could not live with myself as a drugs cheat. I know that I won my gold medal "clean"; I am proud of my achievement and nobody can ever take it away from me.

Some people will be shocked that I was even tempted to cheat. But I knew that if I did not take steroids or some other banned performance-enhancing drug, the chances of my being the best in the world at the shot were remote.

At the Commonwealth Games last year I threw 19.49 metres, which is a good mark, but I knew that I can only achieve that sort of distance once a year, whereas if I took steroids I guess I would be able to throw close to my best in nearly every competition. Steroids enable an athlete to train harder, recover more quickly and therefore become stronger.

I started throwing the shot aged 13 at secondary school in Canvey Island, Essex. Later I represented

---

Matt Simson, a champion shot thrower, explains how his dream of competing in a clean sport soured

---

my country at boys, youth, junior and senior levels. At 19, I became aware of drug taking in athletics when I started coming up against Eastern European countries for the first time. It was easy to see that these people were mainly natural 14- to 15-stone competitors, yet some were coming in at 17 and 18 stones.

When I won the bronze medal in the European juniors competition at 19 I was content that there were only two people in Europe who could throw further than me in that year. But I was naive in thinking that if I just trained hard and worked hard, everything would be fine.

At senior rank, I started getting more disillusioned by the drug-taking that was going on all around me. At 6ft 5ins and 19 stone, I'm pretty strong; but some of the people I had been competing against as juniors began taking drugs.

They started doing bench press weight lifts of 600lbs and above, when my best ever was 400lbs.

Clean away: Simson felt he competed at a disadvantage

Some of these people had the worst throwing technique I had ever seen, yet the shot was still just flying. It was just unbelievable.

Some athletes would be open about taking drugs. Others would be able to list every anabolic steroid in the book and yet claim that they were "clean". I left the sport with many regrets. I have a great talent for throwing the shot and I never got the recognition I deserved. At the end of last year, I could say to myself, "well I believe I'm probably in the top six clean athletes in shot putt this year", but who cares? It did not mean anything to anybody because I might be ranked 40th in the world.

If I had gone on steroids, I honestly believe I could have won the gold at this year's world championships. It's no big deal for someone who has been clean to go on steroids and improve a metre and a half or two metres. But to win the world championship on steroids would mean nothing to me.

Most people look at athletics and think it is a glamorous sport. In reality it is very mercenary. I only ever really got involved in sport because it was fun. But all that has gone. Athletics has created a monster that is out of control; there seems little commitment to the fight against drugs when some countries call for a reduction in drug bans from four to two years. Life bans should be mandatory. Club athletics is still wholesome and enjoyable, but at international level the sport is very different. The need for sensation and new records to maintain the flow of money comes first, the health of the athletes a poor second. I am left with simple but depressing advice for young athletes: don't go into athletics at the highest level.

The Sunday Times

Fuelled by drugs and

Almost everyone is on something that would get an Olympic athlete banne

Even though it's not in the *Radio Times* schedule for the Olympics, we know that there is one event that is guaranteed plenty of TV exposure: the naming of the first athlete to be sent home after testing positive for drugs – or, more accurately, "banned substances".

Those athletes who do test positive – such as Andrew Davies and Andrew Saxton, the Welsh weightlifters sent home from Barcelona in 1992 – can expect to return home to a hail of abuse.

When (and it almost certainly is when) it happens this time, let us hope that none of the strong language comes from any of the 14 male MPs and lords who, we hear, have been taking artificial testosterone shots in order, as one prescribing doctor, Malcolm Carruthers, puts it, to "rev the engine and take the handbrake off". Apparently, our rulers had been finding the pressures of maintaining their seats and the long hours at the House too telling, and discovered that they needed something extra to keep them going.

And we can be sure, can't we, that no female representative taking hormone-replacement therapy (HRT) to artificially fend off the effects of aging

---

MPs and lords, we hear, have been taking testosterone shots to 'rev the engine and take the handbrake off'

---

will be first to the media barricades to condemn somebody for taking an artificial performance enhancer.

But – on the principle that it should be those without sin who cast the first stone – who is really in a position to lob the first chunk of abuse? Although we choose largely to ignore it, the fact is that Olympic (or aspiring) athletes stand apart from the rest of society not only for their abilities. The rest of us now comprise a society that depends so deeply on drugs to give us just that little bit extra to get us through the day that perhaps not a single one of us could reasonably expect to make the grade if we, like those athletes, were subjected to random urine testing.

Leave aside testosterone and HRT: how many people do you know who suffer from asthma and have to use an inhaler regularly? Or who take hay-fever tablets or remedies so that they can work or drive or go for a walk without their eyes and nose streaming? Sorry, that would test positive under the Olympic rules.

Perhaps you're one of the 2 million people on Prozac – now prescribed to many young mothers, who find the first five years of their children's lives exhausting. Or maybe you are on some other antidepressant.

Writing

1 Imagine that you are the parent of a child who does not enjoy taking part in competitive sport in school. However, your child does like exercise. Write a letter to the school outlining your objections and explaining why you think competitive sport is not a good thing for children to be encouraged to take part in. You may wish to use some of the ideas in the articles above, but try to include your own ideas as well.

2 Describe a time when you have taken part in a sport and really enjoyed it, or taken part in a sport and hated it. You could write about both occasions but you should concentrate on giving a detailed description of the event.

hypocrisy

says **Charles Arthur**

Not for nothing was Valium so well known as "mother's little helper".

85 Or are you one of the million people taking Ecstasy regularly, to give you that pep to get through a long night? Or one of the uncounted millions smoking

90 cannabis to relax after an infuriating day at work? Perhaps you're about to start a long drive home after a tiring day. Why not pop one of those concentrated

95 caffeine tablets to give you an amphetamine lift without the illegality? You know, of course, that all of those would get you banned from amateur sports.

100 Maybe you can pass all those tests – you treat your body as a temple, or nearly. But you want to have a drink after work, or over a business lunch to seal

105 that contract? You'll all have to go to the back of the queue of people lining up to be rude about so-called "disgraced" athletes.

110 If the drug is available, we'll find a way to use it. Stimulants to cope with the pressures of down sized offices, narcotics to escape the pressures of city life,

115 antidepressants to let us fit in when otherwise we'd be kicking and punching people off the pavement. Let's accept it, despite what Nancy Reagan

120 might have hoped for, we all long ago just said "yes".

But where do all these advances, which

125 take the rest of us forward into a world where we can manipulate our moods and our memory at

130 will, leave athletes? Rather than being the cream of our society, they are left somewhere outside.

135 They are living in a world where they have to dodge the drugs that lie in wait for them at every turn, in all those remedies and pick-me-

140 ups. It is as challenging as being a matador who evades a herd of raging bulls. One wrong move, and the testers will gore you.

145 Bearing that in mind, it's clear that the athletes who test positive don't deserve our scorn. They have already submitted to an existence

150 which is wholly outside that which the rest of us can imagine. Nowadays, to be an Olympic athlete takes not just talent and training, but all the

155 mental strength to live like an ascetic. The drug-takers aren't outcasts, except from this strange world of athletics.

The drugged Ben Johnson wins at the 1988 Olympics, only to be disqualified

They're not pariahs they're just

160 like all the rest of us. And we should welcome then back into the fold, not scorn them for leaving an artificial existence outside our own. Anything else

165 is just hypocrisy.

The Independent

Key Points

♦ You will find help with writing letters on page 226.

♦ You will find help with personal writing on pages 19–31.

♦ Use page 192 onwards to help you to check your grammar, punctuation and spelling.

The Village that lost its Children

This passage has been chosen to help you focus on the language used by a writer to show mood. Writers choose language carefully to convey emotions and build up an impression in our minds. You should read the passage carefully, noting especially how it has been written, and then answer the questions.

The Village that lost its Children

1 Few people had ever heard of Aberfan until disaster struck it. It was just another of the small mining ghettos lying tucked away in the sump of the South Wales valleys – a huddle of anonymous terraced houses of uniform ugliness unrelieved except for a chapel and pub.

2 Its heart was the coal-pit, and its environment like the others – the debris of a slowly exhausting industry: a disused canal, some decaying rail-tracks, a river black as the Styx, a general coating of grime over roofs and gardens, and the hills above blistered with a century of slag-heaps.

3 Such villages learned to accept a twilight world where most of the menfolk worked down the pits. Many died early, with their lungs full of coal-dust, and the life was traditionally grim and perilous. Disaster, in fact, was about the only news that ever came out of the valleys – the sudden explosion underground, miners entombed alive, or the silent death in the dark from gas. Wales and the world were long hardened to such news. But not to what happened in Aberfan…

4 A colliery sends to the surface more waste than coal, and a mining village has to learn to live with it. It must be put somewhere or the mine would close, and it's too expensive to carry it far. So the tips grow everywhere, straddling the hillside, nudging the houses like black-furred beasts. Almost everyone, from time to time, has seen the danger in them, but mostly they are endured as a fact of life.

5 On the mountain above Aberfan there were seven such tips. The evening sun sank early behind them. To some of the younger generation they had always been there, as though dumped by the hand of God. They could be seen from the school windows, immediately below them, rising like black pyramids in the western sky. But they were not as solid as they looked; it was known that several had moved in the past, inching ominously down the mountain.

6   What was not known however was that the newest tip, number 7, was a killer with a rotten heart. It had been begun in Easter 1958, and was built on a mountain spring, most treacherous of all foundations. Gradually over the years, the fatal seeping of water was turning Tip 7 into a mountain of moving muck.

7   Then one morning, out of the mist, the unthinkable happened, and the tip came down on the village. The children of Pantglas Junior School had just arrived in their classroom and were right in the path of it. They were the first to be hit by the wave of stupefying filth which instantly smothered more than a hundred of them.

8   The catastrophe was not only the worst in Wales but an event of such wanton and indifferent cruelty it seemed to put to shame both man and God…

9   The tragedy of Aberfan was to be of inertia – of danger which grew slowly for all to see, but which almost no one took steps to prevent. Now that the worst has happened, the process of healing also seems infected by the inertia of public authority and private grief – a dullness of shock and apathy which freezes the power of action.

10   Even today, a year later, the visitor needn't search hard for reminders; the stain of what happened is still nakedly visible. One sees the ineffectual little bulldozers, high on the mountain, patting and smoothing the remains of the tip. The black trail down the hillside left behind by the avalanche – a series of gigantic descending waves – is now covered by the fresh false innocence of grass which doesn't conceal its revolting power.

11   Where the waves broke on the village remains a terrible void, and little has been done to soften the horror. Sheered-off houses, broken walls and polluted back-gardens, a heap of smashed and rusty cars; these form a rim of wreckage around a central wilderness – the site where the school once stood.

12   Immediately after the disaster, in a kind of frenzy of outrage, all that was left of the school buildings was savagely bulldozed. It seems to have been the last attempt to obliterate the pain. The scene of the tragedy today, where a hundred and sixteen children died, is just a sloping area of squalid rubbish, a trodden waste – lying derelict in the rain.

13   Someone, over the months, has aimlessly tried to enclose it with a few old railings and bits of broken wire. The barrier is ineffective and almost obscene and only adds to the desolation. Walk across the site and the ground itself seems stifled, choked and littered with trash – old shoes, stockings, lengths of iron piping, lemonade cartons, rags. Fragments of the school itself still lie embedded in the rubbish – chunks of green-painted classroom wall – all gummed together by the congealed slime of the tip and reeking sourly of sulphurous ash.

14   Even more poignant relics lie in a corner of the buried playground, piled haphazardly against a wall – some miniature desks and chairs, evocative as a dead child's clothes, infant-sized showing the shape of their bodies. Among the rubble there also lie crumpled little song-books, sodden and smeared with slime, the words of some bed-time song visible on the pages surrounded by drawings of sleeping elves.

15   Across the road from the school, and facing up the mountain, stands a row of abandoned houses. This must once have been a trim little working-class terrace, staidly Victorian but specially Welsh, with lace-curtained windows, potted plants in the hall, and a piano in every parlour – until the wave of slag broke against it, smashed in the doors and windows, and squeezed through the rooms like toothpaste.

16   Something has been done to clear them, but not very much. They stand like broken and blackened teeth. Doors sag, windows gape, revealing the devastation within – a crushed piano, some half-smothered furniture. You can step in from the street and walk round the forsaken rooms which

still emit an aura of suffocation and panic – floors scattered with letters, coat-hangers on the stairs, a jar of pickles on the kitchen table. The sense of catastrophe and desertion, resembling the choked ruins of Pompeii, hangs in the air like volcanic dust.

17 But the raw, naked, inexplicable scar on the village remains the site of the school itself – that festering waste of sombre silence from which no one can take their eyes. Why, one wonders, after all this time, has it not been cleared or decently covered? It seems that the people of Aberfan are made powerless by it, spellbound, unable to move. The ground is so seared with memory it has become a kind of no-man's land, a negative limbo paralysing the will, something poisoned, sterile and permanently damned, on which nothing can be planted, nothing built.

18 The aftertaste of the macabre which still affects the village is strengthened further by its attraction for sightseers. The streets of Aberfan are narrow, and not built for traffic, so the bulldozed site of the Junior School itself has become the most convenient carpark for tourists. Almost any fine afternoon you will see them arrive, parents and children with cameras and balloons, clambering over the ruins and up and down the railway embankment eating ice-creams and photographing each other.

19 I remember young lovers arm-in-arm, wandering around the devastated waste; a green-suited blonde posing against a slag-heap; another in shorts hitching a ride on a bulldozer; an elegant old lady poking at pieces of rubble.

20 They had come, they had seen it – the shock of Aberfan for an outing, to take home with their snaps and seaweed. Visitors from America, Canada and Australia, too, tip-toeing carefully with large round eyes. With a certain eagerness also exclaiming, 'My, wasn't it just terrible?' Approaching a miner with a hushed enquiry. 'Excuse me, please,' – pointing down – 'but are they still under there?…' 'What was it like – were you here that day?'

21 Most of the villagers seem in no way distressed by this, visitors are a comfort rather than an intrusion. The stories begin again for each newcomer, recited in a kind of dream.

22 … Yet the trippers, scrambling over the slag in their bright holiday clothes, are on the whole not a lovely sight. As one old miner exclaimed, 'Why don't they bring their buckets and spades? There's plenty of dirt for them to dig.'

23 But some of the Welsh visitors, one notices – those from the neighbouring coal-valleys – are subtly different from any of the others.

24 They come in silent families, without questions or cameras, but bring their children too – walking them quickly over the ruins and hold on to their arms, feeling their living flesh …

I Can't Stay Long by Laurie Lee

Reading

Group or individual response

Discuss, or make notes in response to the following questions:

a) Look at paragraphs 1, 2 and 3.

   What picture does Laurie Lee paint of this place and the people who lived there? Would you wish to go there?

b) Look at paragraphs 4, 5 and 6.

   What do you learn about the coal tips and especially tip number 7? How does the writer use language to show that these tips were dangerous?

FOCUS

Looking at imagery

Pick out words and phrases that show how dangerous this tip was.

How does the writer use language to create images in our minds? Can you find any **similes** or **metaphors** in the writing?

Laurie Lee makes the mountain seem alive and human by giving it human characteristics. We call this **personification**. Can you find an example of this?

Look at the way some phrases start with the same letter 'a mountain of moving muck'. This is called **alliteration**. The use of alliteration can make a description more vivid and easier for a reader to imagine. Why do you think this author uses alliteration?

What else does the writer compare the tips with?

---

c) Look at paragraphs 7, 8 and 9.

   What happened on the morning of the disaster? How does the writer use language to express his anger to the reader?

d) Look at paragraphs 10, 11 and 12.

   In the passage as a whole Laurie Lee builds up a depressing picture of Aberfan. How do these three paragraphs add to this picture? Pick out anything in these paragraphs that might sadden a reader. You need to look carefully at how he describes the disaster scene.

e) Look at paragraphs 13, 14 and 15.

   Why do you think the writer includes such a detailed description of the disaster site? How does the language used by the author emphasise the tragedy?

f) Look at paragraph 16 to the end.

   What does the writer think generally of the visitors who go to Aberfan? How do some of the Welsh visitors differ? What do you think about the way this passage ends?

2 Write your own response to the article. Explain briefly what caused the tragedy at Aberfan. What impression of Aberfan does the writer create and how does he do this? How does he portray his own feelings about the events? Use these prompts to help you:

♦ Summarise briefly the events that led up to the disaster and its results.

♦ Think closely about your response to the questions on the previous page, which helped you to focus on the writer's language.

♦ Think about the description of Aberfan before and after the tragedy.

♦ Study how the writer conveys his own feelings about the tragedy.

Writing

1 Describe and write about a place that you find distressing or disturbing because of the way it looks. This might be a place that has had a profound effect on you, as Aberfan obviously had on Laurie Lee.

2 Write an article for a newspaper that describes a place that has been transformed, or one that should be. Explain what it was like and how it has changed, or if it is yet to be done, how you would transform it.

> ### Sue Davies writes…
>
> 'As a child I lived very near to Aberfan. The morning of this disaster remains vivid in my mind. I was in the car with my father when we heard about it over the radio and the sheer horror of it affected both of us. I remember that he hugged me. I was only eight at the time, but like most children I understood death.
>
> 'Later, my father and I spent evenings collecting for Aberfan. It seemed a strange thing to do, to give money, and a poor way of saying 'Sorry'. It was one way however, of showing that the suffering of Aberfan was a shared one, a communal grief.
>
> 'I have agonised over using this passage. To focus on the language of the passage and to use it as an exercise could seem callous to some. This is not the intention. The intention is to remind people of a tragedy that cost a village more than we can possibly imagine and to remind people why it happened.'

Key Points

♦ You will find help with personal writing on pages 19–31.

♦ You will find help with writing description on pages 24–25.

♦ For help with grammar, punctuation and spelling, turn to 'Get it right' starting on page 192.

Read the articles that follow: **Cancer charity falls victim to Lottery fever**, **Just like Santa!** and **Lottery profits are in wrong pockets**.

Cancer charity falls victim to Lottery fever

JENNY WALFORD and NICK HORTON

CANCER charity Tenovus has become the first major victim of the National Lottery placing the future of pioneering medical
5 research in serious doubt.

The Welsh-based group has been forced to scrap its own lottery, which raises £1.5m annually – half its total income –
10 for studies into the disease.

And there were warnings last night that many other charities face a crisis because of the runaway success of the Lottery.

15 The Government was accused of ignoring fears that the game would kill off rivals which offer much smaller winnings.

Labour Welsh health spokesman
20 Rhodri Morgan said, 'We want a National Lottery, not a national steamroller.'

Tenovus organisers blame the launch of the National Lottery's
25 £50,000 Instants scratch card for the collapse of its own scheme, which carries a top prize of £5,000. Though the Government has increased charities' maximum
30 possible payout to £25,000, it is too late for Tenovus.

It has lost most of its shop sales, and seen a 25 per cent drop at remaining stores.
35 Many supermarkets like Asda and Tesco, previous Tenovus

lottery territory, now stock the Instants cards instead because of their 'vast' profits.
40 More than 500 mainly part-time workers will be made redundant, Tenovus will announce this morning.

It plans to ask the Government
45 for compensation.

Some of the main victims could be scientists in Wales, who often rely on grants from charities to fund their work. A Tenovus
50 scientist said funds were already squeezed, and researchers were having to apply for extra grants from elsewhere.

One said the research they had
55 been undertaking into breast and prostate cancer could not now expand.

Michael Downs, Tenovus organising secretary, said, 'The
60 decision to close was almost inevitable once the Government chose to ignore our arguments that National Lottery scratch cards would kill off not only our lottery,
65 but the majority of other lotteries in the UK.'

Tenovus, which last year celebrated its 50th anniversary,

has become one of Britain's
70 biggest independent cancer charities from small beginnings in Cardiff. Its lottery raised £10m in the last 15 years.

It says it is 'not in immediate
75 danger'. It may open more shops, adding to the 28 it has. But Mr Downs said these would never earn as much as its lottery, and it would have to rely more than ever
80 on supporters.

Cardiff West MP Mr Morgan urged National Heritage Secretary Stephen Dorrell to persuade Camelot to donate some of its
85 profits towards medical charities which have suffered.

Other forms of gambling have also been badly affected, such as the pools companies, whose
90 donations to good causes will also fall as a result.

Welsh Secretary John Redwood declined to comment yesterday, and said it was a matter for the
95 Department of National Heritage.

A Heritage spokesman said the department was monitoring the situation but added if Tenovus felt it could no longer compete, 'it is
100 their decision to stop operating.'

● A record jackpot of £19m for Saturday's National Lottery was forecast yesterday by organisers Camelot.

Western Mail

JUST LIKE SANTA!

Family's joy at lottery win

A FAMILY of five from Llanharan is celebrating a £72,656 win on the National Lottery today.

David and Jayne Cox and their three children, Rebecca, nine, Laura, six and eight-month-old Mark, collected their winnings this morning.

Mrs Cox, 30, told the Echo: "David was in the pub and I was dressed in my nightie watching the draw with the girls.

"When we got three numbers I thought we had won £10, we missed the fourth and then we got the fifth. I went to phone my mum and then Rebecca called out that we had got the bonus ball too. We spent an anxious time until 9.30pm, waiting to find out how much we had won. We will bank the money until after Christmas and then look at buying a new house."

BRYAN THICKINS has handed out more than £33m to lottery winners over the last 12 months and he says it makes him feel like Santa Claus all year round.

Former television engineer Mr Thickins has been the regional manager for Camelot's Cardiff office since the Lottery began a year ago today and he is the one who gets to meet all the winners.

"It is a terrific job," he said. "I must be one of the only people in the country who never gets that Monday morning feeling. It is our busiest day and you never know who is going to walk through the door.

"They come in penniless and leave a lot better off."

Mr Thickins says the job isn't without its downside – and he has sometimes had to explain to would-be winners that they are not as rich as they might have thought.

"When it first started some people didn't seem to fully understand the rules and they came in thinking they had won when they hadn't. Fortunately that doesn't happen so much now," he said.

By Sarah Dutton

Mr Thickins may be the man with the money, but he is keen to point out that all winnings are paid out in a cheque and cash is never handed out.

"The smallest cheque I have ever written is £1 and I can't tell you how many jackpot cheques because the winners have all opted to keep their success quiet.

"We do keep in touch with our big winners, and they often send us postcards from their exotic holidays.

"One of my favourite moments in this job was just before Christmas last year.

"A man came into our office in tears. He had won £4,700, and it was enough to save his home from being repossessed and to buy his kids some Christmas presents. That is when I felt like Santa Claus and I thought this is what the job is really all about.

"I also had a bloke come in whose marriage had ended, he had lost his job and his life was in ruins. He came in on New Year's Eve with a largish claim and he was able to build a new life for himself."

Lottery cash boost for Diversions Dance

A CARDIFF-BASED dance company can hit the road and take its productions to venues throughout Wales and Europe thanks to a grant from the National Lottery.

Diversions Dance has been given £22,500 to buy a new lorry, which will replace an unreliable old truck that the company had been using.

Artistic director Roy Campbell Moore, who set up Diversions Dance 12 years ago, said: "The old truck left us in some doubt about whether or not we would get to the next venue. The National Lottery award has been terrific fillip to the company."

Bryan Thickins, Cardiff's regional manager for Camelot said: "I'm very pleased that Diversions Dance has been able to benefit from the success of the National Lottery."

Was it you? The story so far...

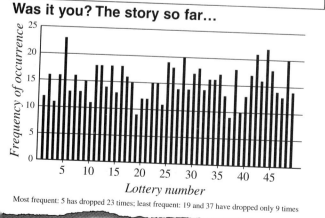

Most frequent: 5 has dropped 23 times; least frequent: 19 and 37 have dropped only 9 times

South Wales Echo

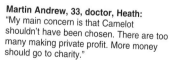

Lottery profits are in wrong pockets

Dan O'Neill

IF Tony Blair wins the next election I hope that one of his first acts is to find some way – any way – of booting Camelot
5 out of the lottery business.

I am still wondering how they got the franchise in the first place, considering that Richard Branson would have given ALL the profits to charity and what are generally
10 referred to as "good causes".

And make no mistake. Those profits are colossal.

Just 18 weeks after the start I see that Camelot have already picked up an astonishing
15 £121m – only four million quid short of the cash they invested to start those bingo balls rolling. The consortium predicted that it would take about £80m of the lottery money in the first year. Instead the figure looks set to be
20 closer to £350m, with the new scratch cards adding another £85m. By the time the franchise runs out in 2001 we are talking hundreds of millions of pounds profit.

Cash which would – under Branson – have
25 gone into the communities.

Libraries need help to survive

I recently came across another story which is relevant. The library service faces a terminal crisis if some £611m isn't found – soon. Like our schools, library buildings are crumbling,
30 there's no cash for book-buying, and essential equipment is missing.

Yet there is no National Lottery cash available. In fact, the attitude towards this most necessary public service beggars belief. The
35 Arts Council's lottery director Jeremy Newton delivered himself of the cretinous remark that libraries did not qualify "because they did not promote literature as an art form."

If he's typical of the men running the lottery
40 we've backed a loser in Camelot. So while libraries close for lack of funds, millions go to the Camelot Consortium of five companies who are already awash with cash.

So there you are Tony. Sort things out – and
45 give Branson a second chance at the lottery franchise.

As things stand the National Lottery is just one more example of this government's determination to make the very rich very much
50 richer.

NATIONAL LOTTERY: Huge profits are being made.

South Wales Echo

Group oral work

In a group make a list of the disadvantages and advantages of the Lottery highlighted in these articles. Decide whether you think the disadvantages outweigh the advantages. Reach a consensus and report back to the class.

Reading

1 Re-read **Cancer charity falls victim to Lottery fever** (page 64) and **Lottery profits are in wrong pockets**, above.

Look at the way these two articles are written. How do they try to persuade us to think badly of the Lottery? Which article is the most effective and why? Use the following prompts to make notes to help you plan your answer.

Focus on 'Cancer charity falls victim to Lottery fever'.

♦ Read paragraph 2, in particular. What are Tenovus scrapping and why?

♦ What else does Tenovus say has been affected by the Lottery?

♦ How many people will lose their jobs?

♦ Who will be the main victims?

♦ What research will be affected?

♦ What might the long term affects of the Lottery be on Tenovus?

Focus on 'Lottery profits are in the wrong pockets'.

♦ How much money did Camelot make in 18 weeks?

♦ Why does the writer of this article mention Richard Branson?

♦ Why does the writer mention the library service?

Comparison

♦ Look at the language used in both extracts. Which one uses the most emotion/emotive language?

♦ Which one gives the most information about the Lottery and how it is run?

♦ Which one tells you most about how the Lottery has affected charities?

2 Read the article **Just like Santa!** again.

♦ Which parts of the article show the Lottery in a positive light?
  Which parts of the article show the Lottery in a negative light?

♦ Why do you think Sarah Dutton chose to portray a positive view of the Lottery in this article?

♦ How does the article create a sense of excitement about the Lottery?
  Think about:
  – use of layout and pictures
  – the headlines and sub-headings
  – use of language.

3 Now read the article **Numbers prove Lottery's success** and the charts provided by Camelot, on pages 68–69.

♦ How does this article try to persuade you that the Lottery is a good thing?

♦ Is there anything in this article that would make you doubt its reliability?

♦ Do the charts encourage you to think well or badly of the Lottery?

4 Compare **Just like Santa!** and **Numbers prove Lottery's success**.
  How does each article try to convince you that the Lottery is a good thing?
  Think about:
  ♦ content   ♦ layout   ♦ organisation   ♦ use of language.

Writing

Write two letters to one of the newspapers from which the articles have been taken. One letter should be written by a person in favour of the Lottery and one written by a person who is against it. You will need to support your ideas with evidence taken from the news stories and any other ideas of your own.

Key Points

♦ You will find help with writing letters on page 226.

♦ You will find help with personal writing on pages 19–31.

♦ For help with grammar, punctuation and spelling, turn to 'Get it right' on page 192.

Numbers prove Lottery's success

Research shows that the National Lottery is not only the biggest in the world but also makes the second highest contribution in tax and donations to good causes as a percentage of sales.

Camelot hands over 41 per cent, just behind the New Jersey lottery on 42 per cent.

Camelot, which has said it is among the most efficient, has looked at most of the other 165 lotteries around the world to see how it ranks.

The company comes first in sales per employee, at $14.3m (£9.1m). It fares worse, however, on operating expenses as a percentage of total sales. Its figure of 13.1 per cent compares with 6.8 per cent in Puerto Rico and 8.3 per cent in New Jersey. The UK lottery is 12th by contribution to government on a per capita basis.

The figures emerged yesterday as Camelot marked the first anniversary of the launch of ticket sales. By the time the 52nd set of numbers is drawn on Saturday the National Lottery will have sold 4.5bn £1 tickets for the online draw and the Instants scratchcards. Prizes will have totalled more than £1.2bn, the five 'good causes' will have benefitted by more than £1.2bn and the Treasury will have collected £500m in duty.

So far 132 millionaires have been created.

But although the National Lottery has been more successful more quickly than almost anyone imagined, and sales from the online game have increased from £63m a week to £65.8m on average in the past three months, there is still some way to go if predictions are to be met.

Camelot will not only have to maintain its current level of sales but increase the total.

It forecast that lottery sales would peak at £5.5bn a year and that over the seven years of the licence £9bn would go to the "good causes" – the arts, charities, the national heritage, a Millennium Fund and sports.

While admitting that the National Lottery meant competition for other parts of the gambling industry, Camelot said that thousands of jobs had been created and the businesses of many independent retailers rejuvenated.

The Henley Centre, the economic forecasting organisation, had warned that in the first year the damage for competing industries, such as off-course betting, could turn out to be a 35 per cent fall in profits and 7,400 jobs lost.

On the more positive side, Henley believes lottery outlets have seen sales rise by between 6 per cent and 20 per cent, generated by an extra 10m to 12m "lottery shopping trips" a week.

Camelot yesterday also issued data on who plays the National Lottery, how often and to what extent.

Two-thirds of the UK population play weekly, although 90 per cent have played at some time.

The average spending is £2.33 a week, low by continental European standards. It varies little across social groups, with the biggest spending by the C2 group of skilled workers at £2.49. The unskilled DEs spend £2.30 on average and the AB professionals £2.33.

Camelot believes that players divide into four characteristic types. The biggest group – 40 per cent – are the 'fun-loving moderates' who are middle market and spend an average amount on the lottery because they enjoy it.

A further group of 26 per cent, mainly young males aged 16 to 34 who enjoy pubs, clubs and takeaways, are 'the big prize dreamers' who are playing for the large jackpot.

A 19 per cent group, spread across all age groups, are quite anti-gambling but play because everyone else is and it is something to talk about.

The final 15 per cent are likely to be older than 55 and unenthusiastic about many things. They play the lottery as something to do.

Regional sales per head also vary across the UK, with Northern Ireland recording the lowest and London the highest.

The statistics show that the unluckiest place to play the online National Lottery game seems to be Wales. Welsh players have spent £238m and got only £78m back in prizes. The Yorkshire region has spent £307m and won £171m in prizes.

Amid the celebrations yesterday the darker side of the National Lottery intruded briefly.

Mr David Rigg, Camelot's director of communications, said the company would be prepared to help fund, together with gambling addiction organisations, independent research on the effects of the National Lottery and scratchcards in particular.

The Financial Times

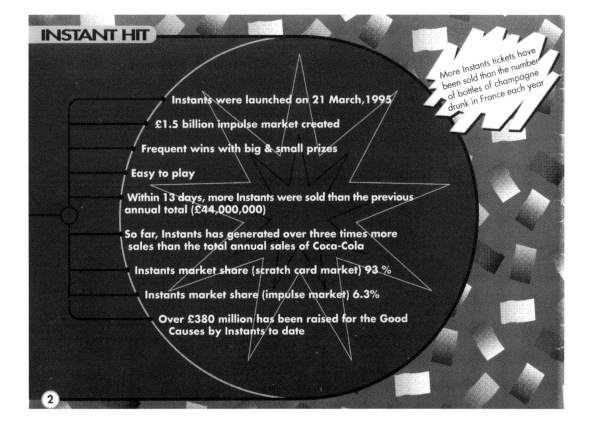

INSTANT HIT

Instants were launched on 21 March, 1995

£1.5 billion impulse market created

Frequent wins with big & small prizes

Easy to play

Within 13 days, more Instants were sold than the previous annual total (£44,000,000)

So far, Instants has generated over three times more sales than the total annual sales of Coca-Cola

Instants market share (scratch card market) 93 %

Instants market share (impulse market) 6.3%

Over £380 million has been raised for the Good Causes by Instants to date

More Instants tickets have been sold than the number of bottles of champagne drunk in France each year

2

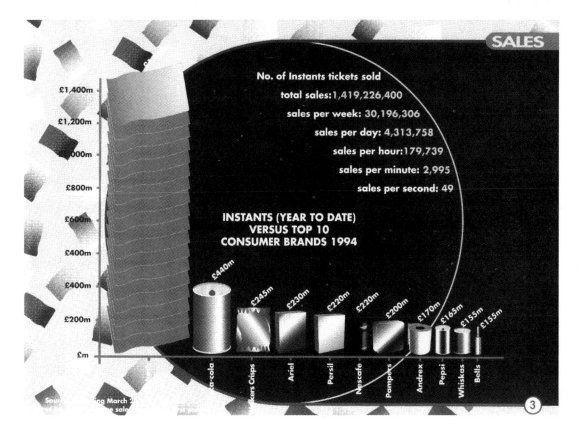

SALES

No. of Instants tickets sold

total sales: 1,419,226,400

sales per week: 30,196,306

sales per day: 4,313,758

sales per hour: 179,739

sales per minute: 2,995

sales per second: 49

**INSTANTS (YEAR TO DATE)
VERSUS TOP 10
CONSUMER BRANDS 1994**

£1,400m
£1,200m
£1,000m
£800m
£600m
£400m
£400m
£200m
£m

£440m — Coca-cola
£245m — Walkers Crisps
£230m — Ariel
£220m — Persil
£220m — Nescafe
£200m — Pampers
£170m — Andrex
£165m — Pepsi
£155m — Whiskas
£155m — Bells

3

Is he keeping the tourists away?

This is the face of Heritage Britain the Government would rather visitors did not see. It is not a feature of the glossy travel brochures that will attract 20 million foreign visitors to this country – and keep afloat a £25 billion-a-year industry that employs 1.5 million people.

But it is what tourists can look forward to when they visit Britain's historic cities and towns this summer – being hounded by a new plague of young beggars.

They demand money, sometimes with menaces, from unsuspecting visitors whose idyllic image of Britain's past is being rapidly shattered.

Whether taking in the medieval streets of York, the Regency splendour of Brighton, or the historic heart of London, overseas holidaymakers have become the new target for the growing army of scroungers.

Now Ministers are to launch a crackdown on these ugly gangs – with their torn and filthy T-shirts, matted hair and pitiful stories – who are feeding on the rich pickings of Britain's tourist industry.

Heritage Minister Iain Sproat is examining ways to stop the hordes of beggars, often working in large groups, setting up camp in the shadow of our most historic cities.

Last night Mr Sproat told *The Mail on Sunday*: 'We cannot let our great heritage fall foul of this. People come from all over the world to enjoy our history and it is being tarnished beyond belief by beggars who home in on tourists.'

'The current laws on begging are unsatisfactory. But I am determined to stamp this out before it destroys a valuable industry.'

He will tell local authorities to use dormant local by-laws to tackle the beggars.

And if that fails, he is expected to back a tough new clampdown – so far resisted by Government lawyers – to bring in a new offence of 'aggravated begging' to stop the pests.

But the new menace goes much further than the traditional begging grounds of the capital.

Police have told us that targeting tourists can be highly lucrative, with beggars earning up to £100 a day in the high season.

City officials in York say beggars are threatening to ruin its image as a tourist haven.

More and more are pouring into the city's tight network of medieval streets, an unwanted deterrent for its two and a half million yearly visitors.

'It is threatening to ruin tourism in the city,' said York council city centre manager, a former police superintendent.

'Begging used to be a rarity, but now it's become commonplace. In the tourist high season the police are constantly having to deal with people who have frightened, intimidated or harassed visitors.'

'They sit on the streets or in shop doorways with their dogs frightening women and older people. We even had an American tourist who had a small denomination coin thrown back at him.' Last year the city's police launched a crackdown, clearing the streets of beggars and trying to encourage them to leave town.

Beggars making £100 a day who threaten Britain's visitors – and a £25 bn industry

Superintendent Steve Green, of York police, said: 'We were arresting six or seven in a week and found some who appeared to be professional beggars, taking advantage of the tourists.' But the beggars keep coming. Homeless Dave, 36, came to York from his hometown of Stourbridge, in the West Midlands.

He said: 'I came here because York is a good patch for begging – I can make about £20 a day from the visitors. The foreigners are the best catch.'

German car-worker Hans Dietter, on holiday from Stuttgart, said: 'I just tell them to get lost. But the problem is way beyond what we have at home. These people are quite menacing. They hang around outside the hotel and target foreigners.'

Reading

1 Read the newspaper article and discuss the impression of beggars that is being built up.

2 Using evidence from the article, explain:
- **a)** what the writer thinks of the beggars
- **b)** how the writer conveys those feelings to the readers.

Use these prompts to help you:
- ♦ Make notes on what the writer says about the beggars and how they live.
- ♦ Think about how the writer conveys his thoughts.

It is a similar story in Exeter where
10 the cathedral is a magnet for tourists and
beggars alike.

Visitors' illusions of the magnificent
building are soon shattered as they find
its precincts littered with used condoms,
15 broken bottles, lager cans, syringes
and human excrement – the residue of

the vagrant population. Chief
Superintendent John Lilley, head of
Exeter police, said: 'We have our fair
20 share of dossers and beggars around the
cathedral. There is no doubt they put
tourists off.

'There are two centres for homeless
people nearby and in summer an influx
25 of New Age travellers makes the
problem worse.'

Exeter Tourism Information officer
David Burkimsher said: 'Exeter has a
problem with beggars who give visitors
30 a very bad impression of a beautiful city.

'They are bad for trade, and bad for the
image of Exeter.'

In Bath, where two million visitors
were attracted to the city's Roman
135 baths and magnificent abbey last year,
the council, police and shopkeepers
have been working together to try to
discourage beggars and shake off its
image as a popular centre for New Age
140 travellers.

David Pratley, Bath's director of
leisure and tourist services, said: 'We
have worked strenuously over the last
two years to reduce the number of
145 threatening beggars.

'We launched *The Big Issue,* a
newspaper to help the homeless, and
that has made a major difference
because it has sorted out those who are
150 genuinely destitute and homeless from
those opportunistic beggars who move
in during the tourist season.'

Similar problems in Bristol were
brought to the Government's attention in
155 January when public relations
consultant Tim Stanley asked visiting
Home Secretary Michael Howard what
the Government was doing about the
homeless scaring away tourists.

160 Mr Howard's response disappointed
Mr Stanley. 'He said if we were
asking for practical advice we should
keep our pressure on the police, and that
it was up to us to see the police resolve
165 the problem.'

Yesterday Mr Stanley, a member of
the Bristol Tourist Forum – made up of
officials and business people – said he
would welcome any Government action
170 to rid the streets of beggars.

'This is a major problem. We have
been told by the police that something
would be done about it, but, as far as I
am aware, there is no evidence that
175 either the police or the council are doing
anything.

'If you are trying to present a
favourable image, people begging on the
streets makes it unpleasant and un-
180 attractive, and visitors are likely to go
somewhere else.'

The message is stark for Ministers.
Britain will open its doors this summer
to millions who want to soak up our
185 heritage. They should not let them
leave with an image more Times Square
than Middlemarch.

The Mail on Sunday

Shelter

Now read this material published by Shelter. As you read, think about how this information about the homeless contradicts the information in the newspaper article, then turn to page 74.

FIVE FACES OF HOMELESSNESS...

WHO IS IN PRIORITY NEED?

Local councils have a legal duty to help homeless people. For some groups of people that help might just be referring them to an advice centre, but for those they consider to be in priority need they have a legal duty to provide temporary housing immediately.

You are unlikely to be accepted as 'in priority need' if you are a single person or a childless couple.

Even if you are accepted by a council as 'in priority need', you then have to prove that you are not 'intentionally homeless'. For example, a family which feels unable to live in a council house because of racial harassment packs its bags and turns to its local authority for help. If the family can't prove harassment it may be considered 'intentionally homeless'. Even if the council does decide that you are intentionally homeless, it is still obliged to provide you with temporary accommodation and help and advice in finding a home.

Priority Need is defined as covering:

1 families with dependent children

2 pregnant women

3 people who are vulnerable because of old age, physical disability or mental health problems

4 people vulnerable for other reasons which might include young people 'at risk' or survivors of violence in the home

5 people made homeless by an emergency (such as a fire)

'For three years I was sexually abused by my brother. My parents didn't believe me, so I left to get away from it.'

'My landlord threw me out when he found out I was pregnant.'

'I found it impossible to manage my money. Before long I got behind with the rent and I was evicted.'

'My mother kicked me out because she didn't want me there. She'd got a new boyfriend.'

'I was made redundant twice, and couldn't keep up the repayments on my mortgage. Our home was repossessed.'

THE TRUTH ABOUT HOMELESSNESS

1 **People sleeping rough are scroungers – they don't want to work.** Most people who beg do so as a last resort. They have no choice. Would you sit in the rain and beg if there was another way of getting money? Don't forget that if you don't have a family to go home to and you are 16 or 17 years old, then you don't have an automatic right to help from the state.

2 **People who sleep on the streets spend their money on drink and drugs.** It is true that some people who sleep rough do have drink or drug problems. But so do many people who are not homeless.

3 **It's a great life sleeping on the streets. No wonder people choose to do it.** 30% of people who sleep out have been sexually and/or physically abused at some time in their life. Women who sleep out are at greater risk of sexual assault and rape.

4 **Squatters are vandals.** Very few squatters damage their squats. Nearly a third of squatters are parents. They want to provide a clean and safe home for their children. They don't want to vandalise it – often they carry out repairs on unused properties. People squat because they have no alternative, because there are not enough affordable homes to go around.

5 **Women get pregnant to get a place to live.** Pregnant single women do not have any priority over couples with children. Evidence shows that when a pregnant woman or young mother becomes homeless it is generally because her relationship with the child/children's father has broken down.

6 **Why don't homeless people go home?** Because they haven't got a home to go to. In Wales, between a quarter and a third of young homeless people have left council care so they have nowhere to go. Others have been forced to leave home because of rows with their parents who can't afford to keep them – or worse still because of violent fathers.

7 **Homelessness only happens in cities.** Homelessness is a major problem in rural villages and small towns too – it is just not so visible. Many rural properties have been bought by more wealthy people from the cities. This forces up property prices in the area, making it more difficult for local people to afford to live there.

8 **Council housing is unnecessary.** Many people cannot afford the rent that private landlords charge, nor can they afford to buy their own homes. So it is vital to provide affordable housing in some other way. Shelter Cymru estimates that another 10,000 affordable rented homes are needed in Wales each year for the next five years, simply to stop matters getting worse. These should come from councils, housing associations and private landlords all providing homes for rent.

9 **Providing enough accommodation for everyone would cost the taxpayer too much.** Wrong. Too much money is already being spent on mortgage subsidies and temporary accommodation such as bed and breakfast. This money could be better spent on providing affordable, long-term accommodation.

10 **It's better to buy a home of your own.** Home ownership is right for some people, but others simply can't afford it, particularly when times get hard. Other people simply prefer not to buy their own homes.

HOMES COST LESS THAN HOMELESSNESS

The average cost of keeping a family in bed and breakfast accommodation per year is £14,196 versus £9,000 which is the annual cost of building a new home to rent.

So offering a family an affordable permanent home is much cheaper than providing insecure temporary accommodation.

All figures and statistics are correct at the time of going to press.

Group oral work

In a group you will take part in a discussion about homelessness on
The Breakfast Show, using the article on pages 70–71 and the Shelter leaflet on
pages 72–73. Allocate these roles:

♦ a celebrity to chair the discussion
♦ the writer of the newspaper article
♦ York council's city centre manager (page 70, line 71)
♦ Chief Superintendent John Lilley (page 71, line 118)
♦ David Pratley, Bath's director of leisure and tourist services (page 71,
  line 141)
♦ tourists who were mentioned in the article – optional
♦ a former homeless person/s – these could be the people mentioned on the
  information sheet published by Shelter
♦ a mother whose child has left home and is living on the streets in a large city.

Try to imagine how each of these people will talk about the homeless problem.
Will they be sympathetic? Before you start, make a few notes to help you.
  Remember that in a discussion you should:

♦ listen carefully to what others have to say – you do not have a monopoly on
  good ideas
♦ attempt to persuade others through logical argument – do not get too heated
  and resort to personal attacks, verbal or physical, on a person who holds a
  different point of view to yours
♦ be clear in your mind about the points you are trying to make
♦ adopt an appropriate register in the discussion.

Your lecturer or teacher may be assessing you during this discussion. In
'Approaching oral coursework' starting on page 13 you were given ideas about
what would gain you a high mark for speaking and listening. Refer to this
again, if necessary.

Reading

1 What two opposing views on homelessness are presented in the two extracts?

2 How does the material from Shelter try to make you sympathise with
  homeless people? How successful is it in doing so?

3 How does the writer of the newspaper article try to influence you and how
  successful do you think he is?

4 Look at the content of both extracts and how the writers' ideas are reinforced by:
  ♦ layout and use of headings and sub-headings
  ♦ use of photographs or illustrations
  ♦ use of language.

Writing

1 Write a letter to the newspaper in response to the article **Is he keeping the tourists away?**, in which you criticise the viewpoint the writer of the article has taken. Use some of the material from the Shelter leaflet to support your points.

2 Write a description of a city street or monument which has become a gathering place for homeless people. You might like to base your description on a real place near you. You may wish to be sympathetic towards homeless people in your writing – you may decide that their presence is inevitable and not necessarily an eyesore, or you may like to write opposing their presence.

Key Points

♦ When writing sentences, you must make sure that your subjects and verbs are in **agreement**.

What is the grammatical error in each sentence below?

He were freezing out on the street last night.
They is very upset to see so many people living on the streets.

It is quite easy to spot the errors in these sentences: the subjects and verbs do not agree.

He is the subject of the first sentence. To agree with *he* the verb should be *was*.

They is the subject of the second sentence. To agree with *they* the verb should be *are*.

♦ Now try these:

My friend and I was/were shocked by the news.
The people in the shelter was/were delighted to see him.

♦ You will find more about agreement on page 197.
♦ You will find help with writing letters on page 226.
♦ You will find help with personal writing on pages 19–31.
♦ For help with grammar, punctuation and spelling, turn to 'Get it right', starting on page 192.

Television is bad for the brain

Look at the article **Turn-off switched on our brains** and the letter by Mrs Brownlow, written to the newspaper in response to it. This was used as a specimen paper for an examination board.

Turn-off switched on our brains

WHEN the Sheppards began their 12 days without television it was like a bereavement. Deep in suburban Staines, Middlesex, the TV-addicted family – computer manager David, wife Denise and sons Peter, 11 and Jonathan, 14 – were frantic.

"When the sets were taken away it was like a depression had set in, like the death of somebody close to us," says Denise, who used to switch on at seven in the morning and off at midnight. "I didn't know what I was doing. I didn't feel right.

"I kept saying to myself 'Why do I feel so awful?' The answer was because we had suddenly had television removed from our lives."

But after six days without constant invasion of TV personalities and games shows, something strange happened.

"We started talking, yes really talking, to each other. We had to use our brains.

"We did things together like swimming and weird and wonderful games. We discussed things together. We became a family. It was quite wonderful," says Denise.

She was also astonished at the change in her quiet, younger son Peter who up to this had been a total television addict.

"He became much more friendly, much nicer.

"He used to get up in the morning and watch TV, come home and watch it again until late.

"Now he doesn't watch it at all in the morning and when he does in the evening he'll often switch it off and do something else."

When the televisions did return, the Sheppards were no longer ruled by the box in the corner of the room.

"Television used to be the centre of attention in our lives," says Denise.

"Everything revolved around it. Cured might not be the right word but we don't want to go back to the bad old days."

Denise, 36, has made every effort to ensure that she doesn't do so. She has started writing a romantic novel – something she would never have found the time to do when every night held the bait of another soap opera or detective series.

Despite new-found togetherness, the family won't be throwing away the Sky dish or the videos.

"If the sets weren't there we would miss them," she says. "But we have all learned a lot."

In fact the whole family was amazed by the change in their lifestyles.

"The experiment wasn't meant to wean us off television – but that's what it did," says Denise.

And it's something that they are extremely grateful for.

"Television stops you doing things and stops you appreciating your family. I really thought we'd be tearing each other apart waiting for the sets' return," says Denise.

"That didn't happen. The funny thing was that we went to bed thinking about people on radio phone-in programmes and their problems. Television never kept us awake like that.

"For me TV was company. People don't like to admit how much they watch. They feel guilty. They feel they should be doing something."

Now the Sheppards keep themselves company. On a typical evening they are just as likely to be seen sitting in the kitchen listening to the radio, or playing a game of Scrabble, as glued to another episode of EastEnders.

Whatever they do, it's done together – as one big family.

Today

Dear Sir,

Having read your article about the Sheppard family, which suggests that being without a television is good for you and your family, I felt I had to write in defence of television.

I am a mother of five children who range in ages from three to sixteen years old, and without television my life would be a misery.

I know that people will criticise me for using the television as a baby-sitter, but it offers them good entertainment safely in a way that a busy mum could not possibly match, particularly with such a range of ages.

A lot of what they watch is purely entertainment – and I don't see anything wrong with that – but a lot is also very educational. They learn about science and nature as well as watching programmes that inform them about news and current affairs in a way that they can understand. They can travel to places around the world and see things that I would never be able to afford to show them. They watch drama series and soaps that deal with issues that matter to them in an imaginative way. They often discuss the things they have seen with each other and with me. It gives me a valuable opening to talk about subjects which I would find awkward to bring up, and to give them my views and some parental guidance. They also see serialisations of good books which they have studied at school. They can see their pop idols perform and watch sports events without the danger of being crushed in crowds or beaten up. That certainly reduces my worries.

I also think that without television my children's homework would suffer. It is the television that keeps my sixteen year old boy sitting down and concentrating long enough to do it. I have tried sending him to his room and he gets far less done. My thirteen year old girl likes to study quietly on her own. Without the television her seven year old sister, who shares her room, would never leave her alone long enough for her to study.

I for one am glad, for myself and for my children, that I live in this modern world with the marvel of television. So let's hear less about what a dreadful thing television is.

Yours

Mrs Sharon Brownlow

Reading

What do you think about the ideas in the article and the arguments in Mrs Brownlow's letter, and the ways in which they were put across?

In your answers you should consider:
♦ how much people watch and use television
♦ the language each writer uses to present his or her ideas
♦ how effective each piece is in persuading you that their viewpoint is right.

Support your ideas by referring to the text.

Writing

Mrs Brownlow argues that even programmes which many people would regard as trivial, like 'soaps', raise issues which are of educational value to her children.

Do you think this is true? Write an article for a young people's magazine in which you argue the educational value of soaps.

You could comment on:
♦ examples of issues raised in soaps which you believe have been dealt with effectively
♦ how a soap might be a better way of dealing with certain issues than a documentary.

Imaginative writing

Imagine a time when there was no television. Write a diary describing how you and your family might have spent your evenings at home together. You could include information about:
♦ family relationships
♦ entertainment
♦ whether you as a member of the family were satisfied with the lifestyle.

Read the passages again if you wish, to give you some ideas.

Television and violence

Now read the article **Television and the culture of violence**, then turn to the questions on page 80.

Television and the culture of violence

HOUR after hour, day after day, brutality invades our senses and our homes. Nightly, our living rooms are awash with blood and stacked high
5 with corpses.

As we loll or eat or even lie in bed, we are bombarded by images of violence and death.

From Bosnia comes news footage
10 of rotting bodies exhumed by one side to vilify the other. Addicts of Casualty are regularly treated to gore by the bucketful. Fans of black comedy – or should it be red? –
15 gawp at Saunders bludgeoning French to pulp.

That's news, we're told. That's life. That's a laugh.

Fact, fiction, faction … tragic,
20 comic … television, argue its promoters with a suitably concerned furrow to their brows, surely has a duty to report or dramatise the world as it is. Their plea in
25 mitigation is that of the gritty realist. Their line is that TV is the mirror of a grim world.

If you believe that, you will believe anything.

30 How many people, even today,

ever see in their whole real lives one tiny fraction of a week's violence as screened on television, let alone that merchandised by video?

35 Television is a distorting mirror, grotesquely and gratuitously exaggerating the violence in modern society. In this respect, it is far more powerful than the Press, 40 which Parliament is at present, apparently, so anxious to curb. For images and sounds that are broadcast constitute the very atmosphere in which modern man 45 exists.

What effect does the ceaseless bombardment of brutal images have on the sensibilities and the proclivities of we who watch? What 50 impact does it have on the immature moral reflexes of our children?

For too long TV producers, directors and administrators have been allowed to shrug off their 55 responsibility. One of the most terrifying aspects of television is how habituated we have become to its ever more coarsening influence.

60 Desperately late, there are signs that people, shocked by callous crimes, are coming out of their trance; beginning to question the pervasive power of the box that is 65 forever drip-feeding violence to the imagination of the millions slumped before it.

The Prime Minister does well to voice rising public concern. He 70 condemns 'the relentless diet of violence on TV'. John Major is a decent man, here tuned in to the worries of decent families.

He speaks convincing common 75 sense when he says that 'what we watch is the biggest influence on many people's thinking'. He commands respect when he calls on programme-makers to have a care, 80 not just about what time they show their vicious wares – before 9pm or after – but whether they should show them at all.

The response by Alan Yentob, the 85 new controller of BBC1, is as typical as it is inadequate.

Displaying PR tact, he apologises for an especially brutal episode of Casualty. Yet continues to defend 90 what he deems the 'quality' of this massively popular hospital series and repeats the standard hand-washing patter of the Corporation that it is the 95 responsibility of parents to monitor what their children see.

Nobody denies that parents have a duty; that they can, and should, do more to stop their children viewing 100 unsuitable programmes.

The Daily Mail acknowledges this, as does the Prime Minister.

But it is the BBC and the other television channels, satellite and 105 terrestrial, which have the overriding responsibility.

They make the stuff or buy it. They pump it out.

They know that in many homes 110 the TV is on from dawn till midnight. It is a drug; a sedative (side-effects perilously ignored). Babies are weaned on it. Children hooked on it; placated by it.

115 Their fathers may abandon them, the box never does.

That is how it is out there, Mr Yentob, in the inner-city where hard-faced juveniles turn early to 120 crime and thuggery.

Television violence may not directly cause that crime and engender that thuggery. But only blinkered fools (who can be 125 sophisticated as well as stupid) would deny its indirect impact.

Broadcasters are ready enough to claim credit for prestigious programmes they make, which they 130 readily extol as an influence for good. Yet they remain reluctant to accept blame for the blood-lust that dominates all too much of the material they screen. Indeed, they 135 shy away from acknowledging that it has any influence at all.

If we concentrate our criticism on the BBC, that is not because its output is more violent than that of 140 commercial television. It is not.

But the BBC is the custodian of public-service broadcasting. Only as defenders of standards can Alan Yentob or John Birt justify the 145 continuation of a Corporation financed by licence fee.

When they seek to excuse violence or pornography by the 'integrity' or 'quality' of this or that film, they 150 represent the cultural establishment that has held sway in Britain since the 1960s.

The test case judgment of the permissive years was in favour of 155 the publishing of D.H. Lawrence's novel Lady Chatterley's Lover: You can't ban it because it's literature.

In the demoralised Nineties, these times of blood-drenched and 160 sexually obsessed television, that judgment has been inverted. Now it would seem, in the eyes of writers and producers, no TV series can be considered culturally valid if it does 165 not contain challenging scenes of violence or perversion, or both.

At last, there is a growing recognition that the permissive pendulum has swung too far; a 170 realisation that there is an unsavoury relationship between violence on television and violence in society.

That does not mean we can put the 175 clock back to a cosy world that no longer exists. TV cannot be compelled or constrained to churn out latter-day versions of Dixon of Dock Green rather than The Bill; 180 Emergency Ward Ten instead of Casualty.

But television should be shamed into shouldering responsibility for the violent totality of its present 185 output. It must mop up some of the blood and tone down some of the sex. Let TV truly reflect, not corrupt, the public it should serve.

This most potent medium of 190 communication must clean up its act.

Reading

1 Make a list of the arguments the journalist uses in **Television and the culture of violence** to persuade you that television violence is bad for you.

2 Now look at the language and structure of the argument:
   ♦ What effect do the first three paragraphs (lines 1–16) have?
   ♦ Why is the fourth paragraph (lines 17–18) so short? What is the effect of repeating 'That's ...' three times?
   ♦ Do you have an answer to the question in the last paragraph of the first section (lines 30–34)? What is the effect of the question – does it make you want to read on?
   ♦ Which words in the middle section (lines 35–140) do you find particularly emotive?
   ♦ Why does the journalist often use very short paragraphs in this article?
   ♦ Does the article convince you? Why/why not?
   ♦ Make a list of the **facts** in this article.

3 *'This article uses emotional language to whip up hysteria about violence on television, but it is based on very little fact and therefore it is not convincing.'* Do you agree or disagree with this statement? Use the notes you made in response to question 2 to help you.

Writing

Use the Focus box opposite to help you answer the following question in which you need to argue a point of view.
   'Violence on television is a primary cause of violence in real life.'
Discuss whether you agree or disagree with this statement.

Key Points

   ♦ When you are writing, a common error is to confuse **Its** and **It's**.
     – *Without* an apostrophe *its* means *belonging to it.*
     – *With* an apostrophe, *it's* means *it is.*
   ♦ Now try these:
     Its/It's a fine day today.
     Look at the horse tossing its/it's head.
     It's/Its not violence on television that matters but how people react to it.
     Television has had it's/its fair share of criticism over the years.
   ♦ You will find more about apostrophes in 'Get it right' on page 206.

Writing to argue a point of view

♦ Always be clear about what you feel before you begin to write.

♦ Ask yourself whether you agree or disagree with the statement made in the title. For instance, Are we made violent by what we watch on television? What is your answer – yes, no, or are you unsure? Look at the following possible standpoints. Which one is closest to your own thinking?

a) Yes, violence on television is bad and creates a violent society.

b) No, violence on television does not cause us to commit acts of violence.

c) Unsure, violence could have an effect on some people but on most it has no effect.

d) None of these views, but you believe …

♦ Once you have decided on your point of view, you have to prove it. To argue your own case means you state your case and use evidence and persuasive language to prove it is strong and valid. You need at least five or six points to make. Write down your points and plan how you will back them up.

♦ In addition, you may also attack the arguments used by the opposition. For instance, if you think that violence on television has nothing to do with increasing violence in society, those who are against violence on television may say 'How do you account for the increase in violent crime?'. You will need to suggest other reasons why society has become more violent. You may feel there are social or economic reasons. What might these be?

♦ If, however, you think television violence is increasing the amount of violence in society, what evidence could you use to support this? You could refer to violent crimes that are copies of violent acts in films. If you are opposed to something, you sometimes need to suggest reforms. What would you want banned from television? Would you want to remove violent deaths from the news – like those seen from Bosnia? Would you want to ban Mickey Mouse, Power Rangers and so on? Where would you want to draw the line?

♦ Plan your essay before you start writing. Decide the order in which you will make your points. Good essays make clear the writer's viewpoint. You should not change your mind halfway through unless you have clearly stated that there are reasons for being unsure about an issue, or you are presenting both points of view.

You will find more information about writing a point of view or argument on pages 41–44.

The rainforest

Read the two extracts that follow on pages 84–85 and 86–88. One is an advertisement by Friends of the Earth and the other is taken from an information leaflet for schools, produced with the aid of the Brazilian Government.

Reading

1 How do the writers attempt to influence the reader and why do you think they do this? Which article are you inclined to believe and why?
Make notes in response to this question, using these prompts:

Friends of the Earth advertisement
♦ What is the purpose of the advertisement?
♦ Why is it written in the first person? What effect does this have on you?
♦ Do you believe what you are being told?
♦ Does any of the information in the advertisement shock you? Does it have any other effect on you?

Rainforest article
♦ What is the purpose of the article? Does it succeed?
♦ Why does the article provide you with so much statistical data?
♦ How does the article try to persuade you that something is being done to slow the rate of deforestation? Does it succeed?

Comparison
♦ How does the tone of the non-fiction article on the rainforest differ from that of the advertisement?
♦ What information does the article provide that the advertisement does not?
♦ What is the purpose of the photographs in each?

2 Now write your answer to the main question above.

Writing

1 Imagine that you work at the Brazilian Embassy. The Friends of the Earth advertisement has been shown to you and you have been instructed to write to Friends of the Earth to complain about its content. When writing the letter, you could think about:
♦ what the Brazilian Government might object to in the content and tone of the advertisement
♦ why and how the Brazilian Government might wish to stop the advertisement being used as part of a campaign to prevent the cutting down of mahogany.

2 Write a letter to your local MP complaining about Britain's financial interest in the rainforest. In the letter you could discuss:

♦ why we should not support the cutting down of the rainforest
♦ what effect we in Britain have on the deforestation in progress
♦ how an MP might be able to help.

Address: Friends of the Earth, 56–58 Alma Street, Luton LU1 2YZ.

Key Points

♦ When you are writing, always check your **spelling**. The words underlined in the paragraph below are amongst the top 100 words most often spelled incorrectly. Can you correct them?

It was a real <u>suprise</u> when Dave and Ali arrived at the party <u>seperetely</u>. I was convinced they were <u>definitly</u> still together. It turns out that they had an argument when Ali <u>recieved</u> a Valentine card from someone else in <u>Febuary</u>. Dave didn't speak to her <u>untill</u> he found the card had been sent to the wrong <u>adres</u> – it wasn't meant for Ali at all.

♦ Turn to page 223 for other common spelling errors and watch out for these words in your own writing.
♦ You will find help with writing letters on page 226.
♦ You will find help with personal writing on pages 19–31.
♦ For help with grammar, punctuation and spelling, turn to 'Get it right' starting on page 192.

PLEASE WILL YO
HAVE MY PEO

There was only one possible name for Friends of the Earth's report on the Amazonian mahogany trade: "Mahogany is Murder". What follows has been pieced together from the evidence of many different Indians.

Let me tell you how it is with us Indians, and the mahogany cutters.

On March 28th, 1988, about 100 Indians met in a house by a river, to discuss what to do about the timber thieves who were cutting and stealing mahogany trees from their lands.

A boat came up the river. It was the timber cutter, Oscar Branco, with 16 hired gunmen. The men got out and shouted that they had come to kill everyone. They started firing.

The Indians tried to flee in canoes, but many were gunned down. Fourteen Indians, including children, were killed. Twenty two more were wounded.

Everyone knew who the killers were. Branco was named as the ringleader by Brazil's chief of Federal Police. Eleven of the sixteen gunmen have been identified.

Yet four years have passed and not one has been prosecuted.

Those Indians and their children – their deaths didn't count.

The Indian lands are ours by right forever. No outsider is meant to come into them without our permission. Nobody is supposed to clear the land, or cut trees for timber or break the ground open looking for gold. The law is supposed to protect us and our land.

But they do come, the timber cutters. They come because the mahogany is so precious.

They try all kinds of tricks to get us to part with the timber. Men came in trucks to some Indian villages. They gave out radios, torches, T-shirts, biscuits and tins of food. The villagers were very grateful for these gifts.

Some weeks later the men returned. They said that the goods had been given on credit and they had come to collect payment – in trees.

In our Kayapo lands, the timber cutters know the Indians are hostile. So they sneak in and out as quickly as they can. Then they send messengers who say that, as the trees have already been cut down, the Indians can only gain if they take a share of the profits and allow the timber cutters to remove the trees.

Some Indians have been fooled into agreeing to contracts which are not at all to their benefit. Two young Xikrin Indians, who had no authority to speak for their tribe, were persuaded to sign a deal with a big timber company. One of those companies which supplies your British importers.

The deal said that half the wood taken from the forest would be granted free to the company to cover the cost of cutting the trees.

It is the first time anyone's heard of a timber company being paid to cut down trees.

The rest of the trees, worth about £300 each, were to be bought from the Xikrin Indians for just £10 each.

But when the final settlement came the Indians got no money, only a bill claiming that they owed the timber company £6,000 for 'merchandise'.

It is when we Indians resist the invasion of our lands that the killing starts.

During an argument, a timber cutter threw an Indian woman's baby into a river where it drowned.

STOP PAYING TO
ᴇ MURDERED?

A film crew met eleven timber cutters armed with shotguns and entering the forest at the start 30 of an Indian hunt.

Even if the timber cutters do not murder us with guns, they have other ways to kill our people.

The mahogany trees grow far apart so the 35 timber cutters hack roads through the forest to reach them. Nearly half of our people have died from diseases brought by the timber cutters since first contact with the outside world.

While our people die, the forest disappears 90 forever.

Many other trees are damaged in the death struggles of the big mahoganies.

We should not cut the trees. The trees give the fruit we eat. We want the honey from the trees, 95 the fruits and all there is to be eaten in the forest. Without the trees there is no game for us to hunt.

It is greed that is killing us, and the trees and the animals.

100 Your greed for mahogany. You in Britain buy more than half the mahogany Brazil produces.

Look! That deep red glow in your mahogany dinner table is the blood of murdered Indians.

Listen! The clatter of your mahogany luxuries 105 is the gunfire that killed Indian children. You must do all you can to help those who are fighting to end this evil trade.

We don't believe that after reading this you could ever contemplate buying 110 **mahogany again. But if we are to halt the illegal trade you must help us force importers and retailers to change their attitudes.**

We have to awaken MPs and 115 **Government to the scandal. Friends of the Earth campaigns locally, nationally, internationally and tirelessly against the cynical timber trade which is accelerating the demise of the Earth's** 120 **last rainforests and their peoples. We've already helped persuade the World Bank to stop funding logging projects in primary rainforest areas. Since our campaign began, British importers of** 125 **tropical timber have dropped by a third. But we need to do so much more. Time is running out. People are dying. The forest is vanishing. Please join us. Please do it now.**

Friends of the Earth

What is happening to the rainforest resource?

Although agriculture produces 14% of Brazil's gross domestic product (GDP), there are large areas of the country where there is very little farming, especially in 5 the north where rainforests still cover huge areas of land. But the soils there are not very suitable for farming. The best areas for farming are on the fringes of the rainforest in Mato Grosso, Mato Grosso 10 do Sul, Goiás, Tocantins and Maranhão.

The Amazon's rainforest is a vast natural resource. It could provide timber and a wide variety of plants, food crops and medicines.

15 The forest also has an important effect on the world's weather. It is also home to hundreds of thousands of unique wildlife species.

However, the government has a 20 responsibility to bring development to the 14 million people who live in the Brazilian Amazon and to find ways of improving the lives of all its people by using its resources sensibly. All the 25 industrialising countries have achieved their prosperity in this way.

How quickly is the Amazon rainforest being cleared? Figures published by the World Bank in 1988 stated that 12% of the 30 Amazon had been cleared. The Brazilian National Space Research Institute reached a much lower estimate of 5%. A figure reached by NASA (the US space agency) suggested that the forest is being cleared 35 at only 0.3% each year. This is less than the rate at which forests are being cleared in the United States.

It is estimated that by 1970, 100,000 square kilometres of forest had been 40 cleared mostly in Pará and Maranhão. The figures below show that the annual rate of clearance fell from 1978 onwards.

Seeding trees being reared for forest regeneration

Average rate of clearance (sq km)	
1978–88	21,500
1988–89	18,824
1992–93	11,000

At the current rate, it would take 300 years to remove all the Amazon
45 rainforest, even ignoring the fact that many forest clearings are abandoned each year. In the most deforested state, Rondônia, not more than 12.6% of the forest has been lost.

50 It is easy for people living outside Brazil to imagine that the forest is being destroyed and nothing is being done to protect it. Given the vast size and remoteness of the Amazon basin, it is
55 difficult to control what is happening there. However, some important steps have been taken in recent years. Here are just some of them.

◆ In 1987, the POLAMAZONIA
60 programme for setting up 'development' areas in the Amazon was suspended.

◆ The 1988 Brazilian Constitution emphasized the need to protect the environment.

65 ◆ In 1989, the 'Nossa Natureza' (Our Nature) programme established a Natural Environment Fund. This programme is backed by the Institute for Environmental Resources
70 (IBAMA).

◆ In 1989, tax incentives for agriculture and livestock developments in the Amazon were suspended.

◆ By 1995 all companies using wood as
75 raw material or energy source must get their supplies from planted and managed forests.

◆ The rate of deforestation has also been reduced through lack of public funds
80 for road building. Of nine projects planned for 1992, six have been postponed, one suspended and only one went ahead.

LANDSAT 5 Satellite deforestation maps of Amazonia

INPE obtains precise information about deforestation on the Brazilian Amazonia through the analysis of satellite images.
The result comprises 334 maps, at the 1 to 250 thousand scale, stored in a computerised data base, showing deforested areas.
The capture of deforestation data proceeds as follows. First, conventional maps are transferred to the computerised data base, in parallel satellite images are selected and processed to correct distortions and to highlight the different types of vegetation cover.

The images are carefully analysed to identify new deforestation areas. All deforested areas are then transferred to the computer, generating the deforestation maps.
Repeating the previous steps for the satellite images obtained during the last two decades, researchers using INPE created a set of maps stored in the computer, showing the true dimension of deforestation in the Brazilian Amazonia.

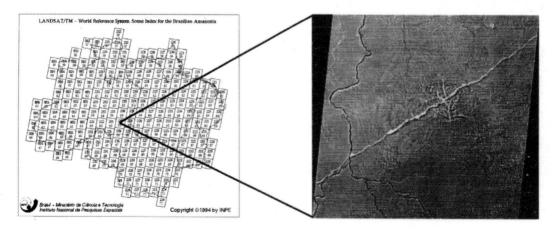

Today in the Amazon there are:

85
♦ Eight national parks.
♦ Seven biological reserves.
♦ Ten ecological stations.
♦ Three ecological reserves.
♦ 24 national forests.
90
♦ Four extractive reserves.
Altogether, these cover 28.3 million hectares, an area well over the size of the entire United Kingdom.

95
So, Brazil's resources, renewable and non-renewable, are being used to develop the economy and create better living standards all round. And steps are being taken to ensure that the environment is also protected.

An area of ecological interest close to Brasilia, protected by forestry police

Xingu territory, Pará

Brazil

All examination boards test your response to either one non-fiction extract, like the one we are going to use, or to two or more extracts which you have to compare.

All the boards test your ability to:
♦ Find and select points from the text. You may be asked to summarise these points.
♦ Follow an argument and explore suggestions within the argument.
♦ Distinguish between fact and opinion.
♦ Make judgments on how information is presented.
♦ Understand and make judgments on how writers use words and present their articles or advertisements, using headlines, sub-headings, inserts and captions to achieve the effects they desire on their readers.

Exam questions

Exam boards vary in their approach to questions.

Some boards, for example SEG, prefer long questions such as these:

> Summarise briefly the writer's arguments...
> Describe the attitude of the writer/s...
> Comment on the writer's use of words and presentation.

Some exam boards, for example London, also offer one long question but help you with prompts:

> Write about the ways in which the writer seeks to attract and sustain the reader's interest. You should write one or two paragraphs on each of the following:
> ♦ the writer's choice of content
> ♦ the writer's use of language.

Other boards, for example NEAB and WJEC, tend to ask several short questions.

We are going to look at a newspaper article over the page, about the makers of Ben and Jerry ice-cream, which you may already have tasted. Read it through, and then turn to 'in the exam' on page 92.

Ben Cohen and Jerry Greenfield: the 'caring capitalists' have changed views on how a successful firm can be run

Capitalism with hippy flavours

America's caring capitalist ice-cream makers are attacking the British market
Nicholas Fox meets the men behind the scoop

1 In 1977 Ben Cohen and Jerry Greenfield wanted to set up a bagel business, but they could not afford the machinery. Instead they signed up for a $5 correspondence course in ice-cream making.

2 It was a lucky break. Greenfield admits the bagel business was ahead of its time and would have flopped. Instead, during the next year they pooled their $8,000 savings and got a $4,000 bank loan to buy an ice-cream machine and rent a run-down petrol station in Burlington, Vermont.

3 They converted the petrol

'Almost overnight we became a $4m company'

---

station into a 'scoop-shop' and started making ice-cream that summer. Their quirky flavours, rich ingredients and chunky fillings were an instant hit and sold ou every day.

4 Now 17 years later, tha shop has spawned Ben and Jerry' Homemade, America's secon biggest premium ice-cream make after Grand Metropolitan's Haager Daaz. It has 500 workers, is quote on the Nasdaq over-the-counte exchange, has sales of $140 millio and has made Cohen an Greenfield famous and rich.

5 They have expanded to Canad. Russia and Israel, but Be

and Jerry's is virtually unknown in Britain, where Haagen-Daaz dominates the market. This is set to change. Last week Cohen and Greenfield launched their ice-cream in this country giving out free scoops in Selfridges' food hall. A limited range is on trial in a few shops. This summer it will hit Sainsbury supermarkets.

6 If America's appetite is anything to go by, it will not be long before flavours such as Chunky Monkey, Cherry Garcia, Rainforest Crunch and Georgia Peach are the toast of dinner parties and the cause of children's tantrums.

7 But this successful partnership had the most unlikely of origins. Cohen and Greenfield first met in gym class at school in Long Island, New York, and became best friends. Greenfield says: 'We were the two fattest boys in the class. When the class did laps we were half a lap behind, so we got to know each other well.'

8 After school the pair went their separate ways, and did not cover themselves with success. Cohen dropped out of college several times before trying his hand at jobs ranging from pottery teaching to cleaning, security guarding and taxi driving.

9 Greenfield wanted to be a doctor, but twice failed to get into medical school and ended up as a laboratory assistant. By 1977 he realized his chances of becoming a doctor were slim and decided to join Cohen in a new business venture.

10 They had two aims. Cohen says: 'We wanted to live in a rural college town and we were interested in the food business.

11 Greenfield corrects him. 'No, we were interested in eating – food was only the vehicle,' he says.

12 They looked at what was selling in big towns and what could be easily transferred to a rural town. They came up with two choices – bagels or home-made ice-cream. The bagels were too expensive to make, so they switched to ice-cream.

13 After passing the course with flying colours, they searched for the right site for their shop. But all the warm college towns already had an ice-cream shop, so Cohen and Greenfield moved to Burlington, Vermont – a town with temperatures below freezing for three months a year.

14 But the cold weather was not a problem. In the summer the shop was filled with customers, in winter Cohen would sell their product to local restaurants. Their reputation spread fast and by 1980 the pair had moved to new premises and were selling the ice-cream in pint tubs to shops and restaurants in neighbouring states. Their biggest problems were keeping up with demand and keeping their battered delivery truck on the road.

15 The quantum leap came in 1984, when Ben and Jerry's built a new factory and started to sell in Boston.

16 Haagen-Daaz took exception to its new rival and tried to pressure distributors to limit sales. Without money for a big legal campaign, Ben and Jerry's launched an advertising campaign, distributed T-shirts and car stickers and Greenfield staged a one-man picket outside the offices of Pilsbury, which owned Haagen-Daaz.

17 The publicity worked. Pilsbury backed down and Ben and Jerry's was entrenched in the public's psyche.

18 But Ben and Jerry's is more than just a corporate success story. The pair like to be known as 'caring capitalists' and have done much to change views on how a successful firm can be run.

19 Cohen says: 'It is important that the company supports the local community. It must not become just another cog in the economic machine and exploit its workers.'

20 The Ben and Jerry's salary rule is that the highest paid worker can only earn seven times more than the lowest. It gives 7.5 per cent of profits to charity, hands out free ice-cream at school sports days and hospitals and ensures all its joint ventures donate money to charity.

21 When it floated, the offer was restricted to Vermont people and one in every 100 families bought shares. The caring policy extends to suppliers and ingredients. The company is famed for sourcing nuts from the Brazilian rain-forest, blueberries from Passamaquoddy Indians and peaches from black farmers.

22 Cynics say it all seems too good to be true. They claim the 'right-on' attitude and hippy packaging is just a marketing ploy to woo customers and differentiate the product from rivals'.

23 Greenfield says caring is central to success. He says: 'A caring company is a positive thing for business and it helps profitability. The two do not have to be mutually exclusive.'

24 But this conflict came close to ruining the partnership. After their runaway early success Greenfield found it hard to cope. He says: 'Almost overnight we became a $4 million company and I was no longer scooping ice-cream but had become a businessman. It was not a realisation I liked.'

---

bagel: bread roll   **Nasdaq over-the-counter exchange:** a stock exchange

The Sunday Telegraph

In the exam

Let's go through the process step by step, as if we are working on a question in an examination hall.

First reading

Whether you are answering short or long questions you will need to take the same initial step. Look at the article, taking in the picture and its caption and the headlines. These give us an idea of what to look for in the article. They give us a reading purpose. We now know who the main characters are: Ben Cohen and Jerry Greenfield.

As we read the article, we must find out more about:
♦ who they are
♦ what they have done, are doing or will do
♦ what happens to them
♦ their ideas, thoughts and attitudes.

If we do this, we are preparing ourselves for the **What?** and the **Why?** questions.

On a clear space on your question paper jot down what you find. This is what I jotted down.

> Ben Cohen and Jerry Greenfield did not shine in school or college.
> They invested the little money they had in an ice-cream business.
> They made unusual, gimmicky ice-cream.
> They moved from being small-time roadside vendors to being nationally and internationally known, and wealthy men with a thriving business.
> They care for the well-being of employees, local communities, third-world people and the environment (or so the writer states).

Short questions

This section takes you through a range of short questions then looks at how you should apply your skills to answering a long question. Even if your exam board offers long questions, you will find it extremely helpful to have worked through these short questions.

> **1** Write the stages by which Ben Cohen and Jerry Greenfield's ice-cream business grew, from the time it started to the time it became an internationally known enterprise. [*10 marks*]
>
> **2** Why, according to this article, are Cohen and Greenfield described as 'caring capitalists'? On the basis of the evidence given, do you agree with this description? [*10 marks*]
>
> **3** How has this article been presented in order to catch the attention and interest of the newspaper reader?
>
> In answering this question you should consider the effect of:
> - the picture
> - the caption under it
> - the main headline
> - the sub-headings. [*10 marks*]
>
> **4** How does the journalist, Nicholas Fox, show his feelings for Ben Cohen and Jerry Greenfield by the way he tells their story? [*10 marks*]

Question 1   Write the stages by which Ben Cohen and Jerry Greenfield's ice-cream business grew, from the time it started to the time it became an internationally known enterprise. [*10 marks*]

Step 1

In 'First reading' you scanned the article to find out about the characters and what they have done. That was Step 1.

Step 2

- Read question 1. This is a 'What?' question.
- Underline the key words in the question.

I would underline:

write

stages

from the time . . . to the time

Step 3

- On your exam paper, highlight all the stages.
- Make sure you find all the stages. Keep looking until you are sure that you have found them all.

  How many did you find? I found ten.

- But have you got them in the right order? I noticed that the stages were not set out in the right order in the article. Did you?

  So you need to do some re-arranging to obtain a good, full-marks answer.

Step 4

Write your answer using a new line for each stage. This helps you and the examiner. (This format would be inappropriate on the 'Reading Literature' paper). These are easy marks if you are prepared to take the trouble to search the text.

GO FOR FULL MARKS! 10!

Question 2	Why, according to this article, are Cohen and Greenfield described as 'caring capitalists'? On the basis of the evidence given, do you agree with this description? *[10 marks]*

This is the 'Why?' question. We still have to find and select points, but now there is an argument to follow, and suggestions in that argument to explore. In addition, we are asked for our opinion based on what we have read.

Step 1

Remind yourself about what you jotted down for Step 1, in question 1.

Step 2

Underline the key words in question 2. I would underline:
Why
caring capitalists
do you agree

Step 3

Underline in the text all the reasons given for why Cohen and Greenfield are 'caring capitalists'.
Make sure you find all the reasons: if you look hard, you could find eight, but you can build a very good answer around five or six.

Step 4

Write your answer to the first part of question 2.

Step 5

Pause to think before you write the second part. You are asked 'do you agree' 'on the basis of the evidence'. You already have the evidence in the first part of your answer to question 2. Ask yourself questions about the evidence, for example: Might there be a reason other than generosity in giving ice-cream free to schools and hospitals? Why might Cohen and Greenfield want it to be known that they help the third world and are concerned about the environment? Think of these and questions of your own and then answer the second part of the question.

Evaluate your answer

Think about your answer and how you might improve it. Ask yourself:

1 Have I copied three or four reasons and given an opinion?
For this you may get 1–3 marks.

2 Have I found five or six reasons and expressed them in my own words? Have I responded thoughtfully to this? For this you might get 4–5 marks.

3 Have I done all the above, linking my ideas and summarising point? Have I developed an argument in response to one or more of the points?
For this you may get 6–7 marks.

4 Have I done all the above and developed a mature argument about 'caring capitalism'? For this you may get 8–10 marks.

Question 3   How has this article been presented in order to catch the attention and interest of the newspaper reader?
In answering this question you should consider the effect of:
- the picture
- the caption under it
- the main headline
- the sub-headings.   [*10 marks*]

Question 3 is testing your ability to make judgments on how information is presented and on how writers use words and present their articles, using headlines, sub-headings, pictures and captions to affect the reader. This is a 'How?' question.

Step 1
Underline the key words in question 3.
I underlined:
catch
attention
interest
Now go through each bullet-point remembering the key words above.

Step 2
Study carefully the large picture, its caption, the headline and sub-headings. It is quicker to think about these features than to read a text of dense writing. There are big features in all of them that stand out.

Step 3
Write your answer.

Evaluate your answer
Read your answer and think about how you might improve it. Ask yourself:

1 Have I described the picture and/or commented on the size of the type?
For this you may get 1–3 marks.

2 Have I commented on the picture and made at least one comment about the headline or caption?

For this you may get 4–5 marks.

3 Have I mentioned details about the face, physique and dress-style of Ben and Jerry and analysed the headline, sub-headings and caption?

For this you may get 6–7 marks.

4 Have I written about how the picture would attract interest? Have I tackled at least two of the expressions like 'caring capitalist', 'attacking the British market', 'Almost overnight', 'hippy flavours', 'Capitalism/hippy'.

For this you may get 8–10 marks.

Question 4   How does the journalist, Nicholas Fox, show his admiration for Ben Cohen and Jerry Greenfield by the way he presents facts and opinions about them?

[10 marks]

Question 4 tests your skill in distinguishing fact from opinion and understanding how writers use words. This is a 'How?' question.

Step 1
Underline the key words:
how... Fox show... admiration
Cohen
Greenfield
way he presents facts and opinions about them

The 'how/way presents' question is designed to allow the best candidates to show how talented they are. If you have worked carefully through all the questions so far, you, too, can approach this kind of question with confidence.

The secret is in the close reading of the text, seeing words and phrases which show in this case how the journalist is influencing you to admire Cohen and Greenfield.

Highlight or circle these words and phrases and jot down ideas round the article itself if you wish.

Step 2
Spend a good five minutes scouring the article for clues and jotting down ideas. These ideas should form the structure of your answer.

Step 3
Write your answer.

Evaluate your answer
You could get 4–5 marks if you can separate facts from the writer's favourable opinion of these men.

For 6–7 marks you have to show that you realise that Fox is telling a success story about two men who are the heroes. You should be able to find where he is emphasising their lovable, admirable, enterprising and caring qualities.

For 8–10 marks you would be expected to comment on two or three details, in addition. For example, the repetition of 'caring capitalists', the climax in paragraph 4, the admiring language in paragraph 6, 'quirky flavours', 'rich ingredients', 'quantum leap' and the very last quotation from Greenfield in the article.

Long questions

You will find it extremely useful to work through the 'Shorter questions' section before you tackle this, as the questions help you to think about the key questions, 'What?', 'Why?' and 'How?'

The following long question consists of several parts: it is the type of question set by the SEG examination board.

> Summarise briefly the achievements of Ben Cohen and Jerry Greenfield. Why were they successful? Describe the attitude of the writer, Nicholas Fox, to these men. Comment on the way this article is presented and on Fox's use of facts and opinion. [*25 marks*]

'Summarise...' is a **What?** question. It tests your ability to find and select points and then to link them and summarise them as you did in question 1 of the short questions (page 93). This is followed by a **Why?** question which tests your ability to find and select points, but also follows an argument as you did in question 2 of the short questions (page 94).

'Describe the attitude...' is a **What?** and **How?** question. It tests your ability to detect opinion and how that opinion is expressed, as you did in question 4 of the shorter questions (page 96).

'Comment on the way...' is a **How?** question. It tests your ability to understand how writers use words and present articles, using headlines, sub-headings, pictures and their captions, inserts, etc. to affect their readers. It is really a mixture of questions 3 and 4 of the short questions.

Evaluate your answer
Look at your answer and ask yourself:

1 Have I identified six or seven stages in the careers of Cohen and Greenfield and two or three examples of their 'caring capitalism'? Also, have I made a statement about the writer's attitude to them? For example: 'He thinks that

they have been successful.'
For this you may be awarded a mark between 1 and 10.

2 Have I done all the above and summarised the article coherently? Have I explained why they were successful? Have I commented on language and presentation?
For this you may be awarded a mark between 11 and 15.

3 Have I covered all the above and commented on **how** the writer has presented his ideas, looking in detail at language and presentation? Have I explored one or two different ways of looking at the writing? For example may the writer be mocking Cohen and Greenfield in certain parts of the article?
For this you may be awarded a mark between 16 and 25.

Here is another long question, similar to those set by the London board:

> Write about the ways in which the newspaper article seeks to attract and sustain the reader's interest.
> You should write one or two paragraphs on each of the following:
> ♦ the writer's choice of content in the article
> ♦ the writer's use of language in the article and its presentation on the page of a newspaper. [*20 marks*]

Answer this question using the skills you learned as you worked through the 'Short questions' section, starting on page 92.

Key Points

♦ Whatever type of question you have to answer, remember to spend nearly half of your allowed time studying the story and thinking about it.

♦ If you write more than $2\frac{1}{2}$ pages in answering the short questions or one long question in this section of the examination, you will be writing far too much.

♦ If you have one long question, it is all the more important to check as you write that you are answering the question the examiner set.
  – Are you answering 'How?' as well as 'What?' and 'Why?'
  – Are you using all the preparation work you did?
  – If there are prompts, are you using them all?

> Remember, take any advice an examiner gives you. It is **always** intended to help you to a good grade. It is **true** that examiners love to give high marks. That is TRUE, TRUE, TRUE.

FICTION AND TEXTS FROM MANY CULTURES

Introduction

Students studying GCSE English need to read a variety of literature and learn to respond sensitively to it. This unit contains extracts from twentieth-century British writers and from writers from many cultures.

As you look at the extracts in this unit, make sure that you read them carefully. Then answer the questions that follow in as detailed a manner as possible. Remember, the more practice you have at reading and responding to a variety of texts, the more successful you will be when it comes to your examination.

You will find help on how to approach this kind of literature in 'An examiner advises…' on page 118.

St Agnes' Stand

Thomas Eidson, who wrote *St Agnes' Stand*, is a senior executive of a large communications firm. His grandparents lived in Oklahoma Territory, Kansas, and Southern Colorado. It is out of the tales told him about family histories that his stories have grown.

In the following story, Nat Swanson had been travelling through the brush when he saw Sister Agnes and her wagon surrounded by Apaches. The Apaches had her trapped in a canyon; behind her lay a steep climb up a sheer cliff face; soon they would attack. Her water had run out and she was sheltering from the sun in a cave. Swanson had never met her, but felt that he should try to save her. Despite this feeling, he continued his journey – until his conscience compelled him to return. Swanson was himself being hunted by gunmen who had shot him.
  This is what happens when he returns and attempts to save her …

He had come down here to save the woman, he thought, nothing more. And now he had three women and seven children to worry about. Even if he could get all ten of them out without the Apaches knowing, which he doubted, there was no way he could hide that many people, especially
5 kids, in the hills. With just the woman and following the hard rocks, moving back through the Apaches at night instead of running from them, he might have been able to escape. But not with seven kids, crying and making noise, falling behind.

  He laid the loaded Hawken down next to him and pulled his pistol. He
10 ran an oiled rag over the weapon, his eyes scanning the space under the wagons as he worked. The Apaches were not likely to charge an armed man in the light of day, but Swanson was not one to be caught off-guard. His head was throbbing. He guessed it was the change in temperature from the cave to the outside, or the wound in his leg, which was
15 beginning to hurt badly again. He let his mind work over the facts a while. Every way he figured it, it came out the same: he was not getting out of here with ten people. For the first time in his life Nat Swanson felt trapped. He could run, but ...

  What had seemed like a fool's errand before, now seemed like a
20 desperate gamble gone terribly wrong; he could almost hear his mother's voice warning him against leaning too hard on a broken reed. He ran his hands through his hair, listening for the sound of her in his memory. There was nothing but the wind. She remained, as always, a shadowy presence in his thoughts. Still, there were things he half-remembered, and
25 he felt she would have done the same thing he had; she, too, would have come for the old nun. He felt a little better. But not much.

Swanson heard a noise to his right and whirled, bringing the pistol up cocked and levelled at the old woman's head. She stared at him for a second and then walked over and returned the canteen to his pack.

30 'That's what guns do,' she said, the words hanging in the hot air.

When she didn't continue, Swanson asked, 'What?'

'They make you afraid.' She stood and walked over to him.

Ignoring the remark, he looked up at her and said, 'You shouldn't stand; you'll be killed.'

35 'Perhaps,' she answered, kneeling down beside him, a candle and a small leather purse in her hands, 'but only if the Lord wants me to die. And I won't die afraid.' She smiled at him. 'Now let me see your leg.'

'It's fine. It's just a hole.'

'Let me see your leg, please,' she said firmly, lighting the candle with a
40 match and sticking it in the sand. 'From the amount of blood on your pants, it's more than just a hole, and the children need you.'

Swanson looked into the woman's face for a few seconds and realised she wasn't going to let him alone; he stretched his leg out so she could see it. The wound was oozing badly. She opened the purse and took out
45 a small knife and heated the blade in the flame of the candle. Swanson watched her thin, delicate hands as she worked. They were old hands, mottled with liver spots but steady, and it was obvious she had dressed wounds before. She was wearing a wedding ring and this surprised him.

Laying the small knife down, she took a pair of scissors and cut the
50 buckskin leggings so she could get at the wound. It wasn't pretty. The
entry hole was small enough, but the bullet had hit bone and flattened out
and the wound was deep and ugly and seeping clear fluid and blood, and
it was dirty. The skin around it was a festering purple colour. The woman
began to reheat the blade of the knife.

55 'What is your plan?' she asked.

Swanson sat staring blindly at the bullet hole for a few seconds. 'I don't
know.'

She seemed a little startled and then went back to heating the knife. He
was thinking that if he'd known about the other nuns and the kids he
60 might not have come at all, but he didn't say it out loud.

She was watching him closely again. 'You would have,' she said after
a few moments.

Swanson jumped. 'Would have what?'

'You were thinking you wouldn't have helped if you'd known there
65 were so many of us.' She waited a second, still staring into his face. 'You
still would have.' Her voice was matter-of-fact.

He looked into her eyes, surprised she had guessed his thoughts. Then
he shrugged it off. He had never not had a choice in his entire life, even
if the choice had been to die. He still had choices. He pulled his eyes
70 away from hers and shook his head, looking out at the brilliant sunlight
and the canyon. Sweat was running down his neck.

'This will hurt. Before I start, I want to thank you for saving the
children. They were dying.'

'How long had they been without water?'

75 'Two days. But it wasn't only the water. It was the fear.'

Swanson didn't understand. He waited for her to explain, but she was
bending over the wound. 'So what's changed?'

'They know God sent you to save them.' She smiled at him.

The words seemed to slap him in the face. She began to run the knife
80 hard around the edge of the wound, leaving a thin trail of blood welting
behind the sharp blade.

'Listen, lady –' Swanson started to say, before the pain slammed him
upside of his head and he went unconscious.

St Agnes' Stand by Thomas Eidson

Reading

Oral work

1 Working either in pairs or groups, discuss the following questions.

♦ Where and when is the story set? Find evidence to support your ideas.

♦ What has happened?

♦ Think about how Sister Agnes and Nat Swanson meet. Is there anything strange about the meeting?

♦ What has Swanson arrived to do and how does he feel about it? Find the evidence in the text.

♦ What have you learned about Swanson? What do you think of him?

♦ How does the writer's use of language build up an impression of the man and the seriousness of the situation?

Written response

2 On your own, spend about 15 minutes writing your own answer to the question: 'What do we learn about Swanson?'

When you have finished, compare your answers with a partner. Have you got all the information you should have, most of it or some of it? Evaluating the quality of your own answers now will help you to write good answers in the future. If you are doing this work at home, check your answer at a later date with another student.

Oral work

3 Again, working in pairs or groups, spend about 15 minutes discussing the text. Focus on Sister Agnes.

♦ What is Sister Agnes like? What evidence do you have to support your ideas?

♦ How does she cope in this situation? What do you think of her?

♦ How does the writer use language to build up an impression of this woman?

Written response

4 On your own, spend about 15 minutes writing your own answer to the question: 'What do we learn about Sister Agnes?'

Imaginative writing

Imagine that you are Nat Swanson and that sometime in the future you tell your grandchildren the story of how you rescued Sister Agnes, the rest of the nuns and the children. Write the story as he might have told it.

Back Home

Back Home was written by Michelle Magorian whose first ambition was to be an actress. She studied speech and drama, and then mime. All this time she had been secretly scribbling stories, and became interested in children's books.

In the extract that follows, Rusty, or Virginia as she is called in the story, has just returned to this country from America where she was evacuated during the war. She has only been back a short time and is finding it hard to get to know her mother and young brother again. The war has ended and Rusty opens the door to find her father, a soldier, unexpectedly returned. Her mother is called Margaret but in the war has gained a nickname – Peggy. Mrs Dickinson Senior is Rusty's grandmother.

After recovering from the shock, Rusty ran up the stairs, yelling. Minutes later, her mother appeared on the landing, her face shining from the steam of the bathroom, her short hair damp and tousled. Charlie was in her arms, wrapped up in a towel, his hair sticking up wildly.

5　　And no one moved.

Her father glanced quickly at her mother's trousers while she gazed down at him, stunned.

Eventually she walked down the stairs. 'I had no idea,' she began weakly. 'Why didn't you let me know you were coming?'

10　'I tried to,' he said. 'But the phone always seemed to be engaged.'

Mrs Dickinson Senior looked a little guilty. 'I'm sorry,' she said, 'I can't stand that thing ringing, so I sometimes just take if off the hook.'

Rusty noticed a flicker of anger pass across her mother's face and then it was gone.

15　'So,' he said abruptly. 'This is Charles.'

'Yes.' She smoothed his hair down. 'Charlie,' she murmured, 'this is your daddy.'

Charlie put his arms round Peggy's neck and buried his face in it.

Mr Dickinson placed his hands awkwardly behind his back.

20　'I'll put him to bed,' said Peggy. 'He'll catch cold in this towel.'

He gave a nod.

'And perhaps you could change into something a little more respectable,' said Mrs Dickinson Senior, lightly.

Peggy blushed. 'We've only just returned from Devon,' she explained.
25　'It was Virginia's half-term.'

'Roger,' gushed Rusty's grandmother suddenly, 'for goodness' sake, let me take your coat and cap, and come and sit in the drawing room. You'll find it just as you left it.'

Rusty followed on behind him. 'Yes,' he said on entering. 'It is.' He
30 looked puzzled. 'I thought this was requisitioned.'

'It was, but I had everything put in storage, and luckily it survived the bombs. I managed to have it all moved back and arranged before Margaret and Virginia and Charles came back. Margaret didn't do a thing. I mean, she didn't have to do a thing. Sit down.'

35 As Rusty sat down in one of the armchairs, she heard her grandmother whisper, 'You've come back just in time, my dear. Your son needs a father's hand.' She leaned back and took a long hard look at him. 'You've changed so much,' she remarked.

'I expect we've all changed a little,' he said, and he glanced at Rusty. 'I
40 hardly recognized Virginia.'

'Oh, you can call me Rusty. Everyone back home does.'

'My dear,' said her grandmother stiffly. 'You *are* back home.'

'I mean,' Rusty stammered, 'back in Connecticut.'

'Rusty?' he repeated.

45 'On account of my hair. Uncle Bruno said it reminded him of leaves in the fall.'

'That's Mr Omsk,' explained her grandmother.

'Well, if you don't mind, I shall continue to call you Virginia. After all, that is what we christened you.'

50 'O.K.' She leaned forward. 'I guess we're a little bit the same, really. I mean, we were both sent away from England. The tea's the worst thing here. I still haven't gotten used to it yet.'

'Well, actually, I wouldn't mind a cup right now.'

'Oh, Roger,' said his mother, 'how foolish of me. I'm afraid it's Mrs
55 Grace's day off. I'll go and make a nice pot for us all.'

As she left, Rusty and her father stared awkwardly at each other.

'And how was your half-term?' he said.

'O.K. We went to Beatie's place.'

He nodded. 'And how is she? Your mother has told me quite a lot about
60 her in her letters.'

'Oh,' said Rusty quietly. 'She died. We had to go hear the will read on Saturday.'

'I see. I'm sorry about that. Your mother sounded very fond of her.'

'Beatie was the tops.' Some instinct told her to steer clear of the subject
of the will. 'I go back to school tomorrow morning,' she said. 'But maybe
they'd let me have a week off – I mean, with you coming back and all.'

'If everyone did that, there'd be chaos.'

'I guess,' said Rusty, disappointed. He could at least have put up a fight.

'Anyway,' she added, 'I'll see you on Friday night.'

'Oh? What's happening on Friday?'

'I come back here for the weekend.'

'You come back here for the weekends?' he said slowly.

Just then her mother walked in. Her father sprang to his feet. Rusty
knew that her mother was wearing her better clothes, but she suspected
that her father did not. Above an old tweed skirt she wore a simple cream
blouse and a grey cardigan that had been darned at the elbows and cuffs.
She drew out a packet of cigarettes from her cardigan pocket.

'Do you have a light?' she asked.

'No. I'm afraid not.' He sat down again.

She walked over to the fire. There was a spill of rolled newspaper by
the grate. She pushed it into the fire, lit the cigarette, and stood leaning
against the mantelpiece.

'I didn't know you smoked, Margaret.' He tapped his fingers on his knee.

She nodded. 'Someone handed me one during a raid in Plymouth.'

The W.V.S. had helped collect half a street of mutilated bodies that
night, and then they had accompanied the surviving relatives and friends
to the mortuary to comfort them as they identified what remained.

'I was as sick as a dog at first,' she said quickly, 'but after that I suppose
I got used to it.'

'I didn't know you had cut your hair either,' he said.

'Well, yes. It was far more convenient.'

They heard the clatter of the tea-trolley in the hall. Peggy hastily placed
her cigarette on the mantelpiece so that the lit end jutted out over the
edge. 'Sit down, Mother,' she said. 'I'll bring it in.'

'Thank you. I thought I'd been forgotten.' And she gave a short laugh.

To Rusty's surprise, her grandmother sat down beside her father, almost
as if she was a chaperone.

Peggy drew out two low tables and laid the cups and saucers out.

'I'll be mother,' said Mrs Dickinson Senior.

At first Rusty didn't understand, but then she realized that 'being
mother' meant that you were the one who poured out the tea.

Back Home by Michelle Magorian

Reading

1 What are your first impressions of the characters in the passage? How does the writer create these impressions in the reader?
   ♦ Look at the reaction of the family to the father's return.
   ♦ Look at the way Mrs Dickinson Senior talks and behaves to Margaret.
   ♦ What do you learn about Virginia? Why is she disappointed?
   ♦ How does the father react when his wife enters the room? Look at the way he is described at this point.

2 What impression do you have of the relationships between these characters?

3 How do you think Mr Dickinson will cope with the way his family has grown up and changed since he has been away to war? Focus on behaviour and on what the characters say to each other.

Writing

'*No matter how young at heart the older generation seems to be, there will always be a generation gap.*'
How far does your experience show this statement to be true?
♦ Is a generation gap a good thing? Does it cause any problems?
♦ Young people are constantly being maligned in the press by older people. What characteristics of the older generation do you find irritating? What positive things can you find to say about the young and the old? What irritates you about some young people?

Personal writing

Write a story titled 'The relative who stayed and stayed and stayed!'
♦ As you plan, think about *why* the relative stayed with you.
♦ Why did the relative outstay their welcome?
♦ Why did their presence annoy you so much?
♦ Why did they eventually leave? Did you manage to part amicably?

Key Points

When writing **direct speech**, it is very important that you punctuate it correctly. If you are unsure about punctuating direct speech, turn to page 208, to help you complete the writing task above.

The Crossing

Cormac McCarthy, who wrote *The Crossing*, lives in El Paso, Texas. *The Crossing* is his seventh novel and the second book in the Border Trilogy.

The Crossing is set in Hidalgo County, New Mexico, and is about two teenage brothers, Billy and Boyd Parham. They are both seeking adventure but neither realise that they live on the cusp of unimaginable events. First comes a trespassing Indian and the dream of wolves running wild amongst the cattle lately brought onto the plains by the settlers. This extract is taken from the beginning of the novel.

When they came south out of Grant Country Boyd was not much more than a baby and the newly formed country they'd named Hidalgo was itself little older than the child. In the country they'd quit lay the bones of a sister and the bones of his maternal grandmother. The new country was
5 rich and wild. You could ride clear to Mexico and not strike a crossfence. He carried Boyd before him in the bow of the saddle and named to him features of the landscape and birds and animals in both Spanish and English. In the new house they slept in the room off the kitchen and he would lie awake at night and listen to his brother's breathing in the dark
10 and he would whisper half aloud to him as he slept his plans for them and the life they would have.

On a winter's night in that first year he woke to hear wolves in the low hills to the west of the house and he knew that they would be coming out onto the plain in the new snow to run the antelope in the moonlight. He
15 pulled his breeches off the footboard of the bed and got his shirt and his blanketlined duckingcoat and got his boots from under the bed and went out to the kitchen and dressed in the dark by the faint warmth of the stove and held the boots to the windowlight to pair them left and right and pulled them on and rose and went to the kitchen door and stepped out and
20 closed the door behind him.

When he passed the barn the horses whimpered softly to him in the cold. The snow creaked under his boots and his breath smoked in the bluish light. An hour later he was crouched in the snow in the dry creekbed which he knew the wolves had been using by their tracks in the
25 sand of the washes, by their tracks in the snow.

They were already out on the plain and when he crossed the gravel fan where the creek ran south into the valley he could see where they'd crossed before him. He went forward on knees and elbows with his hands pulled back into his sleeves to keep them out of the snow and when he
30 reached the last of the small dark juniper trees where the broad valley ran

under the Animas Peaks he crouched quietly to steady his breath and then raised himself slowly and looked out.

They were running on the plain harrying the antelope and the antelope moved like phantoms in the snow and circled and wheeled and the dry
35 powder blew about them in the cold moonlight and their breath smoked palely in the cold as if they burned with some inner fire and the wolves twisted and turned and leapt in a silence such that they seemed of another world entire. They moved down the valley and turned and moved far out on the plain until they were the smallest of figures in that dim whiteness
40 and then they disappeared.

He was very cold. He waited. It was very still. He could see by his breath how the wind lay and he watched his breath appear and vanish and appear and vanish constantly before him in the cold and he waited a long time. Then he saw them coming. Loping and twisting. Dancing.
45 Tunneling their noses in the snow. Loping and running and rising by twos in a standing dance and running on again.

There were seven of them and they passed within twenty feet of where he lay. He could see their almond eyes in the moonlight. He could hear their breath. He could feel the presence of their knowing that was electric
50 in the air. They bunched and nuzzled and licked one another. Then they stopped. They stood with their ears cocked. Some with one forefoot raised to their chest. They were looking at him. He did not breathe. They did not breathe. They stood. Then they turned and quietly trotted on. When he got back to the house Boyd was awake but he didn't tell him
55 where he'd been nor what he'd seen. He never told anybody.

The Crossing by Cormac McCarthy

Reading

1 What do you learn from *The Crossing* about the characters and the way they live? Which words and phrases tell you this?

2 Which words and phrases give you the most vivid picture of the 'new country'? Why?

3 How does the writer use language to create a picture of the family, the night and the importance of the incident with the wolves? Look at:
  ♦ The description of Hidalgo (lines 1–11).
  ♦ How the person's actions are described (lines 12–20).
  ♦ The description of the night and its events (lines 21–32).
  ♦ The language used to describe the wolves and the man's reaction to them (lines 33–55).

FOCUS

Reading texts from other cultures

When you respond to a text from another culture in an examination, you may be asked what the story or extract reveals about where it is set. It is important not to simply repeat information you have learned about the author's background or about the country in which it is set. You must look carefully at the text to find your answers. Think particularly about the way the author uses language.

Imaginative writing

The Crossing presents a picture of:
♦ the place where the writer saw the wolves
♦ the wolves themselves
♦ the antelope they hunt.

Write about a place that has meant a lot to you and has left an indelible memory. When you describe a place it is important to use all your senses:
♦ describe the way it looked, the sounds you associate with it and the smells
♦ develop your descriptions as this writer has done: '*The antelope moved like phantoms in the snow and circled and wheeled and the dry powder blew about them in the cold moonlight and their breath smoked palely in the cold...*'

Good descriptive writing enables the reader to paint the scene in their mind and to see the picture in the mind's eye.

An Imaginative Experience

Mary Wesley, who wrote *An Imaginative Experience*, was born near Windsor in 1912. Her education took her to the London School of Economics and during the war she worked in the War Office. One of her chief claims to fame is that her first novel was published at the age of seventy! (There is hope for the rest of us!)

In this extract Sylvester has just returned unexpectedly from America. His wife, Celia, has just left him; he was somewhat relieved to see her go. He has been to America on an assignment and also had a much needed holiday. He has employed Julia to clean the house. He has never met her, but has communicated with her via notes. Her son, Christy, and her husband, Giles, have recently been killed in a car accident. She has a flat of her own, but it is Christmas time and she cannot face the party that all the occupants have planned. She escapes and the only place she has to go is Sylvester's house to which she has a key. The woman called Rebecca referred to in the passage is his secretary.

Sylvester Wykes was soon standing on his doorstep with the rugs and his bags round his feet, watching the taxi drive away while he fumbled for his key.

The dolphin knocker was brightly polished and the paintwork
5 gleaming; he turned the key. He was enormously tired, aching for sleep. He put the rolled rugs beside his bags and, shutting the door, listened gratefully to the silence.

From the sitting-room came a rustling sound.

A dog crouched by the sofa; it swept its tail to and fro across the
10 parquet. On the sofa there was a woman asleep.

Overwhelmed by fatigue and surprise, Sylvester sat in the armchair.

The dog rose, came towards him, sniffed his trousers. Sylvester whispered, 'It's all right.' The dog repositioned itself by the sofa. Sylvester stretched his legs, leaned back, tried to think, heard the rustle
15 of the dog's tail. Hadn't Rebecca said something in her letter?

When Joyful barked Sylvester jerked awake with a grunt and the woman on the sofa telescoped her legs to her chin and stared speechless across her knees.

Sylvester said, 'My God. I fell asleep. Who are you?' His heart was
20 thudding.

It was still quite dark; the clatter of the letter-box as the postman pushed in mail ceased and the hair along the dog's back subsided. Sylvester repeated, 'Who are you?'

The woman sprang to her feet. Putting the sofa between them, she said,
25 'How did you get in?'

He could see that she was afraid. He said. 'I let myself in with my key.
I live here.'

'*What?*'

'I live here. This is my house.'

30 Her face was paper white. 'Can you prove it?' She was quite a tall girl,
wearing jeans and a heavy sweater under a black coat.

Irritably Sylvester said, 'Of course I can prove it.'

'*How?*' The dog moved to stand between them. She repeated, 'How?'
and glanced towards the telephone. The dog, infected by her fear, growled.

35 Sylvester said, 'The letters which have just come through the box will
be addressed to me; my name is Sylvester Wykes.'

She said, 'I don't believe you. Don't move. My dog –'

'I hate to undeceive you,' Sylvester said, 'but your dog wagged his tail
when I came in. Why don't you go and look at the letters? I won't move.
40 Go on.'

She hesitated, then edged warily out of the room. Sylvester called after
her, 'Don't run away.'

She came back with the letters and handed them to him. She said, 'Are
you his son?'

45 'Whose son?'

'Sylvester Wykes's.'

'*I* am Sylvester Wykes. Who may you be?' His startled heart had settled
down; he was intrigued.

'I thought he was quite old.' She spoke as of some character in the past.
50 'Quite an old man,' she said.

Irritably Sylvester said, 'I've got jet lag and I feel bloody old, but I am
not all that ancient. You still have not told me who *you* are.'

'Julia Piper.'

'My cleaning lady? Gosh!' He was taken aback. Breaking into laughter,
55 he said, 'I visualized you as on the old side, too. But tell me, do you work
over Christmas?'

Julia said, 'I was taking refuge. Don't worry, I'll go now. I'm sorry I –'

He could see embarrassment flood her face pink. He said, 'Please don't
go. Please stay. Have some breakfast,' he said, 'I'm starving. There's food
60 in the house. There should be bread in the freezer, and butter; there's
marmalade and coffee and dried milk, we can manage.' And as she still
appeared poised for flight, he repeated, 'Please.'

At her feet the dog sat back and began to scratch, its leg thumping on the bare floor. Sylvester said, 'I brought rugs from the cleaners; I left them in the hall with my luggage when I came in. I saw you, I sat down for a moment and fell asleep. I'll take my stuff upstairs. Tell you what, why don't you go and put the kettle on while I do that? I trust you not to scarper,' he said cheerfully.

Half-reassured, Julia said, 'All right.'

Carrying his bags upstairs Sylvester wished that he had watched her instead of dozing off; asleep she would not have looked so wary or so defensive. What was she defensive about? What was she doing here? It was odd. Hadn't Rebecca written something about squatters? Was she a squatter? Far too young to be a cleaning lady. Perhaps she just knew the cleaning lady's name and was using it? He put his bags down in the bedroom and looked about for signs of illicit occupation.

Spotless room, faint smell of Brasso and floor polish, his father's silver brushes gleaming on the dressing table. Clean sheets on bed. Bathroom spotless also. Fresh towels on towel rail, bath and basin gleaming and dry as a bone, new unused cake of soap. What's going on? He opened the bathroom window and looked out. 'Good God! What's happened to the garden?'

Running down the stairs two at a time, arriving abruptly in the kitchen, startling the dog, he shouted, 'What's happened to the garden?'

Backed against the stove, a coffee grinder in her hand, Julia said defensively, 'You arranged – we arranged – I thought it –'

'God! I'd forgotten. Quite forgotten. Hi! Don't look like that. Don't! It's bloody marvellous. It's lovely. There's a snowdrop out, a Christmas rose, winter jasmine. It's a work of genius! Who did you get to do it? It's wonderful.'

'I did it.'

'You?'

'Yes.'

'Oh!'

They stood appraising each other across the room. Julia smiled faintly.

It occurred to Sylvester that it was years, if ever, since he had had such an agreeable homecoming. He said, 'Would your genius stretch to making us both breakfast? And your dog? What's his name?'

'Joyful.'

'Apt.'

An Imaginative Experience by Mary Welsey

Group oral work

Read the extract from *An Imaginative Experience* carefully and explore in groups what you have learned about the characters. Imagine how this story might end.

Reading

1 How does the writer create a feeling of suspense in the passage and encourage us to read on? How does she show the developing relationship between the characters?

 ♦ Look closely at the reaction of Julia when she realises there is a man watching her.

 ♦ Look at Sylvester's reaction to Julia's presence.

 ♦ What do they learn about each other which changes their attitudes? How do we know that their suspicions of each other are gradually vanishing?

 ♦ Look at the way the writer uses language to describe Julia and Sylvester and their reactions.

Imaginative writing

Julia stays for breakfast. Write the conversation they might have. This can be written as a dialogue or as a drama. If you set it out as a dialogue, you will need to use speech marks; if you set it out as a drama, you will need to use play format.

Key Points

 ♦ When you are reading or writing you will find that **adverbs** make the text more interesting. Adverbs provide more information about verbs, adjectives, or another adverb in the sentence. For example in the phrase '*Irritably*, Sylvester said...', *irritably* tells us *how* Sylvester spoke.

 ♦ Adverbs usually answer questions such as: How? When? Where? How much? They are frequently formed by adding '-ly':

 slow – slowly   happy – happily
 emphatic – emphatically   true – truly

A Sunrise on the Veld

Doris Lessing, who wrote *A Sunrise on the Veld*, was born of British parents in Persia in 1919. At the age of five she was taken to Southern Rhodesia (now Zimbabwe), where she spent her childhood growing up on a large farm.

In this extract a young boy wakes at 4.30 a.m. He takes his gun and wanders off into the bush, with only his dogs for company. The painful nature of the death of a young buck sets him thinking about responsibility.

There was nothing he couldn't do, nothing! A vision came to him, as he stood there, like when a child hears the word 'eternity' and tries to understand it, and time takes possession of the mind. He felt his life ahead of him as a great and wonderful thing, something that was his; and
5 he said aloud, with the blood rising to his head: all the great men of the world have been as I am now, and there is nothing I can't become, nothing I can't do; there is no country in the world I cannot make part of myself, if I choose. I contain the world. I can make of it what I want. If I choose, I can change everything that is going to happen: it depends on
10 me, and what I decide now.

The urgency, and the truth and the courage of what his voice was saying exulted him so that he began to sing again, at the top of his voice, and the sound went echoing down the river gorge. He stopped for the echo, and sang again: stopped and shouted. That was what he was! he sang, if he
15 chose; and the world had to answer him.

And for minutes he stood there, shouting and singing and waiting for the lovely eddying sound of the echo; so that his own new strong thoughts came back and washed round his head, as if someone were answering him and encouraging him; till the gorge was full of soft voices
20 clashing back and forth from rock to rock over the river. And then it seemed as if there was a new voice. He listened, puzzled, for it was not his own. Soon he was leaning forward, all his nerves alert, quite still: somewhere close to him there was a noise that was no joyful bird, nor tinkle of falling water, nor ponderous movement of cattle.

25 There it was again. In the deep morning hush that held his future and his past, was a sound of pain, and repeated over and over: it was a kind of shortened scream, as if someone, something, had no breath to scream. He came to himself, looked about him, and called for the dogs. They did not appear: they had gone off on their own business, and he was alone.
30 Now he was clean sober, all the madness gone. His heart beating fast, because of that frightened screaming, he stepped carefully off the rock

and went towards a belt of trees. He was moving cautiously, for not so long ago he had seen a leopard in just this spot.

At the edge of the trees he stopped and peered, holding his gun ready;
35 he advanced, looking steadily about him, his eyes narrowed. Then, all at once, in the middle of a step, he faltered, and his face was puzzled. He shook his head impatiently, as if he doubted his own sight.

There, between two trees, against a background of gaunt black rocks, was a figure from a dream, a strange beast that was horned and drunken-
40 legged, but like something he had never even imagined. It seemed to be ragged. It looked like a small buck that had black ragged tufts of fur standing up irregularly all over it, with patches of raw flesh beneath ... but the patches of rawness were disappearing under moving black and came again elsewhere; and all the time the creature screamed, in small gasping
45 screams, and leaped drunkenly from side to side, as if it were blind.

Then the boy understood: it *was* a buck. He ran closer, and again stood still, stopped by a new fear. Around him the grass was whispering and alive. He looked wildly about, and then down. The ground was black with ants, great energetic ants that took no notice of him, but hurried and
50 scurried towards that fighting shape, like glistening black water flowing through the grass.

And, as he drew in his breath and pity and terror seized him, the beast fell and the screaming stopped. Now he could hear nothing but one bird singing, and the sound of the rustling, whispering ants.

55 He peered over at the writhing blackness that jerked convulsively with the jerking nerves. It grew quieter. There were small twitches from the mass that still looked vaguely like the shape of a small animal.

It came into his mind that he should shoot it and end its pain; and he raised the gun. Then he lowered it again. The buck could no longer feel;
60 its fighting was a mechanical protest of nerves. But it was not that that made him put down the gun. It was a swelling feeling of rage and misery and protest that expressed itself in the thought: if I had not come it would have died like this: so why should I interfere? All over the bush things like this happen, they happen all the time; this is how life goes on, by
65 living things dying in anguish. He gripped the gun between his knees and felt in his own limbs the myriad swarming pain of the twitching animal that could no longer feel, and set his teeth, and said over and over again under his breath: I can't stop it. I can't stop it. There is nothing I can do.

He was glad that the buck was unconscious and had gone past suffering
70 so that he did not have to make a decision to kill it even when he was feeling with his whole body: this is what happens, this is how things work.

It was right – that was what he was feeling. *It was right and nothing could alter it.*

A Sunrise on the Veld by Doris Lessing

Reading

If you are working as an individual make brief notes in response to these questions. If you are working in a group, discuss the questions then make notes to prepare for your own writing.

1 Using the prompts, make notes about what happened to the boy that morning.
   ♦ What is happening at the beginning of the passage? Have you ever felt like this?
   ♦ How old is this boy? What impression do you get of him? Where is he playing?
   ♦ What attracted the boy's attention? How did he react?
   ♦ What does he witness?
   ♦ How would you have felt if you had seen this? What would you have done?
   ♦ Look at the language used to describe the events. What impression does it give?
   ♦ Why did the boy lower the gun? Would you have shot the buck? Why doesn't he?

2 What has happened to the boy during this extract? How does Doris Lessing make us aware that these events are unique in the boy's experience and that the morning's events are deeply significant to him?

   To answer these questions you will need to think about the two things the boy became aware of that morning. You will also need to look closely at the way this extract is written and the way the writer uses language to describe events and mood.

   Use these prompts to help you:
   ♦ What became apparent to the boy at the beginning of the passage?
   ♦ How did the boy feel about the dying buck?
   ♦ Why didn't the boy do anything about it?
   ♦ How does the writer use language to create setting and mood?
   ♦ How does the writer contrast the mood at the beginning of the extract with the mood at the end?

Personal writing

Write about a time when you have been forced to face up to your responsibilities.
   ♦ Think about a time you have learned something from an event you witnessed. Describe what happened and how you think you learned from it.
   ♦ This passage describes a time in this boy's life when he was completely free. Write about a time when you felt free and in control of your own destiny.

The English exam tests your ability to respond to both prose and poetry texts in timed conditions.

Working through the sections in this unit will have helped you to develop your reading and understanding skills. This section shows you how to apply your skills in exam conditions.

Sula

Helene and her daughter entered a coach peopled by some twenty white men and women. Rather than go back and down the three wooden steps again, Helene decided to spare herself some embarrassment and walk on through to the colored car. She carried two pieces of luggage and a string
5   purse; her daughter carried a covered basket of food.

As they opened the door marked COLORED ONLY, they saw a white conductor coming toward them. It was a chilly day but a light skim of sweat glistened on the woman's face as she and the little girl struggled to hold the door open, hang on to their luggage and enter all at once. The
10 conductor let his eyes travel over the pale yellow woman and then stuck his little finger into his ear, jiggling it free of wax.

'What you think you doin', gal?'

Helene looked up at him.

So soon. So soon. She hadn't even begun the trip back. Back to her
15 grandmother's house in the city where the red shutters glowed, and already she had been called 'gal'. All the old vulnerabilities, all the old fears of being somehow flawed gathered in her stomach and made her hands tremble. She had heard only the one word; it dangled above her wide-brimmed hat, which had slipped, in her exertion, from its carefully
20 levelled placement and was now tilted in a bit of a jaunt over her eye.

Thinking he wanted her tickets, she quickly dropped both the cowhide suitcase and the straw one in order to search for them in her purse. An eagerness to please and an apology for living met in her voice. 'I have them. Right here somewhere, sir ...'

25 The conductor looked at the bit of wax his fingernail had retrieved. 'What was you doin' back in there? What was you doin' in that coach yonder?'

Helene licked her lips. 'Oh ... I ...' Her glance moved beyond the white man's face to the passengers seated behind him. Four or five black faces
30 were watching, two belonging to soldiers still in their shit-colored uniforms and peaked caps. She saw their closed faces, their locked eyes, and turned for compassion to the gray eyes of the conductor.

'We made a mistake, sir. You see, there wasn't no sign. We just got in the wrong car, that's all. Sir.'

35   'We don't 'low no mistakes on this train. Now git your butt on in there.'

He stood there staring at her until she realised that he wanted her to move aside. Pulling Nel by the arm, she pressed herself and her daughter into the foot space in front of a wooden seat. Then, for no earthly reason, at least no reason that Nel understood then or later, she smiled. Like a
40   street pup that wags its tail at the very doorjamb of the butcher shop he has been kicked away from only moments before, Helene smiled. Smiled dazzlingly and coquettishly at the salmon-colored face of the conductor.

Nel looked away from the flash of pretty teeth to the other passengers. The two black soldiers, who had been watching the scene with what
45   appeared to be indifference, now looked stricken. Behind Nel was the bright and blazing light of her mother's smile; before her the midnight eyes of the soldiers. She saw the muscles of their faces tighten, a movement under the skin from blood to marble. No change in the expression of the eyes, but a hard wetness that veiled them as they looked
50   at the stretch of her mother's foolish smile.

As the door slammed on the conductor's exit, Helene walked down the aisle to a seat. She looked about for a second to see whether any of the men would help her put the suitcases in the overhead rack. Not a man moved. Helene sat down, fussily, her back toward the men. Nel sat
55   opposite, facing both her mother and the soldiers, neither of whom she could look at. She felt both pleased and ashamed to sense that these men, unlike her father, who worshipped his graceful, beautiful wife, were bubbling with a hatred for her mother that had not been there in the beginning but had been born with the dazzling smile. In the silence that
60   preceded the train's heave, she looked deeply at the folds of her mother's dress. There in the fall of the heavy brown wool she held her eyes. She could not risk letting them travel upward for fear of seeing that the hooks and eyes in the placket of the dress had come undone and exposed the custard-colored skin underneath. She stared at the hem, wanting to
65   believe in its weight but knowing that custard was all that it hid. If this tall, proud woman, this woman who was very particular about her friends, who slipped into church with unequalled elegance, who could quell a roustabout with a look, if *she* were really custard, then there was a chance that Nel was too.

70   It was on that train, shuffling towards Cincinnati, that she resolved to be on guard – always. She wanted to make certain that no man ever looked at her that way. That no midnight eyes or marbled flesh would ever accost her and turn her into jelly.

Sula by Toni Morrison

In the exam

Suppose you had to answer questions on *Sula*. Let's go through the process step by step, as if we were working on it in an examination hall.

First reading

Whether you are answering short or long questions you will need to take the same initial step. Read the story first to find out about the main characters:

1 who they are, and any clues to the kind of people they are

2 what they do and what happens to them

3 how they relate to each other

4 what they think about each other during and at the end of the story.

If you concentrate, you can do all this in nine or ten minutes. In an examination make sure you are always looking for something as you read, so that you don't waste any time.

　　This is what I found in answer to the four questions.

---

1 Characters – who they are

Helene	a black mother
Nel	Helene's daughter
A conductor	a white man who makes sure that all passengers are in the right place with the right tickets
Two soldiers	black passengers on the train

2 What they do and what happens to them

Helene and Nel board a 'whites only' coach by mistake. The white conductor is unpleasant to Helene. In reply Helene humiliates herself to the conductor. The two black soldiers and Nel react to the incident. Nel makes a promise to herself.

3 How they relate to each other

The white conductor despises Helene.
Helene shows her feelings of inferiority by smiling sweetly at him.
Nel sees her mother in a new way.
The black soldiers show their disgust with Helene.

4 What they think about each other

Helene is afraid of the white conductor.
The white conductor sets out to insult Helene and enjoys his authority over her.
Nel is both 'pleased and ashamed' to see the black soldiers hating her mother, unlike her father who 'worshipped' her. Was her mother really 'custard'?

Long questions

Examination boards vary a little in the way they ask questions: Most boards, such as SEG, NEAB, MEG and London, like to ask one or two long questions, carrying as many as 30 or 40 marks. One long question on the story you have just read could be similar to the one below. The really important words in this question are 'What?' and 'How?'

What effects does this incident on the train have on the characters in the story? How does Toni Morrison make these effects fascinating for a reader?

[*30 marks*]

Some boards, like SEG and London, may help you answer this question by adding what examiners call prompts. Their questions may look like this:

What effects does this incident on the train have on the characters in the story? How does Toni Morrison make these effects fascinating for you? It will help you to consider the way Toni Morrison shows:

♦ the feelings of Helene as she boards the train
♦ the way the 'white conductor' treats her and speaks to her
♦ Helene's consequent behaviour to the conductor
♦ the way the two black soldiers react to the incident
♦ Nel's thoughts and feelings about the incident and the characters involved in it.

[*30 marks*]

If you are given 60 minutes to answer a long question like this, you should spend 20–25 minutes reading and planning, and the rest of the time writing.
   You should follow these three steps:

Step 1
In 'First reading' you scanned the article to find out about the characters and what they have done. Now ask yourself what effects the incident has on each character – make brief notes to remind you. If you are given bullet points it will help you to make brief notes for each point.

Step 2
Read the story again. This time think about **how** the author writes and about **how** the author makes the characters' thoughts and feelings vivid to you. Underline or circle key words and images.
♦ **How** do we know about Helene's feelings? Which words and phrases are particularly significant?

- **How** do we learn about Helene and the white conductor's attitudes to each other? Think about how they speak to each other.
- **How** do we learn about Nel's thoughts and feelings? What images are used to describe them?

Step 3
Write your answer.

Now write your answer to the long question on the previous page.

Evaluate your answer
Read your answer and ask yourself:

1 Have I just copied straight from the story the points I underlined?
   If so, you will not achieve a very high grade.

2 Have I tried to put these points in my own words and tried to explain something about each point?
   For example: 'Helene is embarrassed when she finds herself in a Whites Only coach. She wants to please the white conductor. He is nasty to her.'
   If you have done this but not gone very much further you will be achieving a Grade E/D.

3 Have I done more than this? Have I looked at the language and thought about what is suggested by particular details in the text?
   For example:
   line 7 'a light skim of sweat' – sign of fear?
   line 12 'gal' – patronising, insulting, sexist, racist?
   line 24 'sir' – respectful, eager to please?
   - If you are looking at it like this it will have pushed your grade up to a C and possibly to a B.
   - To get higher marks (grades B, A, A*) you need to tackle the parts of the text that make you think and really focus on the author's use of language.
     For example:
     'bright, blazing light of her mother's smile' compared with 'the midnight eyes of the soldiers'
     'custard' compared with 'marbled flesh'.
   - The more detail you discuss, the better your chance of A/A*. Candidates who gain the highest grades frequently quote detail – not large chunks from the story but significant words and phrases about which they can say something interesting and relevant.

Short questions

If you are taking other syllabuses, for example WJEC, you will find that you are more likely to be given several short questions than one long question. If that is the case, follow Steps 1 to 3 above for each question. Look carefully at the marks allowed for each question and divide up your time so you spend most time on the questions which give most marks.

If the short question asks you to look at particular lines make sure you concentrate on the lines specified.

Key Points

♦ Whatever type of question you have to answer, remember to spend nearly half of your allowed time studying the story and thinking about it.

♦ If you write more than 2½ pages in answering the short questions or one long question in this section of the examination, you are writing far too much.

♦ If you have one long question, it is all the more important to check as you write that you are answering the question the examiner set.

– Are you answering 'How?' as well as 'What?' and 'Why?'

– Are you checking that you are using all the preparation work you did?

– If there are prompts, are you using them all?

Remember, take any advice an examiner gives you. It is **always** intended to help you to gain a good grade. It is **true** that examiners love to give high marks. That is TRUE, TRUE, TRUE.

SHORT STORIES FOR COURSEWORK

Introduction

For GCSE English you now have to read literature by a major twentieth-century author and by a pre-twentieth-century author. Most exam boards ask you to read these works for coursework. Short stories are an ideal form in which to study works by major authors.

In this unit there are two short stories. One is by a pre-twentieth-century author, Thomas Hardy, and the other is by Joyce Cary, a respected, well-known modern writer. If you want to compare these stories, you will find an assignment on page 149.

If you want to compare prose with poetry you will find an assignment on page 150 comparing Joyce Cary's short story *Growing Up* (twentieth century) with 'Cousin Kate', page 168 (pre-twentieth-century poem).

Short stories

Characteristics of short stories

Short stories often:

♦ have a small number of main characters (unlike a novel which may have lots of characters)

♦ concentrate on one or two events in the characters' lives rather than tell their whole life stories

♦ spend only a short amount of time setting the scene

♦ give you a great deal of information in a short space using flashbacks or comments which characters make to each other about past events.

What to look out for in short stories

When you respond to a short story you need to think about:

♦ **Content**
What has happened in this story?

♦ **Theme**
What is the main idea being developed in this story?

♦ **Characters and their relationships**
What have I learnt about the characters? You learn about a character in three ways, through:
– what they say
– what they do, their actions in the story
– how they behave and act with others.

♦ **Mood**
How does this story make me feel?

♦ **Structure**
How is this story put together? Does it start at the beginning of the story and work logically to the end? Does it involve the use of flashbacks to help you understand what is happening now? How does the writer build up tension in the story and keep you hooked and reading?

♦ **Style**
Does the writer use images, detailed descriptions or anything else that adds to the story? How does the writer convey information about characters? Does the writer contrast one character with another to emphasise the good and bad points?

To gain a high grade you must comment on structure and style as well as content, theme and character. Remember not to spend too long re-telling the story. Students who gain high grades think about **how** an author achieves certain effects in the story as well as **what** the author says.

A pre-twentieth century story: *The Son's Veto*

Thomas Hardy, who wrote *The Son's Veto*, was a major author writing at the end of the nineteenth century and the beginning of the twentieth century. He wrote novels, short stories and poems. Some of his novels have recently been made into films, such as *Jude the Obscure*. In his novels and stories he explores relationships between men and women and looks at the effects their environments and the circumstances in which they live have upon their lives.

Read this story carefully. Try to do this in a quiet place where you won't get distracted!

The Son's Veto

To the eyes of the man viewing it from behind, the nut-brown hair was a wonder and a mystery. Under the black beaver hat **surmounted** by its tuft of black feathers, the long locks, braided and twisted and coiled like the rushes of a basket, composed a rare, if somewhat barbaric, example of
5 ingenious art. One could understand such weavings and coilings being **wrought** to last intact for a year, or even a calendar month; but that they should be all demolished regularly at bedtime, after a single day of **performance**, seemed a reckless waste of successful fabrication.

    And she had done it all herself, poor thing. She had no maid, and it was
10 almost the only accomplishment she could boast of. Hence the unstinted pains.

    She was a young invalid lady – not so very much of an invalid – sitting in a wheeled chair, which had been pulled up in the front part of a green enclosure, close to a bandstand where a concert was going on, during a
15 warm June afternoon. It had place in one of the minor parks or private gardens that are to be found in the suburbs of London, and was the effort of a local association to raise money for some charity. There are **worlds within worlds** in the great city, and though nobody outside the immediate district had ever heard of the charity, or the band, or the
20 garden, the enclosure was filled with an interested audience sufficiently informed on all these.

    As the strains proceeded many of the listeners observed the chaired lady, whose back hair, by reason of her prominent position, so challenged

topped

made

use

communities in a big city

inspection. Her face was not easily discernible, but the **aforesaid** cunning

25 tress-weavings, the white ear and **poll**, and the curve of a cheek which
was neither flaccid nor sallow, were signals that led to the expectation of
good beauty in front. Such expectations are not infrequently disappointed
as soon as the disclosure comes; and in the present case, when the lady,
by a turn of the head, at length revealed herself, she was not so handsome

30 as the people behind her had supposed, and even hoped – they did not
know why.

For one thing (alas! the commonness of this complaint), she was less
young than they had **fancied** her to be. Yet attractive her face
unquestionably was, and not at all sickly. The revelation of its details

35 came each time she turned to talk to a boy of twelve or thirteen who stood
beside her, and the shape of whose hat and jacket implied that he
belonged to a well-known public school. The immediate bystanders
could hear that he called her 'Mother'.

When the end of the recital was reached, and the audience withdrew,

40 many chose to find their way out by passing at her elbow. Almost all
turned their heads to take a full and near look at the interesting woman,
who remained stationary in the chair till the way should be clear enough
for her to be wheeled out without obstruction. As if she expected their
glances, and did not mind gratifying their curiosity, she met the eyes of

45 several of her observers by lifting her own, showing these to be soft,
brown, and affectionate orbs, a little plaintive in their **regard**.

She was conducted out of the gardens, and passed along the pavement
till she disappeared from view, the schoolboy walking beside her. To
inquiries made by some persons who watched her away, the answer came

50 that she was the second wife of the incumbent of a neighbouring parish,
and that she was lame. She was generally believed to be a woman with a
story – an innocent one, but a story of some sort or other.

In conversing with her on their way home the boy who walked at her
elbow said that he hoped his father had not missed them.

55 'He have been so comfortable these last few hours that I am sure he
cannot have missed us,' she replied.

'Has, dear mother – not have!' exclaimed the public-schoolboy, with an
impatient fastidiousness that was almost harsh. 'Surely you know that by
this time!'

60 His mother hastily adopted the correction, and did not resent his
making it, or retaliate, as she might well have done, by **bidding** him to
wipe that crumby mouth of his, whose condition had been caused by
surreptitious attempts to eat a piece of cake without taking it out of the
pocket wherein it lay concealed. After this the pretty woman and the boy

65 went onward in silence.

Margin glosses:
- talked of before
- head
- thought
- look
- telling

That question of grammar bore upon her history, and she fell into **reverie**, of a somewhat sad kind to all appearance. It might have been assumed that she was wondering if she had done wisely in shaping her life as she had shaped it, to bring out such a result as this.

a daydream

The past

70 In a remote nook in North Wessex, forty miles from London, near the thriving country-town of Aldbrickham, there stood a pretty village with its church and parsonage, which she knew well enough, but her son had never seen. It was her native village, Gaymead, and the first event bearing upon her present situation had occurred at that

75 place when she was only a girl of nineteen. How well she remembered it, that first act in her little tragicomedy, the death of her reverend husband's first wife. It happened on a spring evening, and she who now and for many years had filled that first wife's place was then parlour-maid in the parson's house.

80 When everything had been done that could be done, and the death was announced, she had gone out in the dusk to visit her parents, who were living in the same village, to tell them the sad news. As she opened the white swing-gate and looked towards the trees

85 which rose westward, shutting out the pale light of the evening sky, she discerned, without much surprise, the figure of a man

standing in the hedge, though she roguishly exclaimed as **a matter of** ⁹⁰ **form**, 'O, Sam, how you frightened me!'

expected thing to do

He was a young gardener of her acquaintance. She told him the particulars of the late event, and they stood silent, these two young people, in that elevated, calmly philosophic mind which is **engendered** when a tragedy has happened close at hand, and has not happened to the ⁹⁵ philosophers themselves. But it had its bearing upon their relations.

caused

'And will you stay on now at the Vicarage, just the same?' asked he.

She had hardly thought of that. 'O yes – I suppose!' she said. 'Everything will be just as usual, I imagine?'

He walked beside her towards her mother's. Presently his arm stole ¹⁰⁰ round her waist. She gently removed it; but he placed it there again, and she yielded the point. 'You see, dear Sophy, you don't know that you'll stay on; you may want a home; and I shall be ready to offer one some day, though I may not be ready just yet.'

'Why, Sam, how can you be so **fast**! I've never even said I liked **'ee**; ¹⁰⁵ and it is all your own doing, coming after me!'

forward; thee

'Still, it is nonsense to say I am not to have a try at you like the rest.' He stopped to kiss her a farewell, for they had reached her mother's door.

'No, Sam; you shan't!' she cried, putting her hand over his mouth. 'You ought to be more serious on such a night as this.' And she bade him **adieu** ¹¹⁰ without allowing him to kiss her or to come indoors.

good bye

The vicar just left a widower was at this time a man about forty years of age, of good family, and childless. He had led a secluded existence in this college living, partly because there were no resident landowners; and his loss now intensified his habit of withdrawal from outward ¹¹⁵ observation. He was seen still less than heretofore, kept himself still less in time with the rhythm and racket of the movement called progress in the world **without**. For many months after his wife's decease the economy of his household remained as before; the cook, the housemaid, the parlour-maid, and the man out-of-doors performed their duties or left ¹²⁰ them undone, just as Nature prompted them – the vicar knew not which. It was then represented to him that his servants seemed to have nothing to do in his small family of one. He was struck with the truth of this representation, and decided to cut down his establishment. But he was forestalled by Sophy, the parlour-maid, who said one evening that she ¹²⁵ wished to leave him.

outside

'And why?' said the parson.

'Sam Hobson has asked me to marry him, sir.'

'Well – do you want to marry?'

'Not much. But it would be a home for me. And we have heard that one
130 of us will have to leave.'

A day or two after she said: 'I don't want to leave just yet, sir, if you
don't wish it. Sam and I have quarrelled.'

He looked up at her. He had hardly ever observed her before, though he
had been frequently conscious of her soft presence in the room. What a
135 kitten-like, **flexuous**, tender creature she was! She was the only one of
the servants with whom he came into immediate and continuous relation.
What should he do if Sophy were gone?

Sophy did not go, but one of the others did, and things went on quietly
again.

140 When Mr Twycott, the vicar, was ill, Sophy brought up his meals to
him, and she had no sooner left the room one day than he heard a noise
on the stairs. She had slipped down with the tray, and so twisted her foot
that she could not stand. The village surgeon was called in; the vicar got
better, but Sophy was incapacitated for a long time; and she was informed
145 that she must never again walk much or engage in any occupation which
required her to stand long on her feet. As soon as she was comparatively
well she spoke to him alone. Since she was forbidden to walk and bustle
about, and, indeed, could not do so, it became her duty to leave. She
could very well work at something sitting down, and she had an aunt, a
150 seamstress.

The parson had been greatly moved by what she had suffered on his
account, and he explained, 'No, Sophy; lame or not lame, I cannot let you
go. You must never leave me again!'

He came close to her, and, though she could never exactly tell how it
155 happened, she became conscious of his lips upon her cheek. He then
asked her to marry him. Sophy did not exactly love him, but she had a
respect for him which almost amounted to veneration. Even if she had
wished to get away from him she hardly dared refuse a personage so
reverend and **august** in her eyes, and she assented to be his wife.

160 Thus it happened that one fine morning, when the doors of the church
were naturally open for ventilation, and the singing birds fluttered in and
alighted on the tie-beams of the roof, there was a marriage-service at the
communion-rails, which hardly a soul knew of. The parson and a
neighbouring curate had entered at one door, and Sophy at another,
165 followed by two necessary persons, whereupon in a short time there
emerged a newly-made husband and wife.

A new life

Mr Twycott knew perfectly well that he had committed social suicide by
this step, despite Sophy's spotless character, and he had taken his

yielding

important

measures accordingly. An exchange of livings had been arranged with an
170 acquaintance who was **incumbent** of a church in the south of London,
and as soon as possible the couple removed **thither**, abandoning their
pretty home, with trees and shrubs and glebe, for a narrow, dusty home
in a long, straight street, and their fine peal of bells for the wretchedest
one-tongued clangour that ever tortured mortal ears. It was all on her
175 account. They were, however, away from every one who had known her
former position; and also under less observation from within than they
would have had to put up with in any country parish.

Sophy the woman was as charming a partner as a man could possess,
though Sophy the lady had her deficiencies. She showed a natural
180 aptitude for little domestic refinements, so far as related to things and
manners; but in what is called culture she was less intuitive. She had now
been married more than fourteen years, and her husband had taken much
trouble with her education; but she still held confused ideas on the use of
'was' and 'were', which did not beget a respect for her among the few
185 acquaintances she made. Her great grief in this relation was that her only
child, on whose education no expense had been and would be spared, was
now old enough to perceive these deficiencies in his mother, and not only
to see them but to feel irritated at their existence.

Thus she lived on in the city, and wasted hours in braiding her beautiful
190 hair, till her once apple cheeks waned to pink of the very faintest. Her
foot had never regained its natural strength after the accident, and she was
mostly obliged to avoid walking altogether. Her husband had grown to
like London for its freedom and its domestic privacy; but he was twenty

clergy in charge

there

noise from a

single bell

years his Sophy's senior, and had latterly been seized with a serious
195 illness. On this day, however, he had seemed to be well enough to justify
her accompanying her son Randolph to the concert.

A death in the family

The next time we get a glimpse of her is when she appears in the
mournful attire of a widow.

Mr Twycott had never rallied, and now lay in a well-packed cemetery
200 to the south of the great city, where, if all the dead it contained had stood
erect and alive, not one would have known him or recognized his name.
The boy had dutifully **followed him to the grave**, and was now again at
school.

> attended his funeral

Throughout these changes Sophy had been treated like the child she
205 was in nature though not in years. She was left with no control over
anything that had been her husband's beyond her modest personal
income. In his anxiety **lest** her inexperience should be over-reached he
had safeguarded with trustees all he possibly could. The completion of
the boy's course at the public school, to be followed in due time by
210 Oxford and ordination, had been all **provisioned** and arranged, and she
really had nothing to occupy her in the world but to eat and drink, and
make a business of indolence, and go on weaving and coiling the nut-
brown hair, merely keeping a home open for the son whenever he came
to her during vacations.

> that

> paid for

215 Foreseeing his probable decease long years before her, her husband in
his lifetime had purchased for her use a semi-detached villa in the same
long, straight road whereon the church and parsonage faced, which was
to be hers as long as she chose to live in it. Here she now resided, looking
out upon the fragment of lawn in front, and through the railings at the
220 ever-flowing traffic; or, bending forward over the window-sill on the first
floor, stretching her eyes far up and down the vista of sooty trees, hazy
air, and drab house-facades, along which echoed the noises common to a
suburban main thoroughfare.

Somehow, her boy, with his aristocratic school-knowledge, his
225 grammars, and his aversions, was losing those wide **infantine
sympathies**, extending as far as to the sun and moon themselves, with
which he, like other children, had been born, and which his mother, a
child of nature herself, had loved in him; he was **reducing their compass**
to a population of a few thousand wealthy and titled people, the mere
230 veneer of a thousand million or so of others who did not interest him at
all. He drifted further and further away from her. Sophy's **milieu** being a
suburb of minor tradesmen and under-clerks, and her almost only
companions the two servants of her own house, it was not surprising that

> childish liking

> limiting his interest

> own world

after her husband's death she soon lost the little artificial tastes she had
235 acquired from him, and became – in her son's eyes – a mother whose
mistakes and origin it was his painful lot as a gentleman to blush for. As
yet he was far from being man enough – if he ever would be – to rate
these sins of hers at their true infinitesimal value beside the yearning
fondness that welled up and remained penned in her heart till it should be
240 more fully accepted by him, or by some other person or thing. If he had
lived at home with her he would have had all of it; but he seemed to
require so very little in present circumstances, and it remained stored.

Her life became insupportably dreary; she could not take walks, and
had no interest in going for drives, or, indeed, in travelling anywhere.
245 Nearly two years passed without an event, and still she looked on that
suburban road, thinking of the village in which she had been born, and
whither she would have gone back – O how gladly! – even to work in the
fields.

Taking no exercise she often could not sleep, and would rise in the
250 night or early morning to look out upon the then vacant thoroughfare,
where the lamps stood like sentinels waiting for some procession to go
by. An approximation to such a procession was indeed made early every
morning about one o'clock, when the country vehicles passed up with
loads of vegetables for Covent Garden market. She often saw them
255 creeping along at this silent and dusky hour – waggon after waggon,
bearing green **bastions** of cabbages **nodding to their fall**, yet never
falling, walls of baskets enclosing masses of beans and peas, pyramids of
snow-white turnips, swaying **howdahs** of mixed produce – creeping
along behind aged night-horses, who seemed ever patiently wondering
260 between their hollow coughs why they had always to work at that still
hour when all other sentient creatures were privileged to rest. Wrapped in
a cloak, it was soothing to watch and sympathize with them when
depression and nervousness hindered sleep, and to see how the fresh
green-stuff brightened to life as it came opposite the lamp, and how the
265 sweating animals steamed and shone with their miles of travel.

turrets; swaying
about

seats carried on
elephants' backs

A figure from the past

They had an interest, almost a charm, for Sophy, these semirural people
and vehicles moving in an urban atmosphere, leading a life quite distinct
from that of the daytime toilers on the same road. One morning a man
who accompanied a waggon-load of potatoes gazed rather hard at the
270 house-fronts as he passed, and with curious emotion she thought his form
was familiar to her. She looked out for him again. His being an old-
fashioned conveyance, with a yellow front, it was easily recognizable,
and on the third night after she saw it a second time. The man alongside

was, as she fancied, Sam Hobson, formerly gardener at Gaymead, who
275 would at one time have married her.

She had occasionally thought of him, and wondered if life in a cottage
with him would not have been a happier lot than the life she had accepted.
She had not thought of him passionately, but her now dismal situation
lent an interest to his resurrection – a tender interest which it is
280 impossible to exaggerate. She went back to bed, and began thinking.
When did these market-gardeners, who travelled up to town so regularly
at one or two in the morning, come back? She dimly recollected seeing
their empty waggons, hardly noticeable amid the ordinary day-traffic,
passing down at some hour before noon.

285 It was only April, but that morning, after breakfast, she had the window
opened, and sat looking out, the feeble sun shining full upon her. She
affected to sew, but her eyes never left the street. Between ten and eleven
the desired waggon, now unladen, reappeared on its return journey. But
Sam was not looking round him then, and drove on in a reverie.

290 'Sam!' cried she.

Turning with a start, his face lighted up. He called to him a little boy to
hold the horse, alighted, and came and stood under the window.

'I can't come down easily, Sam, or I would!' she said.

'Did you know I lived here?'

295 'Well, Mrs Twycott, I knew you lived along here somewhere. I have
often looked out for 'ee.'

He briefly explained his own presence on the scene. He had long since
given up his gardening in the village near Aldbrickham, and was now
manager at a market-gardener's on the south side of London, it being part
300 of his duty to go up to Covent Garden with waggon-loads of produce two
of three times a week. In answer to her curious inquiry, he admitted that
he had come to this particular district because he had seen in the
Aldbrickham paper, a year or two before, the announcement of the death
in South London of the aforetime vicar of Gaymead, which had revived
305 an interest in her dwelling-place that he could not extinguish, leading him
to hover about the locality till his present post had been secured.

They spoke of their native village in dear old North Wessex, the spots
in which they had played together as children. She tried to feel that she
was a dignified personage now, that she must not be too confidential with
310 Sam. But she could not keep it up, and the tears hanging in her eyes were
indicated in her voice.

'You are not happy, Mrs Twycott, I'm afraid?' he said.

'O, of course not! I lost my husband only the year before last.'

'Ah! I meant in another way. You'd like to be home again?'

315 'This is my home – for life. The house belongs to me,. But I understand' – She let it out then. 'Yes, Sam, I long for home – our home! I should like to be there, and never leave it, and die there.' But she remembered herself. 'That's only a momentary feeling. I have a son, you know, a dear boy. He's at school now.'

320 'Somewhere handy, I suppose? I see there's lots on 'em along this road.'

'O no! Not in one of these wretched holes! At public school – one of the most distinguished in England.'

'Chok' it all! of course! I forget, ma'am, that you've been a lady for so many years.

325 'No, I am not a lady,' she said sadly. 'I never shall be. But he's a gentleman, and that – makes it – O how difficult for me!'

The acquaintance thus oddly reopened proceeded **apace**. She often looked out to get a few words with him, by night or by day. Her sorrow was that she could not accompany her one friend on foot a little way, and 330 talk more freely than she could do while he paused before the house. One night, at the beginning of June, when she was again on the watch after an absence of some days from the window, he entered the gate and said softly, 'Now, wouldn't some air do you good? I've only half a load this morning. Why not ride up to Covent Garden with me? There's a nice seat 335 on the cabbages, where I've spread a sack. You can be home again in a cab before anybody is up.'

She refused at first, and then, trembling with excitement, hastily finished her dressing, and wrapped herself up in cloak and veil, afterwards sidling downstairs by the aid of the handrail, in a way she could adopt on an

rapidly

emergency. When she had opened the door she found Sam on the step, and
he lifted her bodily on his strong arm across the little forecourt into his
vehicle. Not a soul was visible or audible in the infinite length of the
straight, flat highway, with its ever-waiting lamps converging to points in
each direction. The air was fresh as country air at this hour, and the stars
shone, except to the north-eastward, where there was a whitish-light – the
dawn. Sam carefully placed her in the seat, and drove on.

They talked as they had talked in old days. Sam pulling himself up now
and then, when he thought himself too familiar. More than once she said
with misgiving that she wondered if she ought to have **indulged in the
freak**. 'But I am so lonely in my house,' she added, 'and this makes me
so happy!'

'You must come again, dear Mrs Twycott. There is no time o' day for
taking the air like this.'

It grew lighter and lighter. The sparrows became busy in the streets, and
the city waxed denser around them. When they approached the river it
was day, and on the bridge they beheld the full blaze of morning sunlight
in the direction of St Paul's, the river glistening towards it, and not a craft
stirring.

Near Covent Garden he put her into a cab, and they parted, looking into
each other's faces like the very old friends they were. She reached home
without adventure, limped to the door, and let herself in with her latch-
key unseen.

The air and Sam's presence had revived her: her cheeks were quite pink
– almost beautiful. She had something to live for in addition to her son.
A woman of pure instincts, she knew there had been nothing really wrong
in the journey, but supposed it conventionally to be very wrong indeed.

Soon, however, she gave way to the temptation of going with him
again, and on this occasion their conversation was distinctly tender, and
Sam said he never should forget her, notwithstanding that she had served
him rather badly at one time. After much hesitation he told her of a plan
it was in his power to carry out, and one he should like to take in hand,
since he did not care for London work: it was to set up as a master
greengrocer down in Aldbrickham, the country-town of their native
place. He knew of an opening – a shop kept by aged people who wished
to retire.

'And why don't you do it, then, Sam?' she asked with a slight
heartsinking.

'Because I'm not sure if – you'd join me. I know you wouldn't –
couldn't! Such a lady as ye've been so long, you couldn't be a wife to a
man like me.'

let herself do this odd thing

'I hardly suppose I could!' she assented, also frightened at the idea.

'If you could,' he said eagerly, 'you'd on'y have to sit in the back parlour and look through the glass partition when I was away sometimes – just to keep an eye on things. The lameness wouldn't hinder that … I'd keep you as genteel as ever I could, dear Sophy – if I might think of it!' he pleaded.

'Sam, I'll be frank,' she said, putting her hand on his. 'If it were only myself I would do it, and gladly, though everything I possess would be lost to me by marrying again.'

'I don't mind that! It's more independent.'

'That's good of you, dear Sam. But there's something else. I have a son… I almost fancy when I am miserable sometimes that he is not really mine, but one I hold in trust for my late husband. He seems to belong so little to me personally, so entirely to his dead father. He is so much educated and I so little that I do not feel dignified enough to be his mother … Well, he would have to be told.'

'Yes. Unquestionably.' Sam saw her thought and her fear. 'Still, you can do as you like, Sophy – Mrs Twycott,' he added. 'It is not you who are the child, but he.'

'Ah, you don't know! Sam, if I could, I would marry you, some day. But you must wait a while, and let me think.'

Breaking the news to Randolph

It was enough for him, and he was **blithe** at their parting. Not so she. To tell Randolph seemed impossible. She could wait till he had gone up to Oxford, when what she did would affect his life but little. But would he ever tolerate the idea? And if not, could she defy him?

She had not told him a word when the yearly cricket-match came on at Lord's between the public schools, though Sam had already gone back to Aldbrickham. Mrs Twycott felt stronger than usual: she went to the match with Randolph, and was able to leave her chair and walk about occasionally. The bright idea occurred to her that she could casually broach the subject while moving round among the spectators, when the boy's spirits were high with interest in the game, and he would weigh domestic matters as feathers in the scale beside the day's victory. They promenaded under the lurid July sun, this pair, so wide apart, yet so near, and Sophy saw the large proportion of boys like her own, in their broad white collars and dwarf hats, and all around the rows of great coaches under which was jumbled the debris of luxurious luncheons; bones, pie-crusts, champagne bottles, glasses, plates, napkins, and the family silver, while on the coaches sat the proud fathers and mothers; but never a poor

cheerful

420 mother like her. If Randolph had not **appertained to** these, had not   identified with
centred all his interests in them, had not cared exclusively for the class
they belonged to, how happy would things have been! A great **huzza** at   cheer
some small performance with the bat burst from the multitude of
relatives, and Randolph jumped wildly into the air to see what happened.

425 Sophy fetched up the sentence that had been already shaped; but she
could not get it out. The occasion was, perhaps, an **inopportune** one. The   badly timed
contrast between her story and the display of fashion to which Randolph
had grown to regard himself as **akin** would be fatal. She awaited a better   part of
time.

430   It was on an evening when they were alone in their plain suburban
residence, where life was not blue but brown, she ultimately broke
silence, qualifying her announcement of a probable second marriage by
assuring him that it would not take place for a long time to come, when
he would be living quite independently of her.

435   The boy thought the idea a very reasonable one, and asked if she had
chosen anybody? She hesitated; and he seemed to have a misgiving. He
hoped his stepfather would be a gentleman? he said.

   'Not what you call a gentleman,' she answered timidly.

   'He'll be much as I was before I knew your father;' and by degrees she
440 **acquainted** him with the whole. The youth's face remained fixed for a   familiarized
moment; then he flushed, leant on the table, and burst into passionate
tears.

   His mother went up to him, kissed all of his face that she could get at,
and patted his back as if he were still the baby he once had been, crying
445 herself the while. When he had somewhat recovered from his **paroxysm**   outburst
he went hastily to his room and fastened the door.

   Parleyings were attempted through the keyhole, outside which she   negotiations
waited and listened. It was long before he would reply, and when he did
it was to say sternly at her from within: 'I am ashamed of you! It will ruin
450 me! A miserable boor! a churl! a clown! It will degrade me in the eyes of
all the gentlemen of England!'

   'Say no more – perhaps I am wrong! I will struggle against it!' she cried
miserably.

   Before Randolph left her that summer a letter arrived from Sam to
455 inform her that he had been unexpectedly fortunate in obtaining the shop.
He was in possession; it was the largest in the town, combining fruit with
vegetables, and he thought it would form a home worthy even of her
some day. Might he not run up to town to see her?

   She met him by stealth, and said he must still wait for her final answer.
460 The autumn dragged on, and when Randolph was home at Christmas for

the holidays she broached the matter again. But the young gentleman was **inexorable**.

unyielding

It was dropped for months; renewed again; abandoned under his repugnance; again attempted; and thus the gentle creature reasoned and
465 pleaded till four or five long years had passed. Then the faithful Sam revived his suit with some **peremptoriness**. Sophy's son, now an undergraduate, was down from Oxford one Easter, when she again opened the subject. As soon as he was **ordained**, she argued, he would have a home of his own, wherein she, with her bad grammar and her
470 ignorance, would be an **encumbrance** to him. Better **obliterate** her as much as possible.

impatience

made a vicar

burden; erase

He showed a more manly anger now, but would not agree. She on her side was more persistent, and he had doubts whether she could be trusted in his absence. But by indignation and contempt for her taste he
475 completely maintained his **ascendancy**; and finally taking her before a little cross and altar that he had erected in his bedroom for his private devotions, there bade her kneel, and swear that she would not wed Samuel Hobson without his consent. 'I owe this to my father!' he said.

dominance

The poor woman swore, thinking he would soften as soon as he was
480 ordained and in full swing of clerical work. But he did not. His education had by this time sufficiently **ousted** his humanity to keep him quite firm; though his mother might have led an idyllic life with her faithful fruiterer and greengrocer, and nobody have been anything the worse in the world.

shut out

Her lameness became more confined as time went on, and she seldom
485 or never left the house in the long southern thoroughfare, where she seemed to be pining her heart away. 'Why mayn't I say to Sam that I'll marry him? Why mayn't I?' she would murmur plaintively to herself when nobody was near.

Some four years after this date a middle-aged man was standing at the
490 door of the largest fruiterer's shop in Aldbrickham. He was the proprietor, but to-day, instead of his usual business attire, he wore a neat suit of black; and his window was partly shuttered. From the railway-station a funeral procession was seen approaching: it passed his door and went out of the town towards the village of Gaymead. The man, whose eyes were
495 wet, held his hat in his hand as the vehicle moved by; while from the mourning coach a young smooth-shaven priest in a high waistcoat looked black as a cloud at the shop-keeper standing there.

The Son's Veto by Thomas Hardy

Reading

Some people find reading stories written before the twentieth century difficult because the language is unfamiliar. Do not become disheartened! Take time to read the story carefully and to read it a number of times. If you come across a word that you don't understand and which is not explained, then use a dictionary. Remember that sometimes the meaning of a word might have changed slightly through time.

You may respond to this story either as an individual, in pairs or in groups.

If you are working as an individual read through the questions below and make brief notes.

First thoughts
♦ What is the story about?
♦ What is your impression of the mother at the beginning of the story?
♦ What do you learn about her husband?

Marriage to Mr Twycott
♦ How did Mr Twycott commit social suicide?
♦ How does the couple's life change after the wedding?

Randolph, the son
♦ How would you describe the relationship between the son and mother?
♦ Does it change during the course of the story? If so in what way?
♦ What does Hardy think of the boy's attitude to his mother? What evidence is there?

Friendship with Sam Hobson
♦ How does the renewed friendship with Sam affect the mother?
♦ What would the mother gain by marrying Sam?
♦ What would she lose? What do you think she should have done?

A decision to be made
♦ What do you think of the son's reaction to the news about the possible second marriage and his subsequent actions? Why didn't the son want her to marry this man?
♦ Why does the reader feel sorry for the mother?
♦ How does Hardy want us to feel about the son?

The context
♦ What evidence is there to suggest that this story was written over a century ago?

Coursework assignments

This assignment looks closely at characters and their relationships.

> The mother in this story sacrifices everything for a son who doesn't even seem to care about her. Women today would not act like this.' Do you agree with this statement?
>
> You should explain how you feel about these characters and their relationship with each other. Remember to refer closely to the text.

To help you plan your answer, use the following structure.

Step 1
Start by underlining words in the assignment title that you think are important.

Step 2
Look back at the notes you made under 'Reading'. Make further notes before you begin writing. If you have your own copy of this book you will find it useful to underline significant words and phrases in the text.

Step 3
Look at the details of the story again, using these prompts to help you:
- Why does Hardy open the story with the very detailed description of the woman's hair?
- What are your first impressions of the son? Which particular words and images help you to form your impression of him?
- Look at the way Hardy presents the son throughout the story. Does the son love his mother?
- What evidence is there to suggest that the mother loves the son?
- How is the mother presented throughout the story? Look for words and images used to describe Sophy throughout the story. What do they tell you about her?
- Find the parts of the story in which Hardy gives you his own opinion. How much does this influence your opinion of the mother?

Step 4
Decide what you think about the mother:
- Should she have married against her son's wishes? Why didn't she?
- Does Hardy approve of this? Do you approve of her decision?

Step 5
Decide whether or not you agree with the statement.

Step 6
As you plan and write your assignment, refer closely to the text and use quotations to support your views.

Twentieth century story: *Growing Up*

Joyce Cary, who wrote *Growing Up*, was a male writer who died in 1957. At the time of his death he had become accepted widely as one of our best modern novelists. In this story Cary looks at the subject of growing up and makes us realise that no matter how old we are, we are never too old to learn. Like the other short story in this unit, it is about families and the relationships within them.

Growing Up

Robert Quick, coming home after a business trip, found a note from his wife. She would be back at four, but the children were in the garden. He tossed down his hat, and still in his dark business suit, which he disliked very much, made at once for the garden.

5 He had missed his two small girls and looked forward eagerly to their greeting. He had hoped indeed that they might, as often before, have been waiting at the corner of the road, to flag the car, and drive home with him.

The Quick's garden was a wilderness. Except for a small vegetable patch near the pond, and one bed where Mrs Quick grew flowers for the
10 house, it had not been touched for years. Old apple trees tottered over seedy laurels, unpruned roses. Tall ruins of dahlias and delphiniums hung from broken sticks.

The original excuse for this neglect was that the garden was for the children. They should do what they liked there. The original truth was
15 that neither of the Quicks cared for gardening. Besides, Mrs Quick was too busy with family, council, and parish affairs, Quick with his office, to give time to a hobby that bored them both.

But the excuse had become true. The garden belonged to the children, and Quick was even proud of it. He would boast of his wild garden, so
20 different from any neighbour's shaved grass and combed beds. It had come to seem, for him, a triumph of imagination; and this afternoon, once more, he found it charming in its wilderness, an original masterpiece among gardens.

And, in fact, with the sun just warming up in mid-May, slanting steeply
25 past the trees, and making even old weeds shine red and gold, it had the special beauty of untouched woods, where there is still, even among

closely farmed lands, a little piece of free nature left, a suggestion of the frontier, primeval forests.

'A bit of real wild country,' thought Quick, a townsman for whom the country was a place for picnics. And he felt at once released, escaped. He shouted, 'Hullo, hullo, children.'

There was no answer. And he stopped, in surprise. Then he thought, 'They've gone to meet me – I've missed them.' And this gave him both pleasure and dismay. The last time the children had missed him, two years before, having gone a mile down the road and lain in ambush behind a hedge, there had been tears. They had resented being searched for, and brought home; they had hated the humiliating failure of their surprise.

But even as he turned back towards the house, and dodged a tree, he caught sight of Jenny, lying on her stomach by the pond, with a book under her nose. Jenny was twelve and had lately taken furiously to reading.

Quick made for the pond with long steps, calling, 'Hullo, hullo, Jenny, hullo,' waving. But Jenny merely turned her head slightly and peered at him through her hair. Then she dropped her cheek on the book as if to say, 'Excuse me, it's really too hot.'

And now he saw Kate, a year older. She was sitting on the swing, leaning sideways against a rope, with her head down, apparently in deep thought. Her bare legs, blotched with mud, lay along the ground, one foot hooked over the other. Her whole air was one of languor and concentration. To her father's 'Hullo,' she answered only in a faint muffled voice, 'Hullo, Daddy.'

'Hullo, Kate.' But he said no more and did not go near. Quick never asked for affection from his girls. He despised fathers who flirted with their daughters, who encouraged them to love. It would have been especially wrong, he thought, with these two. They were naturally impulsive and affectionate – Jenny had moods of passionate devotion, especially in the last months. She was growing up, he thought, more quickly than Kate, and she was going to be an exciting woman, strong in all her feelings, intelligent, reflective. 'Well, Jenny,' he said, 'what are you reading now?' But the child answered only by a slight wriggle of her behind.

Quick was amused at his own disappointment. He said to himself, 'Children have no manners but at least they're honest – they never pretend.' He fetched himself a deck chair and the morning paper, which he hardly looked at before his early start on the road. He would make the best of things. At fifty-two, having lost most of his illusions, he was good at making the best of things. 'It's a lovely day,' he thought, 'and I'm free

till Sunday night.' He looked round him as he opened the paper and felt
again the pleasure of the garden. What a joy, at last, to be at peace. And
the mere presence of the children was a pleasure, nothing could deprive
him of that. He was home again.

Jenny had got up and wandered away among the trees; her legs too
were bare and dirty, and her dress had a large green stain at the side. She
had been in the pond. And now Kate allowed herself to collapse slowly
out of the swing and lay on her back with her hair tousled in the dirt, her
arms thrown apart, her small dirty hands with black nails turned
palm upwards to the sky. Her cocker bitch, Snort, came loping and
sniffing, uttered one short bark and rooted at her mistress's legs.
Kate raised one foot and tickled her stomach, then rolled over and
buried her face in her arms. When Snort tried to push her nose under
Kate's thigh as if to turn her over, she made a half kick and murmured,
'Go away, Snort.'

'Stop it, Snort,' Jenny echoed in the same meditative tone. The sisters
adored each other and one always came to the other's help. But
Snort only stopped a moment to gaze at Jenny, then tugged at Kate's
dress. Kate made another more energetic kick and said, 'Oh, go
away, Snort.'

Jenny stopped in her languid stroll, snatched a bamboo from the border,
and hurled it at Snort like a spear.

The bitch, startled, uttered a loud uncertain bark and approached,
wagging her behind so vigorously that she curled her body sideways at
each wag. She was not sure if this was a new game, or if she had
committed some grave crime. Jenny gave a yell and rushed at her. She

95 fled yelping. At once Kate jumped up, seized another bamboo and threw it, shouting 'Tiger, tiger.'

The two children dashed after the bitch, laughing, bumping together, falling over each other and snatching up anything they could find to throw at the fugitive, pebbles, dead daffodils, bits of flower-pots, lumps of
100 earth. Snort, horrified, over-whelmed, dodged to and fro, barked hysterically, crazily, wagged her tail in desperate submission; finally put it between her legs and crept whining between a broken shed and the wall. Robert was shocked. He was fond of the sentimental foolish Snort, and he saw her acute misery. He called to the children urgently, 'Hi Jenny
105 don't do that. Don't do that, Kate. She's frightened – you might put her eye out. Hi, stop – stop.'

This last cry expressed real indignation. Jenny had got hold of a rake and was trying to hook Snort by the collar. Robert began to struggle out of his chair. But suddenly Kate turned round, aimed a pea-stick at him
110 and shouted at the top of her voice, 'Yield, Paleface,' Jenny at once turned and cried, 'Yes, yes – Paleface, yield.' She burst into a shout of laughter and could not speak, but rushed at the man with the rake carried like a lance.

The two girls, staggering with laughter, threw themselves upon their
115 father. 'Paleface – Paleface Robbie. Kill him – scalp him. Torture him.'

They tore at the man and suddenly he was frightened. It seemed to him that both children, usually so gentle, so affectionate, had gone completely mad, vindictive. They were hurting him, and he did not know how to defend himself without hurting them, without breaking their skinny
120 bones, which seemed as fragile as a bird's legs. He dared not even push too hard against the thin ribs which seemed to bend under his hand. Snort, suddenly recovering confidence, rushed barking from cover and seized this new victim by the sleeve, grunting and tugging.

'Hi' he shouted, trying to catch at the bitch. 'Call her off, Kate. Don't,
125 don't, children.' But they battered at him, Kate was jumping on his stomach, Jenny had seized him by the collar as if to strangle him. Her face, close to his own, was that of a homicidal maniac; her eyes were wide and glaring, her lips were curled back to show all her teeth. And he was really strangling. He made a violent effort to throw the child off, but
130 her hands were firmly twined in his collar. He felt his ears sing. Then suddenly the chair gave way – all three fell with a crash. Snort, startled, and perhaps pinched, gave a yelp, and snapped at the man's face.

Kate was lying across his legs, Jenny on his chest; she still held his collar in both hands. But now, gazing down at him, her expression
135 changed. She cried, 'Oh, she's bitten you. Look, Kate.' Kate, rolling off his legs, came to her knees. 'So she has, bad Snort.'

The girls were still panting, flushed, struggling with laughter. But Jenny reproached her sister, 'It's not a joke. It might be poisoned.'

'I know,' Kate was indignant, But burst out again into helpless giggles.

140 Robert picked himself up and dusted his coat. He did not utter any reproaches. He avoided even looking at the girls in case they should see his anger and surprise. He was deeply shocked. He could not forget Jenny's face, crazy, murderous; he thought, 'Not much affection there – she wanted to hurt. It was as if she hated me.'

145 It seemed to him that something new had broken into his old simple and happy relation with his daughters; that they had suddenly receded from him into a world of their own in which he had no standing, a primitive, brutal world.

He straightened his tie. Kate had disappeared; Jenny was gazing at his 150 forehead and trying to suppress her own giggles. But when he turned away, she caught his arm, 'Oh Daddy, where are you going?'

'To meet your mother – she must be on her way.'

'Oh, but you can't go like that – we've got to wash your bite.'

'That's all right, Jenny. It doesn't matter.'

155 'But Kate is getting the water – and it might be quite bad.'

And now, Kate, coming from the kitchen with a bowl of water, called out indignantly.

'Sit down, Daddy – sit down – how dare you get up.'

She was playing the stern nurse. And in fact, Robert, though still in a 160 mood of disgust, found himself obliged to submit to this new game. At least it was more like a game. It was not murderous. And a man so plump and bald could not allow himself to appear upset by the roughness of children. Even though the children would not understand why he was upset, why he was shocked.

165 'Sit down at once, man,' Jenny said. 'Kate, put up the chair.'

Kate put up the chair, the two girls made him sit down, washed his cut, painted it with iodine, stuck a piece of plaster on it. Mrs. Quick, handsome, rosy, good-natured, practical, arrived in the middle of this ceremony, with her friend Jane Martin, Chairman of the Welfare 170 Committee. Both were much amused by the scene, and the history of the afternoon. Their air said plainly to Robert, 'All you children – amusing yourselves while we run the world.'

Kate and Jenny were sent to wash and change their dirty frocks. The committee was coming to tea. And at tea, the two girls, dressed in their 175 smart clean frocks, handed round the cake and bread and butter with demure and reserved looks. They knew how to behave at tea, at a party.

They were enjoying the dignity of their own performance. Their eyes passed over their father as if he did not exist, or rather as if he existed only as another guest, to be waited on.

And now, seeking as it were a new if lower level of security, or resignation, he said to himself, 'Heavens, but what did I expect? In a year or two more I shan't count at all. Young men will come prowling, like the dogs after Snort – I shall be an old buffer, useful only to pay bills.'

The ladies were talking together about a case – the case of a boy of fourteen, a nice respectable boy, most regular at Sunday School, who had suddenly robbed his mother's till and gone off in a stolen car. Jenny, seated at her mother's feet, was listening intently, Kate was feeding chocolate roll to Snort, and tickling her chin.

Quick felt all at once a sense of stiffness. He wanted urgently to get away, to escape.

Yes, he needed some male society. He would go to the club. Probably no one would be there but the card-room crowd, and he could not bear cards. But he might find old Wilkins in the billiard room. Wilkins at seventy was a crashing, a dreary bore, who spent half his life at the club; who was always telling you how he had foreseen the slump, and how clever he was at investing his money. What good was money to old Wilkins? But, Quick thought, he could get up a game with Wilkins, pass an hour or two with him, till dinner-time, even dine with him. He could phone his wife. She would not mind. She rather liked a free evening for her various accounts. And he need not go home till the children were in bed.

And when after tea, the committee members pulled out their agenda, he stole away. Suddenly, as he turned by the corner house, skirting its front garden wall, he heard running steps and a breathless call. He turned, it was Jenny. She arrived, panting, holding herself by the chest. 'Oh, I couldn't catch you.'

'What is it now, Jenny?'

'I wanted to look – at the cut.'

Robert began to stoop. But she cried, 'No, I'll get on the wall. Put me up.'

He lifted her on the garden wall which made her about a foot taller than himself. Having reached this superior position, she poked the plaster.

'I just wanted to make sure it was sticking. Yes, it's all right.'

She looked down at him with an expression he did not recognise. What was the game, medical, maternal? Was she going to laugh? But the child 220 frowned. She was also struck by something new and unexpected.

Then she tossed back her hair. 'Good-bye.' She jumped down and ran off. The man walked slowly towards the club. 'No,' he thought, 'not quite a game – not for half a second. She's growing up – and so am I.'

Growing up by Joyce Cary

Reading

1 *If you are working as an individual make brief notes in response to these questions. If you are working in a group, discuss the questions then make notes to prepare for your own writing.*

♦ Could such events have happened in your family? Try to define the discoveries Robert Quick makes about his daughters and himself.

♦ Does Quick seem to you a good parent?

♦ Why does the writer introduce: a) the tea-party with the Welfare Committee; b) the story about the fourteen-year-old boy; c) Wilkins?

♦ What is Quick's main reason for wanting to go to the club? There is a strong clue in one particular sentence.

2 Make notes in response to the following questions. Your answers will help you to complete your coursework assignment.

First thoughts

♦ What are your first impressions of the family and their relationship with each other? What evidence is there in the text to support your impressions?

♦ What is the mood at the beginning of the story? How does Robert Quick feel? How do you know?

The attack

♦ What do the girls do to the dog? Is the father shocked by their behaviour? How does this action affect the mood of the story at that point?

♦ How fierce was the attack on the dog and then the father? Look at the language that Cary uses to describe these attacks. What halted the attack?

Changes

♦ The writer states: 'something new had broken into his old simple and happy relation with his daughters; that they had suddenly receded from him into a world of their own in which he had no standing, a primitive, brutal world'. What do you think he means by this? What do you think had changed in the way the father viewed his daughters?

♦ Did the daughters' views also change? What evidence suggests this?

♦ How often does the mood of the story change? What prompts each change?

Relationships

♦ What do we learn about Mrs Quick? What type of relationship do she and her husband have?

♦ What type of relationship do the two sisters have?

Growing up

♦ What strikes you about the ways in which the girls' behaviour changes?

♦ Is the account of the fourteen-year-old boy relevant to the story? How?

♦ Can you understand the father's fear? Was he in danger?

♦ What does the father mean when he says at the end of the story 'She's growing up -– and so am I.'

♦ What do you think of the ending? What do you think of this story?

Coursework assignments

1 This assignment asks you to look closely at the relationships explored in *Growing Up*.

> During the course of the afternoon the father's relationship with his daughters and theirs with him undergoes a change. What causes the change to occur? How does the writer Joyce Cary convey this changing relationship to the reader?

You will need to plan your answer to this assignment.

♦ Look at **what** happens and the way it is described.

♦ Show **how** the effect on the father is made clear to the reader. Do not fall into the trap of merely re-telling the story – you need to show how the events in the story affect the characters. Remember that when a question includes the word 'how', this usually means that you are being asked to look carefully at the mood and style, and the way the story is organised.

2 In this assignment you will compare *Growing Up* with *The Son's Veto*, a pre-twentieth-century story by Thomas Hardy. If you have not read *The Son's Veto* you can find it on page 126. Look also at the questions in 'Reading' which follow it on page 140, to help you understand the story's meaning.

> What similarities and differences can you find between *Growing Up* and *The Son's Veto*? You should pay particular attention to the way the relationships between parents and children are presented by the authors.

Use the following prompts to help you:

First thoughts

♦ What are the two stories about?

♦ What do they have in common?

♦ How are the parents made unhappy by the children?

The children

♦ How are the children presented by the writers?

♦ Do you prefer the son in *The Son's Veto* or the daughters in *Growing Up*? Why?

The parents

♦ Which parent do you feel the most sorry for?

♦ Is the author of either story sympathetic to the parent?

♦ What do you think of the parents' reactions to their children's behaviour in these stories? Would you have reacted differently?

The stories

♦ What do you think of the titles of the two stories?

♦ Which story do you prefer and why?

3 This assignment allows you to compare a twentieth-century piece of prose with a pre-twentieth-century poem. You will need to have read the poem 'Cousin Kate' by Christina Rossetti on page 168 and the questions in 'Reading' which follow it on page 170.

> Both *Growing Up* and *Cousin Kate* are about relationships that have changed people and somehow shattered illusions they might have had. What similarities and what differences can you find between the story and the poem?

Use the following prompts to help you.

First thoughts

♦ What has happened to the narrator in the poem 'Cousin Kate'? How does she feel about Cousin Kate?

♦ How does the father feel about his daughters in the story *Growing Up*?

Moods

♦ What is the mood in 'Cousin Kate'? Does it change at the end?

♦ What is the predominant mood in *Growing Up*?

♦ How does the father feel about his children at the end of the story?

♦ How does the narrator feel at the end of 'Cousin Kate'?

Changes

♦ How have these people been affected by what has happened to them?

♦ Think about the narrator in the poem, and the father and daughters in the story. What illusions, if any, have been shattered?

♦ How do the two writers use language to show how the events are influencing and changing characters?

Finally

♦ How do you feel about the poem and the story? Which do you prefer, and why?

POETRY

Introduction

The poems in this section have been carefully chosen to offer opportunities for responding to poetry as practice for examinations or for coursework assignments. You will need to check with your lecturer or teacher to see which combination best suits your coursework demands. In this unit you will find:

♦ Three poems by the well-known twentieth-century poet, Sheenagh Pugh. This provides a twentieth-century poet study.

♦ A selection of poetry by William Blake, a named pre-twentieth-century poet. This provides a pre-twentieth-century poet study.

♦ An assignment comparing William Blake with Sheenagh Pugh. This provides a pre-1900 poet/post-1900 poet comparison.

♦ A comparison between 'Cousin Kate' by Christina Rossetti, a named pre-twentieth-century poet, and a twentieth-century poem with a similar theme, 'The Seduction' by Eileen McAuley. This provides a pre-1900/post-1900 comparison.

♦ Three translations of a poem 'First Ice' from another culture and tradition. This provides a coursework assignment.

How to approach a poem

Poems are much more intense than stories because a poet condenses his or her thoughts and ideas into a few words. You often have to read a poem two or three times to make sure that you understand it. You should also remember that poems are often written to be read aloud. The rhyme, rhythm and language of a poem are important because they are used by the poet to express his or her ideas and to convey emotion.

When you are asked to write about a poem, there are five important areas that you must refer to.

1 Content

You must show the examiner that you have understood the poem and know what it is about.

2 Theme

You should consider the ideas the poet is expressing or the issues the poem addresses.

3 Mood

You should think about the sort of emotions and atmosphere that the poem creates.

Ask yourself how the poet makes you feel – angry, sad, happy, reflective, optimistic, pessimistic?

4 Structure

You must look at how the writer has put the poem together. Is it in verses? Is it a special type of poem – a sonnet, an ode or an elegy? How does one part of a poem lead on to another?

5 Language

You should think about why the poet has chosen those particular words. Are there any words or images which you find surprising?

Every time you respond to a poem you must look at these five key areas. Examiners highly reward those students who show that they are engaging with the language of a poem and are trying to understand why it has been structured in a certain way.

It is also important to know that there are no right or wrong answers to the questions – your own response to the poem is important. However, you must always support your views with evidence from the poem. Imagine that you are in a court of law and you have to prove your case. The same thing has to happen whenever you respond to literature – you must prove your case. You have to say **why** you believe your ideas are correct.

Whenever you are responding to a poem it is useful to write down the five headings – content, theme, mood, structure and language – and put your ideas under the relevant heading.

Sheenagh Pugh

Sheenagh Pugh is a Welsh poet who writes in English. She has won many prestigious poetry awards and is well known throughout Great Britain as a poet of exceptional ability and standing. Her poetry is thought-provoking and its themes of much interest to young and old alike.

Earth Studies

The three poems by Sheenagh Pugh which follow are taken from the 'Earth Studies' sequence, a history of the world in nineteen poems. Set in the future, they explore the rise of human civilisation and the abuse of the Earth that eventually leads to its death. The 'survivors' leave Earth and the children who survive are given lessons, 'Earth Studies', to prepare them for a time when they might return.

  Read the poem 'The Craft I Left in was Called Esau', on page 155, carefully. A common mistake students make when responding to a poem is to under-estimate it. There is a lot to write about here, so be careful to read between the lines.

  Sometimes poets don't *state* things they *imply* them. The word *imply* means to suggest indirectly or to hint. For instance, Sheenagh Pugh called the spacecraft *Esau*. The Bible relates how Esau sold his inheritance for a bowl of soup – could the poet be suggesting that mankind has also made a bad bargain? This is not stated but is *implied* by her naming of the craft. Use the questions in 'Reading' and the Focus box on the next page, to help you study the poem.

Reading

If you are working as an individual make brief notes in response to these questions. If you are working in a group, discuss the questions then make notes to prepare for your own writing.

1 Look at the questions at the side of the poem on the opposite page. Make notes under these headings: content, theme, mood, structure and language. What do you think of the poem? Why is it written in this way? What do you like or dislike about it? Give reasons for your answers.

2 Write in response to this question: *The poem is about a brave, new technological journey into space. What is the poet's attitude to this journey?*

FOCUS

Planning and writing a response

First, make detailed notes on a poem. One way to write about a poem is to comment on content, theme, mood, structure and language separately. However, very often the theme of the poem is closely linked to all areas, so separating them can lead you to repeat yourself.

It is often easier to follow the structure of the poem as you write. Begin by giving a brief overview of the poem, stating what it is about, the mood it creates overall and your first impressions. If you are answering a specific question, address the question at the beginning of your answer.

Then write about the poem looking at each line, group of lines or verses in turn. As you write about each part of the poem, comment on the content, mood and theme *and* how the poet conveys them through the language he or she chooses.

Examiners assess a response to a poem by looking for the following:

G grade – you will show that you have understood the basic storyline and will simply rewrite this.

D grade – you will understand the content of the poem but also the theme. For example, the poet's warning in 'Earth Studies' is about the implications for all mankind. You will convey empathy with (be on a wavelength with) the poet and will make tentative suggestions about language used, referring to a few words or phrases.

C grade and above – you will be more confident. You will do the above in more detail. For example, in 'Earth Studies' you will realise the enormous change and finality of leaving Earth. You will link the name Esau with the last line of the poem. You will write about structure, mood and language. You will engage with the language and address more questions about it, for example, why 'scratched' (line 2) – does this indicate haste? 'A' grade candidates will refer to the difference between the unknown that mankind is heading towards and the safety of the known world by picking up phrases such as 'charted coastlines' (line 23).

All candidates will be expected to explain how they feel about the poem and its effect upon them.

The Craft I Left in was Called Esau

The craft I left in was called Esau
at least that name was scratched on the smooth door
I went in by. Someone said the engineers
gave them all names, I don't know. The stars
5 outside were what I noticed first; they looked
so incongruously normal. People joked
nervously; just like a plane flight.
They found seats, wondered if bags would fit,
gestured at the stars and told each other:
10 'Be seeing those in close-up soon'. No bother,
no big deal. I can't recall feeling sad,
not then. I think I was too interested
in the achievement, the technicalities.
And when we took off, there were the night skies
15 ahead; still, so still, a new ocean.
It seemed natural to look for an horizon,
as a captain would look where he was bound,
not back to port. Then the ship turned,
just slightly, and there was our long bright wake
20 already closing, and we looked back
along it to where you could still trace
charted coastlines on the bluish mass,
quite small really; uncanny with distance,
our late guesthouse; our inheritance.

Annotations:

What impression does the word 'scratched' give? What does this tell you?

How does this traveller feel? Do these travellers realise what they are doing?

Here there are 'charted coastlines'. What about where they are going?

Why use the word 'late' not 'last'? What has 'inheritance' to do with the title? What is the theme?

Why is the craft called Esau? Look at the note at the bottom of the page.

What does 'incongruous' mean? What is the mood of the travellers? How do you know the travellers are on their first journey of this kind? Do you think they are coming back?

Why repeat 'still'? Why a 'new ocean'? Why choose 'natural' – 'normal' was used earlier?

How is this poem written? Could it be a diary? How do you feel?

Note Esau was the eldest son of Isaac and Rebekah in the Old Testament of the Bible. The name in Hebrew means 'rough' or 'covered with hair'. In return for a bowl of potage (thick soup), Esau sold his birthright (inheritance) to his twin brother Jacob.

Seeing Earth

The poem opposite is last in the 'Earth Studies' sequence. The title is the question that one of the pupils asks their teacher. Before you read the poem, read what the poet herself says about it.

'This poem is in the voice of Christie, a teacher, who is an old, moody, earth survivor. This makes it what they call a personal poem – a poem where you write in somebody else's voice. It's liberating, it's interesting and it's a challenge.

'This particular poem was difficult because Christie has to sound like himself, cynical and emotional, but he is, in fact talking about the one thing that makes him emotional and some of that has to come through.

'The repetition of that phrase "Look at it", is as close as I can get in Christie's voice to conveying extreme emotion. It causes a kind of build up of tension throughout the poem towards the end. When you read it aloud you can't help reading it in a more emotional voice.

' "Damascening" is a process of inlaying, to add a pattern to a blade of a sword; the tracery of frost on the leaf is being compared to inlay on a steel or silver sword. And I did wonder about that because it's not a very common word to use and I did wonder whether Christie would put it in. I still do wonder...'

Reading

If you are working as an individual make brief notes in response to these questions. If you are working in a group, discuss the questions then make notes to prepare for your own writing.

Content

♦ What is the poem about?

Theme

♦ Why was the poem written? How does Sheenagh Pugh make us think about what could happen in the future? What could make us leave this planet?

Mood

♦ What mood does the poet convey to the reader? What does the teacher tell the pupil to look out for? Are you surprised by this? Think about the things you would miss if you had to leave this planet. What would they be?

Structure

♦ Look at the structure of the poem. Why does the poet choose to write it in this way? Can you detect a pattern? Read it aloud. Does it have a rhythm?

Language

♦ Why does the poet use the word 'look' so often? How can you look at something with your hands, with your skin?

♦ Read what Sheenagh Pugh has to say about the language of the poem. Are there any words or phrases that you really like or feel you should write about?

Your response

♦ How do you feel about this poem? Explain your own reaction.

Do You Think We'll Ever get to See Earth, Sir?

I hear they're hoping to run trips
one day, for the young and fit, of course.
I don't see much use in it myself;
there'll be any number of places
5 you can't land, because they're still toxic,
and even in the relatively safe bits
you won't see what it was; what it could be.
I can't fancy a tour through the ruins
of my home with a party of twenty-five
10 and a guide to tell me what to see.
But if you should see some beautiful thing,
some leaf, say, damascened with frost,
some iridescence on a pigeon's neck,
some stone, some curve, some clear water;
15 look at it as if you were made of eyes,
as if you were nothing but an eye, lidless
and tender, to be probed and scorched
by extreme light. Look at it with your skin,
with the small hairs on the back of your neck.
20 If it is well-shaped, look at it with your hands;
if it has fragrance, breathe it into yourself;
if it tastes sweet, put your tongue to it.
Look at it as a happening, a moment;
let nothing of it go unrecorded,
25 map it as if it were already passing.
Look at it with the inside of your head,
look at it for later, look at it for ever,
and look at it once for me.

Reading

The two poems you have looked at so far deal with leaving Earth when it has become uninhabitable, and questioning whether mankind will ever be able to return. In **Geography 1** Christie, the teacher, is giving a geography lesson about the island of Surtsey which was 'born' late and lost too soon.

If you are working as an individual make brief notes in response to the questions. If you are working in a group, discuss the questions then make notes to prepare for your own writing. Remember that when you write about a poem you should explore the content, theme, mood, structure and language of the poem.

Read 'Geography 1', opposite, then answer the questions.

Content
♦ What was Surtsey and how was it formed?
♦ Why was Surtsey said to be important?

Theme
♦ Why was Surtsey used as a lesson for these pupils? What message is Pugh trying to get across?

Mood
♦ What is the mood of this poem? How does Sheenagh Pugh make the audience feel? Does the language encourage this mood or is it the subject matter?

Structure
♦ Why is this poem written in verses? What is Christie supposed to be doing as he talks in the poem?

Language
♦ Choose phrases that you particularly like or dislike. Explore areas of the poem that you may find difficult to understand.

Your response
♦ How do you feel about this poem? Do you like it? Are you upset or made angry by it?
♦ How does this poem relate to the two poems by Sheenagh Pugh that you have already read? Which poem do you prefer, and why?

Coursework assignment

Look back at the three poems you have studied. Sheenagh Pugh presents us with a sad view of the future and a grim warning of what could be. Discuss how she does this, paying particular attention to the way she uses mood and language, and how she organises the poem.

Geography 1

We will look today at the island of Surtsey,
preserved for posterity on my colour slides.
Surtsey: off southern Iceland; thrown from the sea
in nineteen-seventy something or another
5 as a result of volcanic activity.

Now here you see the terrific spray, the water
heaved aside as the rock was thrown up.
(Sea-water, that was; a shock of cold
when it struck you.) But the rock was still hot
10 with angry energy; it wanted to shout,

and here's where it told the world, erupting
that flood of colours, all triumph – look at the purple –
and gold warm and living as the sun.
(Look up the sun, someone, for next week.)

15 In this one the colours are cooling, which is why
the man can stand cautiously on the edge,
surveying the prospects. Surtsey was important,
because it was like watching the world begin,

as you can see here. The cooled rock, so black
20 after those colours, hardly bare any time
before the moss inched over. Even birds
nested in a few years. The man here
is a warden, guarding his little world

from any interference, letting it grow
25 as it was meant to. And there's a funny thing,
that men so carefully kept this corner
swept and dusted, while the rest of the house…

I saw it, you know. Surtsey. I saw it
one day in passing, it was a few years old,
30 just an offshore island, a stony outline
softened with lichen. Someone said
that's Surtsey, and I said: fancy that,
but I hadn't time to look properly.

William Blake

The five poems by William Blake in this unit have been taken from *Songs of Innocence and of Experience.*

William Blake was born in London in 1757 and died in 1827. He started drawing at an early age, and his education and early employment was in drawing and engraving. Blake went on to express his vision of the world through writing and illustrating poetry. *Songs of Innocence* was produced in 1789; *Songs of Experience* was produced five years later.

For much of his life Blake's poems remained unread. This was partly because of the limited circulation of his work, and partly because of the rumours put about by his opponents that he was mad (a myth that survived for years after his death). Blake stood out as a dissenter, someone who held different views to most of those around him.

Blake supported the exploited industrial workers, whom he felt had been oppressed by the wealthy, many of whom made huge profits at the workers' expense. Some of his views on the exploitation of the poor can be seen in his poems about chimney sweeps.

In the poem, 'London', Blake paints a grim picture of social deterioration. If he was alive today he would probably have much in common with Sheenagh Pugh, the twentieth-century poet featured in this book starting on page 153.

William Blake believed in God, but was against the Established Church, which he felt was the ally of the landed gentry. Blake suggests in his writing that the church is not doing enough to prevent the misery of the small boys used to clean chimneys. Read **The Lamb** and **The Tiger** on the opposite page, then turn to 'Reading' on page 162.

The Lamb and The Tiger

Although these two poems are both concerned with creation, they form a direct contrast to each other. **The Lamb** is taken from *Songs of Innocence*; **The Tiger** is taken from *Songs of Experience*. 'The Tiger' is probably Blake's most famous poem.

The Lamb

    Little lamb, who made thee?
    Dost thou know who made thee?
Gave thee life and bid thee feed
By the stream and o'er the **mead**;

meadow

5 Gave thee clothing of delight –
Softest clothing, woolly, bright;
Gave thee such a tender voice,
Making all the **vales** rejoice?

valleys

    Little lamb, who made thee?
10   Dost thou know who made thee?

    Little lamb, I'll tell thee,
    Little lamb, I'll tell thee;
He is called by thy name,
For he calls himself a lamb;
15 He is meek and he is mild,
He became a little child:
I a child and thou a lamb,
We are called by his name.
    Little lamb, God bless thee,
20   Little lamb, God bless thee.

The Tiger

Tiger, tiger, burning bright
In the forests of the night,
What immortal hand or eye
Could **frame** thy **fearful** symmetry?

shape; terrifying

5 In what distant deeps or skies
Burnt the fire of thine eyes?
On what wings dare he aspire?
What the hand dare seize the fire?

And what shoulder, and what art,
10 Could twist the sinews of thy heart?
And when thy heart began to beat,
What dread hand and what dread feet?

What the hammer? What the chain?
In what furnace was thy brain?
15 What the anvil? What dread grasp
Dare its deadly terrors clasp?

When the stars threw down their spears
And watered heaven with their tears,
Did he smile his work to see?
20 Did he who made the lamb make thee?

Tiger, tiger, burning bright
In the forests of the night,
What immortal hand or eye
Dare frame thy fearful symmetry?

Reading

If you are working as an individual make brief notes in response to these questions. If you are working in a group, discuss the questions then make notes to prepare for your own writing.

1 Focus on 'The Lamb'. This is a poem that sounds as if it is written by a child. In it the child asks: 'Little lamb, who made thee?'
   - What does this poem tell us about Blake's religious convictions?
   - Does it sound as though he believed in God and Christ?
   - Who was referred to as the 'Lamb of God'? Who became a child on earth?
   - What can you say about the structure and the language used in this poem?
   - What do you think of this poem?

2 Now re-read the poem, 'The Tiger'.
   - Why is this poem regarded as a direct contrast to the poem about the lamb?
   - Who do you think is the immortal person referred to in line 3?
   - Look at lines 13–16. Where does Blake suggest the tiger was created?
   - Look at line 20. What does Blake think of this tiger?
   - How does this poem contrast in mood with 'The Lamb'?
   - What do you think of this poem? It has been published in an anthology of the hundred best loved poems in English Literature, chosen by the general public. Why do you think it is one of Blake's most famous and well liked poems?

The Chimney Sweeper

The first of the two poems which follow, 'The Chimney Sweeper', is taken from *Songs of Innocence*. The second poem over the page, with the same title, is taken from *Songs of Experience*. Read through the poems, then turn to 'Reading' on page 165.

Young boys were sold to master-sweeps to climb up inside the chimneys of large eighteenth century houses to clear the soot. This was dangerous and disease-prone work and many died. Parents were paid for their sons according to age and size – the younger and smaller boys being in greater demand.

The Chimney Sweeper from *Songs of Innocence*

When my mother died I was very young,
And my father sold me while yet my tongue
Could scarcely cry '**weep** weep weep weep!'
So your chimneys I sweep and in soot I sleep.

5 There's little Tom Dacre, who cried when his head,
That curled like a lamb's back, was shaved; so I said,
'Hush, Tom! Never mind it, for when your head's bare
You know that the soot cannot spoil your white hair.'

And so he was quiet, and that very night,
10 As Tom was a-sleeping, he had such a sight!
That thousands of sweepers – Dick, Joe, Ned and Jack –
Were all of them locked up in coffins of black,

And by came an angel who had a bright key,
And he opened the coffins and set them all free;
15 Then down a green plain leaping, laughing they run
And wash in a river, and shine in the sun.

Then naked and white, all their **bags** left behind,
They rise upon clouds, and sport in the wind;
And the angel told Tom, if he'd be a good boy,
20 He'd have God for his father and never **want** joy.

And so Tom awoke, and we rose in the dark,
And got with our bags and our brushes to work;
Though the morning was cold, Tom was happy and warm –
So if all do their duty, they need not fear harm.

street call for 'sweep'

bags of soot

lack

The Chimney Sweeper from *Songs of Experience*

A little black thing among the snow,
Crying 'weep, weep' in notes of woe;
'Where are thy father and mother, say?'
'They are both gone up to the church to pray.

5 Because I was happy upon the heath
And smiled among the winter's snow,
They clothed me in the clothes of death,
And taught me to sing the notes of woe.

And because I am happy and dance and sing,
10 They think they have done me no injury,
And are gone to praise God and his priest and king,
Who make up a heaven of our misery.'

Reading

If you are working as an individual make brief notes in response to these questions. If you are working in a group, discuss the questions then make notes to prepare for your own writing.

1 Look at 'The Chimney Sweeper' from *Songs of Innocence*, on page 163. Discuss these questions:
   ◆ Why did the father sell the boy as a chimney sweep?
   ◆ In verse 2 why is the boy's head shaved? What do you think of the way the other boy tries to soothe his tears? How is his hair described? Does this poem have anything in common with 'The Lamb'?
   ◆ What do you think of the central part of the poem when Tom's dream is described?
   ◆ What does Blake think of what these boys have to do? Does he believe what the boy says in the last line of the poem?
   ◆ What do you think of this poem?

2 Look closely at 'The Chimney Sweeper' from *Songs of Experience*, opposite.
   ◆ Where have the parents gone?
   ◆ Many readers think that placing the parents in church promotes Blake's attack on the authorities of Church and State – for allowing this to happen to young boys. Do you agree?
   ◆ Where else does Blake attack the church in this poem?
   ◆ Why do the people connected with this child think they have not harmed him?
   ◆ What do you think the last line of the poem means?
   ◆ Is the child in this poem better or worse off than the child in the poem taken from *Songs of Innocence*? In the first poem there was some comfort for the boy; is there any comfort in this poem?
   ◆ Which of the two poems is the harshest and strongest outcry against this type of exploitation? Why do you think this?

London

Now look at the poem 'London' from *Songs of Experience*. Blake wants the reader to think about important issues – he thinks that the new freedoms of the changing time have resulted in hardship for many. He believes that the end will be ruin and so finishes the poem with a frightening view of the corrupted future.

London

I wander through each chartered street
Near where the chartered Thames does
   flow,
And **mark** in every face I meet

notice

Marks of weakness, marks of woe.

5
In every cry of every
   man,
In every infant's cry of fear,
In every voice, in every ban,
The mind-forged manacles
   I hear.

How the chimney-sweeper's cry
10 Every black'ning church
   appals,
And the hapless soldier's sigh
Runs in blood down palace walls.

But most through midnight streets I
   hear
How the youthful **harlot's** curse

prostitute

15 Blasts the new-born infant's tear,
And **blights** with **plagues** the marriage

spoils; diseases

   hearse.

Reading

If you are working as an individual make brief notes in response to these questions. If you are working in a group, discuss the questions then make notes to prepare for your own writing.

1 Look at 'London' and discuss the questions that follow.
   ♦ What is the first verse of the poem about? What is the mood of this verse?
   ♦ What are manacles? How can these affect the oppressor and the victim?
   ♦ Why does Blake use the word 'black'ning' to describe the church. It is the time of great industrialization. Is there more to it than this? How else do we use the word 'blacken'?
   ♦ What is the curse that is referred to in the last verse?

2 Think about any differences between the poems in *Songs of Innocence* and those in *Songs of Experience*.
   ♦ Are there any differences? If so what are they?
   ♦ This is what someone said about these two anthologies of poetry:
     'The ideal world of *Songs of Innocence* is threatened by evil and corruption in the *Songs of Experience*.'
     When you have read the poems discuss whether or not you agree with this view.

Coursework assignments

You have now examined five poems by Blake, and should be able to show understanding of the content of his poems and his themes, as well as the way he uses poetic techniques to convey his ideas. Choose one of these assignments.

> 1 Imagine that you have been asked to shorten this section of the book. You are allowed to use only three of Blake's poems. Which ones would you choose to keep and why? You will need to make a strong case for their inclusion and suggest brief reasons for discarding the other two.
>
> 2 Choose one poem from *Songs of Innocence* and one poem from *Songs of Experience*. Explain why they appeal to you. Comment on the themes of the poems and the way Blake uses language to emphasise the themes.
>
> 3 Compare and contrast any two poems in this section. You should pay particular attention to the content as well as Blake's use of image and language.
>
> 4 Compare and contrast the views of creation presented in 'The Lamb' and 'The Tiger'.
>
> 5 Blake's poems impart a powerful social message. With reference to at least two poems show how Blake does this through his use of subject and language.

Comparing poets

On page 160 it was suggested that William Blake has something in common with Sheenagh Pugh, whose poems can be found starting on page 153.

Read the poem **London** by William Blake (page 166). Then read **The Craft I Left in was Called Esau** and **Do You Think We'll Ever get to See Earth, Sir**? (pages 155–156) by Sheenagh Pugh. What similarities and differences can you discover and explore? Remember that when you **compare**, you look for similarities. When you **contrast** you look for differences.

♦ What are these two poets writing about? Can you see any similarities in the subjects they have chosen? Are they interested in people, the environment? When comparing poets it is important to look at **what** they write and, most importantly, **how** they write it.

♦ What themes are present in these poems?

♦ Look at the structure, mood and language of the poems. How do the poets engage the reader's attention?

♦ What is different about these poems? Can you tell that one was written over two hundred years ago? Does this make it more or less effective, or doesn't it matter?

♦ Do you think these poems are effective in getting a message across?

Comparing 'Cousin Kate' and 'The Seduction'

For this assignment you will compare a pre-twentieth-century poem, 'Cousin Kate' by Christina Rossetti with a twentieth-century poem, 'The Seduction' by Eileen McAuley.

Cousin Kate

Christina Rossetti was born in 1830 and died in 1894. She was the daughter of an Italian refugee and was one of four children who were all talented and artistic. She started writing poetry when she was twelve. She also had some poems published by her brothers when she was nineteen but she did not become well known until 1862. Christina Rossetti had two offers of marriage but chose to live as a single woman.

   She is probably best known for her Christmas carol, 'In the bleak midwinter'. Many people believe that Christina Rossetti was an unhappy poet, as many of her poems speak of loss and grief. Her poems are also marked by a love of nature, however, and many have a strong sense of rhyme and rhythm.

   'Cousin Kate' is a narrative poem, which means that it tells a story in verse. Read through the poem carefully, then turn to 'Reading' on page 170.

Cousin Kate

I was a cottage maiden
Hardened by sun and air,
Contented with my cottage mates,
Not mindful I was fair.
5 Why did a great lord find me out,
And praise my flaxen hair?
Why did a great lord find me out
To fill my heart with care?

He lured me to his palace home –
10 Woe's me for joy thereof –
To lead a shameless shameful life,
His plaything and his love.
He wore me like a silken knot,
He changed me like a glove;
15 So now I moan, an unclean thing.
Who might have been a dove.

O Lady Kate, my cousin Kate,
You grew more fair than I:
He saw you at your father's gate,
20 Chose you, and cast me by.
He watched your steps along the lane,
Your work among the rye;
He lifted you from mean estate
To sit with him on high.

25 Because you were so good and pure
He bound you with his ring:
The neighbours call you good and pure,
Call me an outcast thing.
Even so I sit and howl in dust,
30 You sit in gold and sing:
Now which of us has tenderer heart?
You had the stronger wing.

O cousin Kate, my love was true.
Your love was writ in sand:
35 If he had fooled not me but you,
If you stood where I stand,
He'd not have won me with his love
Nor bought me with his land;
I would have spit into his face
40 And not have taken his hand.

Yet I've a gift you have not got,
And seem not like to get:
For all your clothes and wedding-ring
I've little doubt you fret.
45 My fair-haired son, my shame, my pride,
Cling closer, closer yet:
Your father would give lands for one
To wear his coronet.

Reading

If you are working as an individual make brief notes in response to these questions. If you are working in a group, discuss the questions then make notes to prepare for your own writing.

1 a) Think about the whole poem, 'Cousin Kate'.
- What is this poem about?
- What are your first impressions of the woman who narrates the story, cousin Kate and the Lord?
- This poem was written more than a century ago. How would this have affected the way the narrator, an unmarried mother, was treated?

b) Now think about the poem in more detail.
- Did the woman who narrates the story love the man? Did he love her?
- How does this quote make you feel about the woman and the man?
  He wore me like a silken knot,
  He changed me like a glove;
- Is the poet sympathetic to this woman? How do you know?
  Why does the poet use 'dove' (line 16)? What colour is a dove?

c) In lines 25–32 the poem begins to get more difficult.
- Why did the Lord marry the cousin? What do lines 31–34 tell us about cousin Kate?

d) Look at lines 35–48.
- What do lines 39–40 tell us about the woman who is telling the story?
- Which woman do you think the poet has more respect for? Why?
- What do you think of the ending to this poem? Are you pleased for this woman? How does she feel about her son? What words does she use to describe him?

2 Pick out three parts of the poem that you like. Explain *why* you like them.

3 Choose words from this list that best sum up the mood of the poem: *happy, sad, angry, bitter, gloating, philosophical.* Find evidence in the poem to support your view.

Coursework assignment

You have been asked to write about 'Cousin Kate' and show your response to a group of students who are finding the poem difficult. You will need to write about the five areas – content, theme, mood, structure and language.
- Introduce the poem. Explain what it is about and when it was written.
- Talk about the structure of the poem and the narrative style.
- Comment on whether you like poems that tell a story.
- Talk about the language and organization of the poem which enables the reader to react to the woman and feel sympathy. It also allows us to dislike the other characters in the poem.

As you work through the five areas, look back at your notes to help you.

The Seduction

Read 'The Seduction' by Eileen McAuley on pages 172–173, and compare it with 'Cousin Kate'. Use 'Reading' below to help you understand the poem and prepare for the writing assignment.

Reading

If you are working as an individual make brief notes in response to these questions. If you are working in a group, discuss the questions then make notes to prepare for your own writing.

1 Make a list of all the things this poem has in common with 'Cousin Kate' and then make a list of all the differences. Look at more than just the content.
   ♦ Think about the women in each poem. What do you think about what happened to them?

2 Look carefully at the language used in 'The Seduction' to describe events.
   ♦ Look at the second verse. What type of picture is painted of this seduction? How do the poet's words build up this impression?
   ♦ Look through the poem further. How does the poet paint a bleak picture of the night's events?
   ♦ Look at the language the poet uses to describe the setting and the boy. Do you feel sorry for the girl at the end?

3 Now look at the language used in 'Cousin Kate'.
   ♦ Look at the word 'lured' in line 9. What does this suggest about the Lord?
   ♦ Look at the way Rossetti contrasts the good and pure cousin with the woman telling the story. Does Rossetti make the reader feel that the teller is really an 'unclean' thing?
   ♦ How does the last verse sound? Is the woman gloating over cousin Kate? What evidence is there to support the feeling that this verse is spoken triumphantly, emphasising that this woman is pleased to have her son?
   ♦ How does this feeling of triumph about the child compare with the way the girl in the poem 'The Seduction' felt about the prospect of motherhood?

4 What do you think of these two poems? Do you think the attitude to teenage pregnancy has changed between the times that these two poems were written? Is there any evidence of this change in the poem 'The Seduction'?
   ♦ Which poem do you prefer and why?

Coursework assignment

Compare and contrast 'Cousin Kate' by Christina Rossetti with 'The Seduction' by Eileen McAuley. Look closely at the content, theme, mood, structure and language of both poems. Use the notes you have made to help you.

The Seduction

After the party, early Sunday morning,
He led her to the quiet bricks of Birkenhead docks.
Far past the silver stream of traffic through the city,
Far from the blind windows of the tower blocks.

5 He sat down in the darkness, leather jacket creaking madly,
He spat into the river, fumbled in a bag.
He handed her the vodka, and she knocked it back like water,
She giggled, drunk and nervous, and he muttered 'little slag'.

She had met him at the party, and he'd danced with her all night.
10 He'd told her about football; Sammy Lee and Ian Rush.
She had nodded, quite enchanted, and her eyes were wide and bright
As he enthused about the Milk Cup, and the next McGuigan fight.

As he brought her more drinks, so she fell in love
With his eyes as bluse as iodine.
15 With the fingers that stroked her neck and thighs
And the kisses that tasted of nicotine.

Then: 'I'll take you to the river where I spend the afternoons,
When I should be at school, or eating me dinner.
Where I go, by meself, with me dad's magazines
20 And a bag filled with shimmering, sweet paint thinner.'

So she followed him there, all high white shoes,
All wide blue eyes, and bottles of vodka.
And sat in the dark, her head rolling forward
Towards the frightening scum on the water.

25 And talked about school, in a disjointed way:
About O levels she'd be sitting in June
She chattered on, and stared at the water,
The Mersey, green as a septic wound.

Then, when he swiftly contrived to kiss her
30 His kiss was scented by Listerine
And she stifled a giggle, reminded of numerous
Stories from teenage magazines ...

When she discovered she was three months gone
She sobbed in the cool, locked darkness of her room
35 And she ripped up all her My Guy and her Jackie photo-comics
Until they were just bright paper, like confetti, strewn

On the carpet. And on that day she broke the heels
Of her high white shoes (as she flung them at the wall).
And realized, for once, that she was truly truly frightened
40 But more than that, cheated by the promise of it all.

For where, now, was the summer of her sixteenth year?
Full of glitzy fashion features, and stories of romance?
Where strangers could lead you to bright new worlds.
And how would you know, if you never took a chance?

45 Full of glossy horoscopes, and glamour with a stammer;
Full of fresh fruit diets – how did she feel betrayed?
Now, with a softly rounded belly, she was sickened every morning
By stupid stupid promises, only tacitly made.

Where were the glossy photographs of summer,
50 Day trips to Blackpool, jumping all the rides?
And where, now, were the pink smiling faces in the picture:
Three girls paddling in the grey and frothy tide?

So she cried that she had missed all the innocence around her
And all the parties where you meet the boy next door,
55 Where you walk hand in hand, in an acne'd wonderland,
With a glass of lager-shandy, on a carpeted floor.

But, then again, better to be smoking scented drugs
Or festering, invisibly, unemployed.
Better to destroy your life in modern, man-made ways
60 Than to fall into this despicable, feminine void.

Better to starve yourself, like a sick, precocious child
Than to walk through town with a belly huge and ripe.
And better, now, to turn away, move away, fade away,
Than to have the neighbours whisper that 'you always looked the type'.

Eileen McAuley

Ice

Andrei Voznesensky wrote a poem in Russian that has been translated into English by different translators. The translations of his poem show how difficult it can be to translate a poem from one language into another and how different translators have interpreted Voznesensky's words. The aim of this assignment is to find out which poem you prefer and why.

First Ice

A girl freezes in a telephone booth.
In her draughty overcoat she hides
A face all smeared
in tears and lipstick.

5 She breathes on her thin palms
Her fingers are icy. She wears earrings.

She'll have to go home alone, alone.
Along the icy street.

First ice. It is the first time.
10 The first ice of telephone phrases.

Frozen tears glitter on her cheeks –
The first ice of human hurt.

The First Ice

In the telephone box the girl freezes,
her face is smeared with running tears
and lipstick, she huddles, peers
out from her chilly collar, aches –
5 blows upon her thin little paws –
icicle fingers! Earrings flash.
Back – alone as she is, along
the long lonely, icy lane.
The first ice. The first time, it was
10 first ice cracking in phoned phrases –
the frozen track shines on her cheeks –
first ice on her insulting ears.

First Frost

A girl is freezing in a telephone booth,
huddled in her flimsy coat,
her face stained by tears
and smeared with lipstick.

5 She breathes on her thin little fingers.
Fingers like ice. Glass beads in her ears.
She has to beat her way back alone
down the icy street.

First frost. A beginning of losses.
10 The first frost of telephone phrases.
It is the start of winter glittering on her cheek,
the first frost of having been hurt.

Reading

If you are working as an individual make brief notes in response to these questions. If you are working in a group, discuss the questions then make notes to prepare for your own writing.

1 What are the poems about?

2 What differences are there between the poems? Think about:
- ◆ the titles
- ◆ the shape of the poems
- ◆ the words and phrases used in each translation
- ◆ the mood created by each translation.

3 Which poem do you prefer and why?

Writing

1 Imagine that you are the editor of a poetry book and you have been told that you can include one version of this poem. Look at the notes that you made earlier and read the poems again. Write to your publisher explaining which version you would include and why you think it is preferable to the other versions.

2 Write a story about a girl making a phone call as she does in this poem. This could be in the form of a short story or a drama.

SHAKESPEARE COURSEWORK
MACBETH

Introduction

All GCSE Examination Boards now require a coursework assignment based on a Shakespeare play. When you have completed this unit you will have an assignment for your coursework folder.

This unit focuses on one assignment, leading you through all the preparation you need to do. The assignment title is:

'Lady Macbeth is the real driving force behind the murder of Duncan.'

Discuss this statement and decide whether or not you agree.

As you work through the unit you will be asked to write shorter pieces in preparation for writing the assignment. Your shorter pieces may equally well be submitted for coursework. Your tutor or teacher will guide you.

To complete this work you will need:
♦ a good video version of the play
♦ a copy of the text.

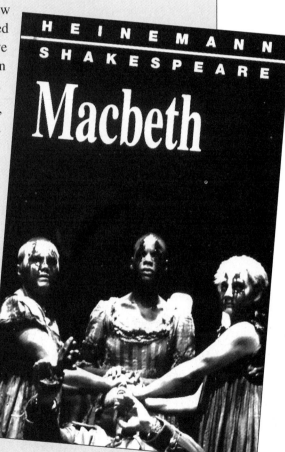

You will also find it useful to have made a summary of what happens in the play. Before you begin the unit, watch the video version of the text carefully.

Macbeth

Getting started

Think carefully about the title for your assignment:

'Lady Macbeth is the real driving force behind the murder of Duncan.' Discuss this statement and decide whether or not you agree.

This title states an opinion and asks you to decide whether or not you agree with it. You will have to prove your point of view using the text to support your ideas.

You will need to decide whether you think Lady Macbeth was entirely responsible for events, whether Macbeth shares some of the responsibility or whether Macbeth was in the hands of fate, and therefore not entirely responsible for his actions. You need to consider Macbeth's character and actions as well as Lady Macbeth's. In this unit you will re-read the text and look at evidence to help you decide.

Discuss

In a group, discuss your first responses to the statement. Use these prompts to help focus your discussion:

♦ Do you think Lady Macbeth forced Macbeth to murder Duncan? Why?
♦ Do you think Macbeth would have murdered Duncan even without Lady Macbeth's persuasion? Why?
♦ If Lady Macbeth was not the driving force behind the murder, how far do you think it was Macbeth himself? How far do you think Macbeth was pushed into murdering Duncan by fate or by events after he heard the witches' prophecy?

Macbeth meets the Witches

Re-read Act 1 scene 3, in which Macbeth and Banquo meet the witches on the heath.

A heath

MACBETH	So foul and fair a day I have not seen.
BANQUO	How far is't called to Forres? What are these,

So withered, and so wild in their **attire**,	40	clothing
That look not like th'inhabitants o' th' earth,		
And yet are on't? Live you, or are you **aught**		anything
That man may question? You seem to understand		
me,		
By each at once her **choppy** finger laying		chopped
Upon her skinny lips. You should be women,	45	
And yet your beards forbid me to interpret		
That you are so.		

MACBETH	Speak if you can. What are you?	
1ST WITCH	All hail Macbeth, hail to thee, Thane of Glamis!	
2ND WITCH	All hail Macbeth, hail to thee, Thane of Cawdor!	
3RD WITCH	All hail Macbeth, that shalt be King **hereafter**!	50 in the future
BANQUO	Good sir, why do you start, and seem to fear	
	Things that do sound so fair? I' th' name of truth	
	Are ye fantastical, or that indeed	
	Which outwardly ye show? My noble partner	
	You greet with present grace, and great prediction 55	
	Of noble having, and of royal hope,	
	That he seems rapt withal. To me you speak not.	
	If you can look into the seeds of time,	
	And say which grain will grow, and which will not,	
	Speak then to me, who neither beg nor fear 60	
	Your favours nor your hate.	

42–43 **aught … question:** Banquo fears they are evil spirits
57 **rapt withal:** carried away with it; also a play on words, *wrapt with all*: involved with everything

1ST WITCH	Hail!	
2ND WITCH	Hail!	
3RD WITCH	Hail!	
1ST WITCH	Lesser than Macbeth, and greater.	65
2ND WITCH	Not so happy, yet much happier.	
3RD WITCH	Thou shalt **get** kings, though thou be none.	
	So all hail Macbeth and Banquo!	
1ST WITCH	Banquo and Macbeth, all hail!	
MACBETH	Stay you **imperfect** speakers, tell me more.	70
	By **Sinel's** death I know I am Thane of Glamis,	
	But how of Cawdor? The Thane of Cawdor lives	
	A **prosperous** gentlemen; and to be king	
	Stands not within the **prospect of belief**,	
	No more than to be Cawdor. Say from whence	75
	You **owe** this strange **intelligence**, or why	
	Upon this **blasted** heath you stop our way	
	With such prophetic greeting? Speak, I **charge** you.	

beget

leaving things unspoken; Macbeth's father

thriving

realms of possibility

get; information

blighted

command

[WITCHES *vanish*

BANQUO	The earth hath bubbles, as the water has,	
	And these are of them. Whither are they	
	vanished?	80
MACBETH	Into the air; and what seem'd **corporal** melted	
	As breath into the wind. **Would** they had stayed.	
BANQUO	Were such things here as we speak about?	
	Or have we eaten on the insane root	
	That takes the reason prisoner?	85
MACBETH	Your children shall be kings.	
BANQUO	You shall be King.	
MACBETH	And Thane of Cawdor too; went it not so?	
BANQUO	To th' selfsame tune and words. Who's here?	

to be flesh

I wish

(Act 1 scene 3)

79–80 **The earth ... are of them:** they disappear like bubbles
84 **insane root:** root of a plant which causes hallucinations

Questions

1 How does Macbeth react to the witches' prophecy? Look at Banquo's speech beginning 'Good sir' (line 51). Why do you think Macbeth seems to fear the prophecy? Why do you think he becomes 'rapt' (*bound up within himself*) (line 57)? Some people think that Macbeth reacts in this way because he is already thinking about murdering Duncan. What do you think?

2 What is the difference between the two men's reaction to the witches? (Look at line 79 to the end of the passage.) Why does Macbeth wish they had stayed?

Macbeth reflects on the prophecies

Macbeth has been informed that he has been made Thane of Cawdor (Act 1 scene 3, line 105). He now thinks about the witches' prophecy. This is the first time that we hear Macbeth talk about how the witches' prophecy has affected him.

The heath

MACBETH	[*Aside*] Two truths are told
	As happy prologues to the swelling act
	Of the imperial theme. – I thank you gentlemen. –
	[*Aside*] This supernatural **soliciting** 130 *prompting*
	Cannot be ill, cannot be good.
	If ill, why hath it given me **earnest** of success, *promise*
	Commencing in a truth? I am Thane of Cawdor.
	If good, why do I **yield** to that **suggestion**, *give in; temptation*
	Whose horrid image doth unfix my hair, 135
	And make my seated heart knock at my ribs,
	Against the use of nature? Present fears *unnaturally*
	Are less than horrible imaginings.
	My thought, whose murder yet is but fantastical,
	Shakes so my single state of man, that function 140
	Is smothered in surmise, and nothing is
	But what is not.
BANQUO	Look how our partner's rapt.
MACBETH	[*Aside*] If chance will have me King, why chance
	may crown me
	Without my stir.

---

128 **happy prologues...imperial theme:** promising forerunners to the increasing splendour of the royal story. (Macbeth sees himself as the central character in a play)

135 **doth unfix my hair:** makes my hair stand on end

137 **Present fears:** real causes of fear

139–141 **My thought...surmise:** murder is only a thought going through my mind, and yet I am so shaken by it that I am unable to act

141–142 **nothing is...is not:** what I imagine is the only thing that exists for me

144 **Without my stir:** without my having to do anything

BANQUO	New honours come upon him,
	Like our strange garments, cleave not to their mould 145
	But with the aid of use.
MACBETH	[*Aside*] Come what come may,
	Time and the hour runs through the roughest day.
BANQUO	Worthy Macbeth, we stay upon your leisure.
MACBETH	Give me your **favour**: my dull brain was **wrought** pardon; troubled
	With things forgotten. Kind gentlemen, your pains 150
	Are registered where every day I turn
	The leaf to read them. Let us toward the King.
	[*To* BANQUO] Think upon what hath **chanced**, and happened
	at more time,
	The interim having weighed it, let us speak
	Our free hearts each to other. openly
BANQUO	Very gladly. 155
MACBETH	Till then enough. – Come friends.

(Act 1 scene 3)

145–146 **strange garments...aid of use:** new clothes do not fit properly until they have been worn for a while
146–147 **Come what...roughest day:** whatever happens, stormy days come to an end
148 **we stay upon your leisure:** we are waiting until it suits you
150 **things forgotten:** things I was trying to remember
151–152 **where every day...read them:** in my memory
154 **The interim...weighed it:** having considered this matter in the meantime

Questions

1 Look at lines 134–138. What is Macbeth thinking about? What 'horrid image' has the witches' prophecy placed in his mind?

2 Which words in the text do you think best sum up Macbeth's confusion?

3 When Macbeth says 'If chance will have me King, why chance may crown me Without my stir' (lines 143–144), do you think he has decided *not* to murder Duncan?

Response

Imagine you are Macbeth. Write a diary entry in which you describe meeting the witches and how you feel now the first part of the prophecy has come true.

Would you have believed the witches and trusted them? Might you feel differently once the first part of the prophecy had come true? How would you feel about murdering someone? Use evidence from the text in your answer.

Macbeth thinks further...

During Act 1 scene 4, Duncan announces that his son, Malcolm, is to be the next king after him. If Duncan had not named Malcolm as the next king, the thanes would then have met and elected a new king after Duncan's death. This might explain why Macbeth had put such faith in the prophecy of the witches. He had thought that as a good general he might have been elected king after Duncan.

Lady Macbeth's reaction to the prophecy

In Act 1 scene 5, Lady Macbeth receives a letter from Macbeth telling her about the witches and their prophecy.

Macbeth's castle
Enter LADY MACBETH, *reading a letter*

L. MACBETH	'They met me in the day of success; and I have	
	learned by the perfect'st report, they have more in	
	them than mortal knowledge. When I burned in	
	desire to question them further, they made	
	themselves air, into which they vanished. Whiles I	5
	stood rapt in the wonder of it, came **missives** from	messengers
	the King, who all-hailed me "Thane of Cawdor", by	
	which title, before these weird sisters saluted me,	
	and referred me to the coming on of time with	
	"Hail King that shalt be!" This have I thought	10
	good to **deliver** thee, my dearest partner of	tell
	greatness, that thou mightst not lose the **dues** of	due share
	rejoicing by being ignorant of what greatness is	
	promised thee. Lay it to thy heart, and farewell.'	
	Glamis thou art, and Cawdor, and shalt be	15
	What thou art promised; yet do I fear thy nature,	
	It is too full o' th' **milk of human kindness**	inner goodness
	To catch the nearest way. Thou **wouldst** be great,	want to be
	Art not without ambition, but without	
	The **illness** should attend it. What thou wouldst	evil
	highly,	20
	That wouldst thou holily; wouldst not play false,	
	And yet wouldst wrongly win. Thou'dst have,	
	great Glamis,	
	That which cries 'Thus thou must do, if thou	
	have it';	

And that which rather thou dost fear to do
Than wishest should be undone. **Hie** thee hither,   25   hurry
That I may pour my spirits in thine ear,
And **chastise** with the **valour** of my tongue   whip; boldness
All that **impedes** thee from the **golden round**,   prevents; crown
Which fate and **metaphysical** aid doth seem   supernatural
To have thee crowned withal.   30

(Act 1 scene 5)

2 **perfect'st report:** most reliable
   information
18 **catch the nearest way:** take by
   the most direct method
20–21 **What thou...holily:** you want
   greatness, but only by fair means

22 **wouldst wrongly win:** would take
   what you should not have
23 **That which cries...have it:** the
   crown which cries 'You must do
   this' if you want it
24 **that which...to do:** i.e. murder

Questions

1 Look at lines 15–20. What does Lady Macbeth fear about Macbeth? What do
you think of her reaction?

2 Look at lines 26–30. What is Lady Macbeth planning to do? Do you think
she wants to become queen
more than Macbeth wants to
be king?

3 Why do you think Macbeth
sent her the letter? Did he
want her to think of a
murder plan?

Lady Macbeth learns that Duncan is to visit

Shortly after reading Macbeth's letter, Lady Macbeth receives the news that Duncan is to stay with them in their castle.

L. MACBETH	The raven himself is hoarse
	That croaks the fatal entrance of Duncan
	Under my battlements. Come you spirits 40
	That tend on mortal thoughts, unsex me here,
	And fill me from the crown to the toe top-full
	Of **direst** cruelty; make thick my blood,
	Stop up th'access and passage to remorse,
	That no compunctious visitings of nature 45
	Shake my fell purpose, nor keep peace between
	Th' effect and it. Come to my woman's breasts,
	And take my milk for gall, you **murd'ring ministers**,
	Wherever in your **sightless substances**
	You wait on nature's mischief. Come thick night, 50
	And **pall thee** in the **dunnest** smoke of hell,
	That my keen knife see not the wound it makes,
	Nor heaven peep through the blanket of the dark,
	To cry '**Hold**, hold!'

Enter MACBETH

L. MACBETH	Great Glamis, worthy Cawdor,
	Greater than both, by the all-hail hereafter, 55
	Thy letters have transported me beyond
	This ignorant present, and I feel now
	The future in the instant.
MACBETH	My dearest love.
	Duncan comes here tonight.
L. MACBETH	And when goes hence?

Glosses (right margin):
- most bitter
- spirits of murder
- invisible state
- cover yourself; darkest
- stop

---

38 **The raven...hoarse:** the croaking raven, a bird of ill-omen, is more hoarse than usual because it signals Duncan's death (bird imagery)

40–41 **spirits...mortal thoughts:** evil spirits that serve murderous thoughts

41 **unsex me:** take away my femininity

43–47 **make thick...and it:** prevent pity from flowing in my veins; make sure that I feel no compassion so that no feelings of humanity upset my ruthless intention, nor stop me from carrying it out

48 **take my milk for gall:** replace my milk with bitterness

50 **wait on nature's mischief:** look after humanity's evil deeds
Come thick night: a plea for darkness

57 **ignorant present:** the present does not know what will happen in the future

MACBETH	Tomorrow, as he purposes.
L. MACBETH	O never 60
	Shall sun that morrow see.
	Your face, my Thane, is a book where men
	May read strange matters. To beguile the time,
	Look like the time; bear welcome in your eye,
	Your hand, your tongue; look like th' innocent
	flower, 65
	But be the serpent under't. He that's coming
	Must be provided for; and you shall put
	This night's great business into my dispatch,
	Which shall to all our nights and days to come
	Give solely sovereign sway and masterdom. 70
MACBETH	We will speak further.
L. MACBETH	Only look up clear;
	To alter favour ever is to fear
	Leave all the rest to me.

(Act 1 scene 5)

60–61 **O never...morrow see:** (Duncan) will not see the sun again
63 **beguile the time:** deceive the world
64 **Look like the time:** wear a suitable expression
67–68 **provided for...great business...dispatch:** play on words, all relating to murder
69–70 **Which shall...masterdom:** two meanings apply:
    (a) tonight ensures our royal future
    (b) this is the most important night of our lives
72 **To alter...fear:** an inappropriate expression always arouses suspicion

Questions

1 Look at Lady Macbeth's first speech, 'The raven himself...' (lines 38–54). Why does she invoke spirits to make her evil? Which images are the most horrific? Do you think she is naturally more evil than Macbeth?

2 Look at Lady Macbeth's second speech, 'O never shall sun...' (lines 60–70). What is she telling Macbeth to do?

3 Why do you think Macbeth says 'We will speak further?' (line 71). Is he trying to put off the decision?

4 Think of the assignment title that you were given at the beginning of this unit. At this point in the play, who seems to be the driving force behind the murder plot?

Lady Macbeth persuades Macbeth ...

Macbeth then tells Lady Macbeth to forget about their plan – he will not kill Duncan. He says, 'We will proceed no further in this business.' This extract from Act 1 scene 7 shows Lady Macbeth's angry reply.

L. MACBETH	Was the hope drunk	35
	Wherein you dressed yourself? Hath it slept since?	
	And wakes it now to look so green and pale	
	At what it did so freely? From this time	
	Such I account thy love. Art thou afeard	
	To be the same in thine own act and valour	40
	As thou art in desire? Wouldst thou have that	
	Which thou **esteem'st** the ornament of life,	regard
	And live a coward in thine own esteem,	
	Letting 'I dare not' wait upon 'I would,'	
	Like the poor cat i' th' adage?	
MACBETH	Prithee peace.	45
	I dare do all that may become a man;	
	Who dares do more is none.	
L. MACBETH	What beast was't then,	
	That made you **break this enterprise** to me?	suggest this plan
	When you **durst** do it, then you were a man;	dared
	And to be more than what you were, you would	50
	Be so much more than the man. **Nor** time nor place	neither
	Did then adhere, and yet you would make both.	were convenient
	They have made themselves, and that their fitness now	
	Does unmake you. I have given suck, and know	
	How tender 'tis to love the babe that milks me –	55

35–38 **Was the...freely:** has hope woken with a hangover, regretting what it said when it was drunk
39 **Such:** worthless as a drunken promise
41–42 **that/the ornament of life:** references to the crown
44 **Letting...would:** letting fear get the better of desire
45 **adage:** proverb (the cat wanted fish, but would not wet her paws)
47 **none:** two meanings apply:
   (a) there is no-one
   (b) not a man, but a superhuman
   beast: contrast with 'man'
50 **to be more...were:** to become king
52 **would:** were determined to
53–54 **that their...unmake you:** time and place are here and now, and you are unmanly/cowardly
54 **I have given suck:** I have had a child (Lady Macbeth was Macbeth's second wife, and she had a son to her first husband)

I would while it was smiling in my face
Have plucked my nipple from his boneless gums,
And dashed the brains out, had I so sworn as you
Have done to this.

MACBETH   If we should fail?

L. MACBETH   We fail?
But screw your courage to the sticking-place,   60
And we'll not fail. When Duncan is asleep —
Whereto the rather shall his day's hard journey
Soundly invite him — his two chamberlains
Will I with wine and wassail so convince,
That memory, the warder of the brain,   65
Shall be a fume, and the receipt of reason
A limbeck only; when in swinish sleep
Their **drenched** natures lie as in a death,   drowned
What cannot you and I perform upon
Th' unguarded Duncan? What not put upon   70
His spongy officers, who shall bear the guilt
Of our great **quell**?   enterprise

MACBETH   Bring forth men-children only,
For thy undaunted mettle should compose
Nothing but males. Will it not be **received**,   accept as true
When we have marked with blood those sleepy two   75
Of his own chamber, and used their very daggers,
That they have done't?

L. MACBETH   Who dares receive it **other**,   otherwise
As we shall make our griefs and clamour roar
Upon his death?

MACBETH   I am settled, and **bend up**   80   like a bow
Each corporal agent to this terrible feat.
Away, and mock the time with fairest show:
False face must hide what the false heart doth know.

(Act 1 scene 7)

56–59 **I would...to this:** Lady Macbeth contrasts her womanliness with her husband's manliness
60 **But screw...sticking-place:** only wind up your courage to its strongest point (as on the string of a cross-bow)
63–67 **his two chamberlains...only:** his attendants will be so overcome by drink and making merry that memory, which is supposed to protect the brain, will melt in an alcoholic haze; they will be so drunk they will remember nothing
70–71 **What not...officers:** we can blame the drunken guards for anything
72–74 **Bring forth...males:** Macbeth is full of admiration for Lady Macbeth's determination
80 **Each corporal agent:** every power in my body
81 **mock the time:** deceive the world

Questions

1 In the speech you have just read from Act 1 scene 7, what arguments does Lady Macbeth use to make Macbeth change his mind?

2 What does this speech tell you about Lady Macbeth? Does she want to kill Duncan more than Macbeth does? Look back over Act 1 scenes 3 to 7. Does she ever show any doubt about what she wants Macbeth to do?

3 Do you think Lady Macbeth has more 'mettle' than Macbeth – is she more courageous? Or is she less moral?

4 How do you think Macbeth feels about the murder at the end of this scene? What evidence do you have for your answer?

The murder

Now read the beginning of Act 2 scene 2.

A courtyard in the castle

L. MACBETH	That which hath made them drunk hath made me bold;
	What hath quenched them hath given me **fire**.
	Hark! Peace!
	It was the owl that shrieked, the fatal bellman,
	Which gives the **stern'st** good night. He is about it.
	The doors are open; and the **surfeited grooms**
	Do mock their charge with snores. I have drugged 5
	their **possets**,
	That death and nature do contend about them,
	Whether they live or die.
MACBETH	[*Within*] Who's there? What ho!
L. MACBETH	Alack, I am afraid they have awaked,
	And 'tis done. Th' attempt and not the deed 10
	Confounds us. Hark! I laid their daggers ready,
	He could not miss 'em. Had he not resembled
	My father as he slept, I had done't.

Enter MACBETH

	My husband!
MACBETH	I have done the deed. Didst thou not hear a noise?
L. MACBETH	I heard an owl scream and the crickets cry. 15
	Did not you speak?
MACBETH	When?
L. MACBETH	Now.
MACBETH	As I descended?
L. MACBETH	Ay.
MACBETH	Hark! Who lies i' th' second chamber?
L. MACBETH	Donalbain.
MACBETH	This is a **sorry** sight. [*Looks on his hands*
L. MACBETH	A foolish thought, to say a sorry sight.
MACBETH	There's one did laugh in's sleep, and one cried
	'Murder!' 20
	That they did wake each other. I stood and heard
	them.
	But they did say their prayers, and **addressed them**
	Again to sleep.

Glossary (margin notes):
- **fire** — courage
- **stern'st** — cruellest
- **surfeited grooms** — drunken servants
- **possets** — hot drinks
- **sorry** — wretched
- **addressed them** — prepared themselves

3 **fatal bellman:** a man paid to ring a bell outside the condemned cell of Newgate Prison, London, at midnight before an execution
4 **He is about it:** he (Macbeth) is commiting the murder
10–11 **Th'attempt…us:** if he has failed (to kill Duncan), we are ruined

L. MACBETH	There are two lodged together.
MACBETH	One cried 'God bless us!' and 'Amen!' the other,
	As they had seen me with these **hangman's** hands.
	Listening their fear, I could not say 'Amen',
	When they did say 'God bless us!'
L. MACBETH	Consider it not so deeply.
MACBETH	But wherefore could not I pronounce 'Amen'?
	I had most need of blessing, and 'Amen'
	Stuck in my throat.
L. MACBETH	These deeds must not be thought
	After these ways; so, it will make us mad.
MACBETH	Methought I heard a voice cry 'Sleep no more!
	Macbeth does murder sleep,' the innocent sleep,
	Sleep that knits up the ravelled **sleave** of care,
	The **death of** each day's life, sore labour's bath,
	Balm of hurt minds, great nature's second course,
	Chief nourisher in life's feast.
L. MACBETH	What do you mean?
MACBETH	Still it cried 'Sleep no more!' to all the house.
	Glamis hath murdered sleep, and therefore Cawdor
	Shall sleep no more, Macbeth shall sleep no
	more.
L. MACBETH	Who was it that thus cried? Why worthy Thane,
	You do **unbend** your noble strength, to think
	So brainsickly of things. Go get some water,
	And wash this filthy **witness** from your hand.
	Why did you bring these daggers from the place?
	They must lie there. Go carry them, and smear
	The sleepy grooms with blood.
MACBETH	I'll go no more.
	I am afraid to think what I have done.
	Look on't again I dare not.
L. MACBETH	**Infirm of purpose!**
	Give me the daggers. The sleeping and the dead
	Are but as pictures.

Line numbers: 25, 30, 35, 40, 45, 50

Glosses:
executioner's
hearing
thread of silk
rest after
comfort
give way
evidence
weak-minded

(Act 2 scene 2)

28–30 **But wherefore...throat:** the inability to say a prayer was thought to be
a sign of being bewitched
35 **sore labour's bath:** relief after hard work
36 **second course:** other form; the first course is being awake, i.e. we spend
our lives either awake or sleeping
37 **Chief nourisher:** i.e. meat – the second course of a meal
51 **but as pictures:** only representations of the living person

Questions

1 Why didn't Lady Macbeth kill Duncan herself? What does this tell us about her?

2 Look at the length of the speeches after Macbeth's entry. What do they tell us about Macbeth's and Lady Macbeth's state of mind?

3 What is Macbeth most worried about? Do you think Macbeth regrets what he has done or is he more worried about what is going to happen to him in the future?

Response

Imagine you have heard all of these speeches between Macbeth and Lady Macbeth as you performed your duties as a servant. You are now worried for your own safety. Write a letter to a friend in which you explain what you have observed and what you have overheard. In the letter you ask for advice about what you should do. Try to convey your feelings about the events that have occurred.

Coursework assignment

'Lady Macbeth is the real driving force behind the murder of Duncan.'
Discuss this statement and decide whether or not you agree.

You are now ready to start planning your answer to the assignment. To help you plan your answer, use this structure:

1 Note briefly what you have learnt about Lady Macbeth since the beginning of the play.

2 Re-read the extracts and the notes you have made in response to the questions. Decide why Macbeth killed Duncan. Would he have committed the murder without Lady Macbeth? Did the witches influence him at all?

3 Decide whether or not you agree with the statement. Select the evidence you will use from the text to support your ideas.

4 As you write your assignment, refer closely to the text and use quotations to support your views.

GET IT RIGHT

Mistakes in grammar, punctuation and spelling will cost you marks in your GCSE exam but learning to write accurately is not just useful for examinations or, indeed, for writing letters to future employers! Writing accurately helps people to communicate with one another more effectively.

This unit will help you to improve the technical accuracy of your writing. You will see cross-references to it in other parts of the book. It is a good idea to refer to this unit throughout the course either when you come across 'Key Points' within a unit or when your tutor or teacher points out errors in your writing. Writing accurately is too important to leave until the end of the course! However, once you have completed your course and just before the exam you may find it useful to work through this unit for revision. The unit covers and gives practice for:

Sentences

- ♦ What is a sentence?
  - – verbs
  - – subject

- ♦ What goes wrong with sentences?
  - – main verb
  - – using commas
  - – agreement

Punctuation

- ♦ Questions
- ♦ Exclamations
- ♦ Capital letters

- ♦ Commas
- ♦ Apostrophes
- ♦ Quotation marks

- ♦ Colons and semi-colons
- ♦ Hyphens and dashes
- ♦ Paragraphs

Spelling

Formats

- ♦ Writing letters and CVs
- ♦ Drafting and editing

- ♦ Writing a report

Sentences

Which of the following are complete sentences?

1 My cousin is about eighteen.

2 I often see him out and about enjoying himself.

3 Out on the town every Saturday.

4 Last week I met him at about 10.30 in the evening.

5 It was a cool evening.

6 Already dark, roads quite wet.

Can you say *why* you think the sentences you have chosen are complete? Don't worry if you can't – we will come back to this later.

What is a sentence?

♦ A sentence is a group of words arranged in a way that is grammatically complete and makes sense.
♦ A sentence always begins with a capital letter and ends with a full stop.

Look at the following:

Was excellent concert the.
The concert was excellent.

Both of the above 'sentences' begin with a capital letter and end with a full stop. The reason the second sentence makes sense is that it follows patterns everyone understands.

Verbs

♦ A full sentence must have a main verb. Verbs have sometimes been referred to as 'action words' because it is often easier to recognise the verb in a sentence if you think of it as a word that describes an action:

swim float dive run jump talk dance read write

♦ However, not all verbs are action words. Some verbs, like to be and to have, describe a state or condition:

*My mother **is** 38 years old.*
*I **was** at home all day yesterday.*
*Peter **has** a really nice sense of humour.*

♦ Other verbs which perform the same kind of function are *seem*, *become* and *appear*:

> *It **seems** that there has been a mistake.*
> *Uncle Simon **appears** to be enjoying himself tonight.*
> *You **have become** quite grown-up since I last saw you.*

♦ *Be* and *have* are also described as auxiliary verbs, which means that they often combine with the forms of 'action words' to create a complete main verb.

> *Richard **is running** in the London Marathon next year.*
> *Tara can't come out – she **is tidying** her bedroom.*
> *'**is running**' and '**is tidying**' are the main verbs of the sentences.*

PRACTICE 1

Write six sentences using *was*, *were*, *have*, *has been* and *had* in combination with action verbs, for example:

*She **was swimming** in the pool.*

Subjects

A full sentence also has a subject. The subject usually tells you what or who the sentence is about:

Daniel *kicked the ball into the trees.* **My sister** *has long black hair.*

PRACTICE 2

1 Identify the subjects of these sentences.

   a) John seemed to be enjoying himself this evening.

   b) Why don't you pay for the tickets for a change?

   c) I really don't want anyone to get hurt.

   d) My doctor says there is nothing to worry about.

   e) The train driver arrived just in time to leave on schedule.

2 Find the main verbs in these sentences.

   a) We really wanted our team to win the match.

   b) Isn't the weather horrible today!

   c) Why can't you be more like your sister?

   d) I put the kettle on to make a mug of coffee.

3 Look back at sentences 1 to 6 on page 193.

   Can you now identify which sentences are complete and say *why* they are full sentences?

4 Read the following extract. All the full stops and capital letters have been left out, but the commas have been left in to help you. Add the missing capital letters and full stops. There were five sentences in the original.

My face pressed to the sweet-smelling upholstery, I imagine what is happening ahead I can't tell how far we have gone, how many blind corners we have taken if we meet something, on this narrow country lane, we will have to reverse past all the cars we have just overtaken that's if we can stop in time I wait for the squeal of brakes, the clash of metal

What goes wrong with sentences?

Forgetting the main verbs

Simon stared out of the train window. The leaves falling, the sky looking grey and dull.

What is wrong with the second sentence? Although the sentence has verbs, it doesn't have a complete main verb. Falling and looking need to be combined with auxiliary verbs (forms of be and have–see pages 193–194) to make a main verb:

*The leaves **were falling**. The sky **was looking** very grey and dull.*

PRACTICE 3

Complete these sentences by filling in the missing auxiliary verb which makes a main verb.

a) An old man _____ getting out of the car.

b) The women _____ watching the car pass by.

Using commas instead of full stops

This is one of the errors students make most frequently, whatever type of writing they are doing (see also page 53).

PRACTICE 4

Look at this example:

Dear Janice

I'm writing this in a hurry before I go out tonight. I was hoping you'd be home next weekend, it's my birthday and I'm going to go out with Lisa and Jane, we were hoping you would be able to come too, I have just heard that you aren't coming home until Monday, I hope you can make it earlier, we'd really love to see you.

It begins to make you feel breathless just to read it, doesn't it? Where should the commas be replaced by full stops?

There is more information about how to use commas in **Punctuation** on page 203.

Agreement of person, tense and number

When you are writing a long sentence, it is sometimes easy to lose the thread of your argument halfway through and forget how you began the sentence. This is where mistakes can creep in, and it is a good idea to try to keep an overall mental 'picture' of how your sentence starts and what you want it to say. If you are unsure, the best method is to look back quickly over what you have written so far, and to do it often.

There are three kinds of basic agreement in English: agreement of person, agreement of tense and agreement of number.

Agreement of person

When you start a piece of writing, you have to choose which 'person' you want to write in. For instance, if you start an essay talking about a character, 'he', then you must use 'he' throughout. You should not change to 'I' or 'They' halfway through the story. You might hear teachers or lecturers refer to stories written in the first or third person. In the list below you can see what they are referring to.

First person singular	*I*
Second person singular	*you*
Third person singular	*he/she/it*
First person plural	*we*
Second person plural	*you*
Third person plural	*they*

> I, you, he/she/it, we, you, they, are words which can be used to replace names or nouns.
>
> They are called **pronouns.**

PRACTICE 5

1 Complete the following sentences. Make sure you include a pronoun which is consistent with the start of the sentence. The first one has been done for you.

a) **He** was sure that **he** had seen the film.

b) She intended to go to the market then...

c) The boy wasn't happy that...

d) The man was annoyed because...

e) You would be surprised if...

f) When we go on holiday...

g) He wasn't going to go...

h) She wanted to tell someone...

i) I want to buy a new...

j) Today it was raining and...

2 Choose a day from last week and write a diary entry for it.

Make sure you write something you are happy to share in small groups. Read your diary entries aloud and, as a group, identify and correct any agreements of person that don't match.

Agreement of tense

It is also important to be consistent in your use of tenses. Many pieces of writing go wrong because students begin writing in one tense and change to another.

♦ Look at the sentences below, for example:

It is very dark. We're creeping along the old path behind the wall. Suddenly something jumped out behind us.

It was very dark. We were creeping along the old path behind the wall. Suddenly something jumps out behind us.

The first version starts in the present and moves to the past. The second starts in the past and moves to the present. Most of these errors occur in stories or in personal writing. One way to avoid such errors is to tell stories using the past tense rather than the present tense.

♦ Agreement of tense can be summed up in two sentences:
a) If you start your writing in the present tense, stay in the present.
b) If you start your writing in the past tense, stay in the past.

Don't forget to check your work as you go along!

PRACTICE 6

1 Write the first paragraph of a personal description of a frightening event, using past time.

2 Write the first paragraph of a brief commentary on an imaginary sporting event, using present time. It can be anything you like, from a football match to a horse race.

Agreement of number

It is important that the **subject** of the sentence and the **verb** of the sentence agree.

For example:

Subject	Verb
I	*was going*
Hannah and Rachael *(They)*	*were going*
We	*were going*

♦ However, problems may occur in longer sentences:

*Hannah and Rachael, who live in the town next door to Natalie, **was** hoping to move to the country.*

In this sentence *was* should be *were* to agree with the subject of the sentence: ***Hannah and Rachael.***

♦ Now look at another example:

*My friend and **I was going** to the cinema.*

The subject is made up of two people, so the verb should be ***were going***.

Ask yourself: 'If I replace the subject words (here, my friend and I) with a pronoun (such as 'we'), which word would I use?' Here the answer is 'we', so the verb must be plural.

♦ Some subjects, such as *Everyone/everybody* and *No-one/nobody* can be a problem because they look as though they ought to be plural (*Everyone* = lots of people), but they are in fact singular and take a singular verb:

Everyone *knows that the earth goes round the sun.*
No-one *is to leave this room without permission.*

PRACTICE 7

1 Complete the following extract by putting was or were in the correct appropriate spaces.

Yesterday, I _____ hoping to go to the fair. I asked Jane if she wanted to go. We _____ deciding what time to go when Jane's brother arrived. He and his friend _____ planning to go to the fair as well. We _____ pleased that they wanted to come as they had a car and could give us a lift.

2 Correct the mistakes in agreement of number and tense in the following passage.

The small party of men came to a halt at the top of the hill at a signal from its leader. Everyone in the party, especially the youngest of the soldiers, are very tired because they have been marching all day. All the men except the leader dropped wearily to the ground and lay there without moving. The leader is a tall, bearded man who wears a cap with a peak which shade his face and eyes from the sun. As he was standing there, he was scanning the countryside from left to right through binoculars which is slung from a leather strap round his neck. He is hoping he will see some sign of movement.

Other common errors

The following errors are made by so many students that it is worth taking special note of them to make sure you avoid them in your own writing.

1 Have/of

Many students write *of* when they should write *have*, for example:

*I could **of** caught the bus*   should be   *I could **have** caught the bus.*

This is because when you say '*I could have caught the bus*' you shorten *have* so you say '*I could've caught the bus*'. The shortened form of *have* sounds like *of*.

2 Who/which

Who is always used to refer to people. *Which* is always used to refer to things. For example:

*That is the man **who** stole my car.*
*That is the bag **which** I bought last week.*

PRACTICE 8

Fill in the blanks in the following passage using *have* or *of*.

I could _____ caught the bus but I put too many eggs in the cake and I couldn't take it out _____ the oven in time. I should _____ 'phoned you but my 'phone was out _____ order. I could _____ 'phoned you from the corner kiosk but I didn't have any money with me.

Punctuation

Questions

Not all sentences end with a full stop. Remember that when you ask a question you should put a question mark **?** at the end:

Where is Shelagh going tonight?
Just what do you think you're doing, young lady?
Why did Joe refuse to come out with us?

Questions often begin with a question word: *What, Where, When, Why, How.* This makes them easy to recognise.

PRACTICE 1

Where should the question marks go in the following extract?

It was still quite dark; the clatter of the letter-box as the postman pushed in mail ceased and the hair along the dog's back subsided. Sylvester repeated, 'Who are you.'

The woman sprang to her feet. Putting the sofa between them, she said, 'How did you get in'.

He could see that she was afraid. He said, 'I let myself in with a key. I live here.'

'What.'

'I live here. This is my house.'

Her face was paper white. 'Can you prove it.'

Exclamations

You can also end a sentence with an exclamation mark **!** . You often use an exclamation mark when you begin a sentence with the words *Oh, What, How,* when you want to emphasise something or when you are giving an order:

What a lovely day it is!
How wonderful she looks in that dress!
I am really fed up with his attitude!
Do it now, please!

PRACTICE 2

Write down ten sentences that could end with an exclamation mark.

Capital letters

Capital letters are not only used at the beginning of sentences. They are used for all proper nouns, that is, names. Remember to use them for:

♦ Personal names: Mel Gibson, Donald Duck, Mrs Allott, Uncle Jim, Lauren, Jack

♦ Names of places, countries, cities: Europe, France, London

♦ Geographical features: Mount Everest, the Amazon

♦ Nationalities and languages: English, Spanish, German

♦ Days, months, festivals: Wednesday, April, Christmas, Ramadan

♦ Religions: Islam, Christianity, Judaism, Buddhism

♦ Names of streets and organisations: High Street, Piccadilly Circus, Barclays Bank

♦ Titles of newspapers, magazines and books: *The Times*, *Esquire*, *Moll Flanders*

♦ For the first word placed inside inverted commas in a sentence, 'Can you give me a lift to work tomorrow?'

♦ The pronoun 'I'.

PRACTICE 3

Punctuate the following extract.

we arrived at longleat about lunch-time hannah was so excited that she hadn't been able to sleep the night before she had read about longleat in the local library in a book called places to visit in england by a.n.explorer rachael and alys wanted to see the hippos on the lake so we booked a ride on the boat which was grandly named s s titanic i wasn't sure about the boat's name and i was glad there were no icebergs around on the boat we were so careful watching the children didn't fall out that we didn't see gran going greener and greener in colour we had forgotten that she gets sea sick on any patch of water bigger than a paddling pool oh the man in the boat was happy to see us get off i'm just glad they didn't make us clean up the mess

Commas

The comma is a useful punctuation mark, second only to the full stop in its importance. The comma helps to separate written language into units of sense which are easy to read and understand. Commas are used to break up longer sentences into small pieces. Look at the text below:

When we got back to the river John a friend of Dave's asked us to get into the boat. Although I can swim I really didn't feel like going out on the river especially as the weather was getting worse. However everyone else wanted to join John so we clambered into the boat. As soon as we got into the middle of the river Dave who was rowing alongside John began to warn us about rapids ahead. Excited and nervous the others began to laugh.

As you can see, the lack of commas makes the text very difficult to read.

PRACTICE 4

Try to put commas where you think they should go, in the paragraph above. Then look at the main uses of the comma, listed below.

1 Commas in lists.

The comma separates items in a list of three or more: you say *bread and butter* but *bread, butter and cheese.*

Jim went to town to buy sausages, satsumas, sealing wax and string.

There is normally no comma between the last two items in the list, which are joined by *and* or *or.*

2 Commas used like brackets.

Commas are used to mark off a part of a sentence which adds information about the subject but is not essential to defining exactly who or what the subject is. This sounds very complicated, and is perhaps easiest to explain by reference to a couple of examples:

The young man, who was only 25, was the most experienced mountaineer in the team.

The Oxford train, which is standing at platform 5, will stop at Reading and Didcot.

In each case, extra information is inserted into the sentence. The sentence would still be complete without the information inside the commas.

3 Commas used to mark off phrases that are separate from the main parts of the sentence.

Meanwhile, in another part of the forest, something stirred.

The lost children, after many adventures, were eventually reunited with their parents.

Hannibal's army, after crossing the Alps, was defeated in battle and driven back.

4 Commas used to indicate a pause in the sentence.

If it is fine tomorrow, I might go swimming

Whenever I hear the music to Phantom of the Opera, I think of the time I went there with the school.

This is the most difficult use of the comma to learn. This is because one of the most common mistakes students make is to use commas instead of a full stops, causing their sentences to run on and on. A sentence should contain one idea. Then you should start a new sentence.

5 Commas and direct (or quoted) speech.
Commas are used to introduce, or signal the end of, quoted speech:

The judge said, 'Let the prisoner be brought in'.

'Let's go to the fair tonight,' said Jake excitedly.

'I don't know,' said Mother, 'how I am going to pay all these bills.'

6 Commas and question tags.
Question tags like *isn't it, didn't I, haven't you*, and so on are separated from the main part of the sentence by a comma:

You've only just come back from Singapore, haven't you?

I told you to go away, didn't I?

It was a really good holiday, wasn't it?

Warning: don't use too many commas

Commas are more difficult to use well than any other punctuation mark. This is because it is sometimes a matter of personal choice whether to use a comma or not.

If you are in doubt, then the best thing to do is probably to leave the comma out.

1 Punctuate the following sentences, putting in the commas and any other punctuation you think is needed.

a) i need to buy the children new shoes trainers and shorts however before that i need to find myself a new understanding bank manager

b) yes you were right i didn't win the lottery but i will one day

c) he is a caring kind and considerate father.

d) i think that restaurant is in such a bad area that success will depend on how efficient the bouncer employed is not how good the chef is.

e) i have got six tickets for the cup final the problem is that I have six good friends I can't take them all so someone is bound to be upset.

f) he turned up for his wedding one and a half hours late he had overslept and then the taxi driver took him to the wrong church.

g) luckily he also got the time of the wedding wrong so all ended well as he was really half an hour early.

h) i wouldn't marry harry if i were her he can't remember anything.

i) only last week harry forgot which train to catch home from work he tried to ring sally to find out but had forgotten her number as well.

2 Now punctuate the following passage.

the bead bangled big chief wingle wangle had three lovely redskin squaws who slept in his wigwam one on a hide of moose one on a hide of reindeer and the third his favourite on a hide of hippopotamus eventually his wives presented him with lovely redskin babies a son from the squaw who slept on the reindeer hide a son from the one who slept on the moose hide but twin sons from the squaw who slept on the hippopotamus hide this all goes to show that the squaw on the hippopotamus hide of the bead bangled wingle wangle was equal to the sons of the squaws on the other two hides.

Apostrophes

Apostrophes are used in writing for two main purposes.

1 They are used to shorten words and replace the letters that have been left out.

it's – it is	*haven't* – have not	*we'll* – we will
won't – will not	*can't* – cannot	*o'clock* – of the clock
I'm – I am	*wouldn't* – would not	*couldn't* – could not
doesn't – does not	*isn't* – is not	*haven't* – have not

2 They are used to show possession by someone, or something. This is the use of the apostrophe that students find the most difficult to understand and use correctly.

the woman's car	*the man's television*	*the boy's shoes*
the Women's Movement	*the men's jobs*	*the Boys' Brigade*

The word that has the apostrophe attached to it is the owner.

PRACTICE 6

1 Look again at the examples of words that have been shortened by use of the apostrophe. Make sentences of your own, using those words.

2 Look again at the list of words where the apostrophe shows possession. Make a list of the owners.

3 Now make a list of what is owned.

Common error

One of the common mistakes is to use an apostrophe in words that don't need it. An easy way to avoid this mistake is to remember that whenever you use the apostrophe, the word that follows it should be owned:

The teacher's scissors were on the desk.
The hairdresser's notice offered haircuts from £5 – Thursdays only

Ask yourself *who* or *what* is the owner. *What* is being owned? Here, the teacher owns the scissors so it is correct to write *teacher's*. The hairdresser owns the notice, so it is correct to write *hairdresser's*.

PRACTICE 7

Explain why it would be incorrect to write:

The teachers scissor's were on the desk.
The hairdressers notice offered haircut's from £5 – Thursday's only

Apostrophes and plurals

♦ The apostrophe for possession usually goes after the word and before the s – **'s**.

♦ However, when the plural of a word ends in s the apostrophe goes after it – **s'**:

singular	plural
lady's bags	*ladies' bags*
boy's ties (one boy)	*boys' ties (many boys owning ties)*

Plurals which don't end in s use an apostrophe after the word and in front of the s.

woman – woman's	*women – women's*
man – man's	*men – men's*
mouse – mouse's	*mice – mice's*

Remember

To show ownership, add an apostrophe s: *Janice's*
but when the plural of a word ends in s the apostrophe goes after it: *Charles'*.

PRACTICE 8

1 Try the following exercises, putting apostrophes where they are needed. Some sentences may not need them.

a) The childrens coats were soaked when the cloakroom flooded.

b) The horses saddles needed cleaning.

c) The ladies bags were on sale in that shop.

d) The mans car radio was stolen.

e) The dogs leads are kept behind the door in the utility room.

f) The kestrels are building their nests early this year.

g) The members badges have not yet arrived and the members are very annoyed.

h) The Christmas Days festivities start whenever the children get up.

i) Holiday bookings for 1997 are already looking promising.

j) Scottish Homes holiday cottages are very good value.

2 Now fill in the apostrophes needed in the following extract.

Bob, Sharon and I were in the middle of a planning meeting when Mr Price-Edwards called.

'You have done it,' he exclaimed.

'Done it?' I asked.

'Last weeks edition sold 10.2 K.'

'Your mams parlour must be floor to ceiling with newspapers,' Sharon said to me.

We returned to the office after a small celebratory lunch and Bob had to attend to some negatives in the dark room.

'Our lord and master is rightly pleased with us,' I said.

'Weve almost doubled the sales in six weeks and we are having to beat off advertisers with a pointy stick.'

'Can we forget the snow then?' Sharon asked me.

'Ive had it up to here.' She held her hand to her throat.

'Thats funny,' I said. 'Because in 1947 there was a snowdrift exactly that deep just outside this very . . .'

I ducked as she threw a pencil at me. Then we laughed, then smiled at each other. We held each others gaze for just a little longer than usual.

Quotation marks or inverted commas

♦ Quotation marks or inverted commas are used to enclose any words written down exactly as they are spoken.

The doctor asked, 'What are your symptoms?'
'I keep on feeling like a horse,' replied the patient.
'Neigh, neigh,' said the doctor, with a grin on his face.

Note that all the words spoken are enclosed by the inverted commas and you must start a new paragraph for each new speaker. It is possible to use either single ' ' or double " " quotation marks for direct speech. However, it is normal to use a single quotation mark to enclose the title of a book or a quotation from a poem.

♦ What do you do when you need to use quotation marks within quotation marks?

a) If you have used single quotation marks elsewhere, your 'quote in a quote' should be in double quotation marks:

'Then she said to me, "What do you think?" and I said . . .'

b) If you have used double quotation marks elsewhere, your 'quote in a quote' should be in single quotation marks:

"Then she said to me, 'What do you think?' and I said . . ."

♦ All punctuation in quotations must be inside the main quotation marks:

'Hello,' said the young girl, 'do you know the way to the zoo?'
'Yes, but why do you want to know?' said the young man.
The girl replied, 'I can't find my brother and I think a zoo is a good place to start looking!'

1 Try punctuating this extract, using capital letters, commas, apostrophes, inverted commas and full stops.

a man was sitting in his kitchen admiring a newly painted white wall have you finished the mural his wife shouted from the hallway yes he said she entered the room and looked at the blank wall thinking she had missed something she asked him what he had decided to call it men drinking beer he said but theres no beer in the picture she said well thats because they drank it all he said but there are no men in it either well thats because theyve gone to the off licence to buy some more he exclaimed

2 When you are writing dialogue, it is important not to use the word *said* all the time. This becomes boring and repetitive. You will find it easier to make your writing interesting (and improve your marks) if you vary the words you choose. Try to think of a word that describes how a character might say something. Look at the list below, and add five words of your own.

whispered	*uttered*	*muttered*	*stuttered*	*shouted*
bawled	*wailed*	*retorted*	*reported*	*replied*
declared	*ordered*	*disclosed*	*informed*	*alleged*
suggested	*divulged*	*exclaimed*	*answered*	*asked*

3 It can also be useful to include further information about the speaker's mood at the time of speaking.

*'The train will be late again,' announced the commuter **angrily**.*

*'I'm afraid the news is not good,' replied the doctor **sadly**.*

'Angrily' and 'sadly' describe *how* something is said or done, and are called **adverbs**. Most adverbs end in 'ly'.

Think of five sentences which include a word giving further information about the speaker's mood.

Colons

We use the colon **:** as a punctuation mark inside a sentence for a number of purposes.

♦ To explain or expand on the statement which comes before it.

The weather was appalling: storm force winds and a temperature of minus 15 degrees centigrade

As the estate agent suspected, the house did not sell: the vendor was asking too much for it.

♦ To introduce a quotation.

I love the end of Othello *where the hero, after fatally stabbing himself, says: 'I kiss'd thee ere I kill'd thee: – No way but this/Killing myself to die upon a kiss.'*

♦ To introduce a list or series of items

To make a lemon meringue pie, you need five things: pastry, eggs, butter, sugar and lemons.

You must remember three things: your passport, your credit card and the safe key.

Remember that, when you use a colon, the two 'halves' of your sentence must be closely related.

Semi-colons

♦ Semi-colons ; are used to divide up sentences into shorter, more manageable sections which are easier to read and to understand. Long sentences which use 'and' or 'but' a number of times can often sound clumsy. You make your writing more elegant by substituting a semi-colon from time to time:

He did not apologize; he did not think he needed to.

We sometimes assume that romantic novels are easy to write; that anyone who writes half-decently can knock out 2,000 words a day and finish a blockbuster in a couple of months.

♦ Semi-colons are also used to punctuate lists where a lot of commas might be confusing:

You must have the following: a degree in a relevant subject; excellent communication skills; at least three years' experience in public relations; a recognized journalistic qualification or training and the ability to travel extensively.

♦ You may find it helpful to think of the semi-colon as the written equivalent of a longish pause – for emphasis or dramatic effect.

Punctuate the following extracts, using all the punctuation necessary.

it was a warm sunny day in late june he walked the dog in the nearby park every day at this time suddenly his peace was shattered oh oh what a wonderful dog an angelic voice exclaimed is she said the man questioningly the woman halted and was suddenly embarrassed as she realized that she was looking at a guide dog well yes actually she is quite beautiful would you describe her to me said the man of course said the young woman as she looked into the depths of his unseeing deep blue eyes

what is the best pick up line you have ever used well i was most impressed with i bet you like bacon and eggs for breakfast did it work no he was a vegetarian what about yours well i dont bother with the line i just pick them up does it work no so far ive had my nose broken twice and have two permanent black eyes oh i wondered how you got those.

Hyphens

There are four main uses for hyphens.

♦ Hyphens are used to join together words, such as:

stand-in	*starry-eyed*
son-in-law	*ice-skate*
hell-bent	*helter-skelter*
hard-headed	*ten-year-old*

♦ Hyphens are used between a prefix (*pre-*, *pro-*, *post-*, *non-* etc) and another word, such as:

post-Renaissance	*Pre-Raphaelite*
pre-twentieth century	*non-aligned*
anti-Europe	*semi-detached*

♦ Hyphens are used to avoid two vowels coming together in a word:

co-operation	*co-ordination*

♦ Hyphens are used to make the meaning of a word clear:

Mother is re-covering the armchair (putting a new cover on)
The patient recovered from his illness (got better)

The barbarian tribes re-formed their alliance against the Romans
(put together again)
He is a reformed criminal (now a model citizen!)

Dashes

The dash looks like a longer version of the hyphen – and is usually laid out with a space on either side of it. Dashes are used (usually in less formal writing) as a substitute for other kinds of punctuation, such as commas, brackets or colons.

♦ Instead of commas or brackets

He sent his shot – a good one – high into the corner of the goalmouth, over the keeper's upstretched arms.

The holiday was – all in all – not unpleasant.

♦ Instead of a colon

You don't understand – I'm not with you on this, I'm against you.

♦ To break or interrupt quoted speech

'There is no use speculating on that subject. Divorces are made in Heaven – please don't touch the cucumber sandwiches!'

♦ To repeat or emphasise

There was nothing in the larder – nothing at all.

♦ To show range

A–Z   1914–1918   pages 46–74

In these examples, the dash replaces the *to* and it does not have a space on either side.

PRACTICE 11

Punctuate the sentences below with hyphens and dashes where they are needed.

1 Jeanie had been working non stop all day. Her friends wanted her to go and see a film with them but she was too tired she just wasn't up to it.

2 After ten minutes at the pre school visit, four year old Ben dissolved in tears. 'I want to go home' he broke off abruptly as the paints were brought out.

3 When David arrived at the hospital he was only semi conscious. He looked bad really awful and we were very worried.

Paragraphs

When you have decided what you want to say, you need to organize your writing into paragraphs.

What is a paragraph?

A paragraph is a group of sentences which deals with a single subject or idea. It can be as long or as short as you like, as long as you are sure that the topic or idea you are exploring has been fully worked out in that paragraph. Once you are satisfied you have nothing further to say on that particular subject, you should move on to a new paragraph.

The following example of paragraphing is taken from *Treasure Island*, a nineteenth-century adventure story by Robert Louis Stevenson.

There was a great, smooth swell upon the sea. The wind blowing steady and gentle from the south, there was no contrariety between that and the current, and the billows rose and fell unbroken.

Had it been otherwise, I must long ago have perished; but as it was, it is surprising how easily and securely my little and light boat could ride. Often, as I still lay at the bottom, and kept no more than an eye above the gunwale, I would see a big blue summit heaving close above me; yet the coracle would but bounce a little, dance as if on springs, and subside on the other side into the trough as lightly as a bird.

I began after a little to grow very bold, and sat up to try my skill at paddling. But even a small change in the disposition of the weight will produce violent changes in the behaviour of a coracle. And I had hardly moved before the boat, giving up at once her gentle dancing movement, ran straight down a slope of water so steep that it made me giddy, and struck her nose with a spout of spray deep into the side of the next wave.

I was drenched and terrified, and fell instantly back into my old position, whereupon the coracle seemed to find her head again, and led me softly as before among the billows. It was plain she was not to be interfered with, and at that rate, since I could in no way influence her course, what hope had I left of reaching land?

♦ You can see how the author uses paragraphs to mark off quite minor but distinct developments in the narrative:

Paragraph 1: The narrator is adrift in a small boat on a heavy sea.
Paragraph 2: Lying flat in the bottom of the boat, the narrator is astonished by how easily it seems to ride the big waves.
Paragraph 3: The narrator sits up and tries to paddle, but the shift in weight makes the boat pitch dangerously.
Paragraph 4: The narrator lies back down in the bottom of the boat again, feeling helpless and despairing of ever reaching land.

♦ Good paragraphing represents a series of ordered stages in a story, or thought-process, which ends in a conclusion of some kind. It makes your work easier to read and understand, and shows that you have put some thought and planning into what you want to say. Before starting a piece of writing, it is always a good idea to make brief notes summarising the points which you wish to make and the order in which they follow each other. It is rather like a storyboard sequence for a film or video, each point represents a new paragraph.

Marking paragraphs

♦ A new paragraph is marked in two ways.
   1) It starts on a new line.
   2) The first word often starts a few spaces in from the left-hand margin.

When you are writing an essay, the first and last paragraphs are especially important.

The first paragraph is used to introduce the subject. You might also like to include a *brief* outline of how you intend to approach it, though don't be tempted to go on at great length at this stage. You will expand your argument in the paragraphs which follow.

The last paragraph sums up the points which you have made, rounds them off with a conclusion and offers an opportunity to say something about how you feel about the subject.

Paragraphing in stories

If you are writing a story which includes direct speech enclosed in quotation marks, (see page 208), you need to start on a new line every time you introduce a new speaker. As with all paragraphing, this is helpful to the reader because it makes it much easier to follow the sequence of the conversation and to tell who is speaking at any time without a lot of tedious repetition of 'said Robert', 'replied Charles', and so on. Paragraphing in speech shows you are introducing a different 'voice' rather than a new idea. It is just as important as paragraphing straight text, to help the reader find their way around the page.

Rewrite the following extract in paragraphs. There were three paragraphs in the original.

She remembered as a girl at the cottage combing her hair in spring sunshine each day taking the dark hairs from the comb and dropping them out of the window with the same fidget of her fingers. A winter gale blew down a thrushes' nest into the garden and it was lined and snug with the black sheen of her own hair. For ages she kept it but it fell apart eventually, what with drying out and all the handling it got as she showed it to the children in class. She lifted her raffia basket and put into it the magnesia, the pack of cards and a handful of teabags. In the hall she put on her heavy overcoat. The driveway to the house had not been made up, even though the house had been occupied for more than three years. It was rutted with tracks which had frozen over. She stopped to try one with the pressure of her toe, to see how heavy the frost had been. The slow ovals of bubbles separated and moved away from her toe. They returned again when she removed her weight but the ice did not break. She shuffled, afraid of falling, the ice crisping beneath her feet. Above her she saw the moon in its last phase shining at midday. The air was bitterly cold. She had a pain in her throat which she experienced as a lump every time she swallowed. She had to chew what little she ate thoroughly or she felt it would not go past the lump. Everyone accused her of eating like a bird. Everyone said that she must see a doctor. But she knew without a doctor telling her that she would not see another winter. In September her son Brian had offered to buy her a heavy coat but she had refused, saying that she wouldn't get the wear out of it.

Spelling

As you can see from the examiner's comments on pages 31 and 45, spelling errors can cost you marks and even help to make a difference between one grade and another. It is important, if you know you have a spelling problem, that you do something about it. Your teacher or lecturer will point out spelling errors in your work, but you need to work to improve your own spelling.

♦ Use a dictionary to check all your work.
♦ If you misspell a word, make sure that you learn the correct version of the spelling. It is silly to repeat mistakes.
♦ Use this section of the book to help you eliminate some errors in your work.
♦ Buy yourself a small notebook. Put all the corrected spellings of words in there. Every week, learn the latest words and test yourself.

PRACTICE 1

1 **On the following pages is a list of words that students frequently mix up.**

Using a dictionary, look up the words you are not sure of and write the meaning in pencil beside them. Make certain that you learn the difference between them.

2 **When you have done that, choose ten pairs of similar-sounding words.**

Write sentences to show that you know what each word means.

accept	. . . .
except	. . . .
all ready	. . . .
already	. . . .
all right	. . . .
alright	. . . .
all together	. . . .
altogether	. . . .
bear	. . . .
bare	. . . .

brake   ....

break   ....

coarse   ....

course   ....

collar   ....

colour   ....

currant   ....

current   ....

cue   ....

queue   ....

defer   ....

differ   ....

draft   ....

draught   ....

fair   ....

fare   ....

fore   ....

for   ....

four   ....

foul   ....

fowl   ....

farther   ....

father   ....

hair   ....

hare   ....

hear . . . .

here . . . .

hole . . . .

whole . . . .

loan . . . .

lone . . . .

meat . . . .

meet . . . .

new . . . .

knew . . . .

no . . . .

know . . . .

now . . . .

your . . . .

you're . . . .

passed . . . .

past . . . .

peace . . . .

piece . . . .

practice . . . .

practise . . . .

quiet . . . .

quite . . . .

right . . . .

write . . . .

their   ....

they're   ....

there   ....

through   ....

threw   ....

to   ....

too   ....

two   ....

witch   ....

which   ....

wear   ....

were   ....

where   ....

weather   ....

whether   ....

Spelling rules

Now look at some of the spelling rules. Understanding these will also help you to overcome any spelling problems you may have.

1 Write *i* before *e*, when the sound is *ee*:

believe, retriever, siege, niece

***except* after *c*:**

receive, perceive, receipt, ceiling, deceive, conceive

exceptions to rule
Some words do not follow this rule, for example: seize, weird, weir, sheik.

note
some words are also spelt ei, but when you read them aloud you will hear that they do not make the ee sound:

neighbour, height, weight, eight, eighty, foreign, their, leisure, forfeit.

1 Write five sentences which include some of the words on pages 216–219. Check them, and make sure that you have learned the rule.

2 Now make a list of ten words that have *ie* in them. Go through the alphabet starting with *believe*.

2 Adding -ed, -ing.

Vowels are *a, e, i, o, u* and sometimes *y*. All other letters are called consonants. Vowels can be short or long:

Short Vowels	Long vowels
lap	loop
hut	hoot
stick	steak
fell	feel

When adding *-ed* or *-ing* to a word, you should look at the last letter of the word.

♦ If the last letter of a word follows a short vowel and is a consonant which is not *w, x* or *y*, you should double it before adding *-ed* or *-ing*:

lap	*lapped*	*lapping*
pat	*patted*	*patting*

♦ If the last letter of the word doesn't immediately follow the short vowel and is a consonant, simply add *-ed* or *-ing*:

part	*parted*	*parting*
limp	*limped*	*limping*

The same rule applies for

glow	*glowed*	*glowing*

as the consonant doesn't follow a short vowel, but a long one.

♦ If a word ends in *e*, you usually take the *e* off before adding *-ed* or *-ing*:

like	*liked*	*liking*
bake	*baked*	*baking*

Add -ing and -ed to the following words:

scrape	mop	till	tile
file	wire	fake	walk
fill	mope	jog	operate
legislate	judge	fine	

3 Adding -*full* to words.

♦ Always drop the last -*l*:

hope   *hopeful*
care   *careful*

♦ where the last letter of a word is *y*

a) If the *y* is pronounced like an *i*, change the *y* to an *i* before adding '*ful*':

beauty   *beautiful*
duty   *dutiful*

b) If the *y* is not pronounced like an *i*, just add '*ful*':

joy   *joyful*

♦ For words such as '*joyfully*' (adverbs – see Practice 9, point 3, page 209) remember to add '*ly*'.

4 Making plurals.

Making words into plurals can cause some spelling errors.

♦ Many plurals are made by just adding an -*s*

toy   –   *toys*
boy   –   *boys*
girl   –   *girls*
tree   –   *trees*

♦ Some plurals need -*es*. These are words which end in sounds such as *s*, *z*, *x*, *sh* and *ch* (as used in the word 'itch')

bush   –   *bushes*
beach   –   *beaches*
loss   –   *losses*
fox   –   *foxes*

♦ Several words which end in *o* need -*es* in the plural, but there are no rules – you will need to learn them as you meet them:

potato   –   *potatoes*

♦ For words that end in -y, turn the -y into an -i and add -es:

country – countries
facility – facilities
try – tries

♦ Some words that end in -f change the -f to -ves:

loaf – loaves

but some do not:

roof – roofs

♦ Some words have unusual plurals:

woman – women
child – children
mouse – mice
goose – geese
man – men

♦ You will come across exceptions to these plural rules – think about child, children and mouse, mice, for example.

PRACTICE 4

Make plurals out of the following words.

apple   box
quiz (be careful with this one – it has an unusual spelling)
tomato   bath   city
land   man   estate
island   ocean   scarf
leaf   people   snake
individual   branch

5 Silent letters can cause some problems.

Silent letters are letters that are written but not said aloud. There are many words with silent letters, so you need to read carefully and remember the spelling patterns of the words that you are reading. For example:

♦ In the word *write* the *w* is not pronounced. The *w* is also silent in *answer*.
♦ In the word *lamb* the *b* is not pronounced.

6 Patterns to remember.

♦ Some words have -ck endings, for example: *brick, lick, pick*.
♦ There are few words that end with just a -c: *picnic, frolic, mimic, panic*.
♦ When you write *q* it always has to be followed by a *u* in English: *quiet, antique, questions*.
♦ When you write a word in the past tense, for example *walked*, there should always be an *e* before the *d*.

1 Below is a list of the most commonly misspelled words. Tick the words you feel confident about spelling and get someone to test you on them.

2 Make a separate list of the words you are unsure about. Set yourself a target of learning some each week, ticking them off as you feel confident about them until all the words are ticked.

A
accelerate
accommodation
achieve
across
address
admire
admission
adventurous
advertisement
aeroplane
afraid
aggression
ammunition
answer
anxiety
anyone
approach
around
autumn
available

B
balloon
barbecue
beautiful
because
before
beginning
believe
below
between
bicycle (bike)
bleed
blood

bodyguard
bonfire
build

C
canoe
casualty
ceiling
character
chocolate
committee
conscience
conscious
consider
co-operate
courageous
cupboard
customer

D
dangerous
daughter
definite
definitely
delightful
difference
disappoint
discover
disguise
doubtful

E
each
eight
either

eleven
eligible
embarrass
employment
engage
engine
enjoy
essential
evening
exaggerate
excellent
extravagant
extraordinary

F
fabulous
famous
familiar
family
fascinate
fashion
February
fierce
force
future

G
garage
general
genius
ghost
government
guilty

H
hair
harass
heart
hectic
helicopter
hello
hidden
holiday
hooligan
hospital

I
ice
idiot
illegal
immediate
incident
incredible
interest
introduce
island

J
jacket
jewellery
jogging
joke
juice

K
karate
kept
kitchen

knew
knowledge

L

label
language
late
leave
leisure
length
library
lieutenant
living
lovely
loving
luxury

M

machine
magazine
magic
magician
manage
manoeuvre
marriage
massacre
measure
media
medicine
minute
mischief
mountain
muscle

N

national
natural
necessary
necessity
neither
niece
noise
nuisance

O

occasion
occupation
ocean
offence
officer
operation
operator
ordinary
outdoors
outstanding
overtake

P

packet
paid
paint
palace
panic
parachute
parallel
paralyse
parcel
parent
patience
peculiar
pedal
penalty
permanent
persuade
photograph
player
playground
plenty
pocket
population
powerful
precious
pressure
privilege
programme
pursue

Q

qualify
quality
question
quotation

R

race
raid
raise
reason
received
recent
recommend
reconsider
recovery
reduction
referee
refuge
refuse
regular
reliable
remember
require
resource
restaurant
right

S

sandwich
salesman
satisfactory
savage
school
science
seashore
season
secrecy
secure
selfish
separately
separation
sergeant

serious
several
shield
shoulder
sincerely
situation
slaughter
sleigh
slow
smile
soldier
somewhere
sophisticated
squalid
strength
suggest
suitable
surprise
surround

T

table
tackle
talent
tangle
taught
teach
technique
television
terrible
thank
their
thought
threat
toilet
tomorrow
tragedy
treasure
tried
triumphant
tyre

U

unavoidable
uncontrollable
unique
unkempt
unmistakable
untidy
until
uprising
usable
useless

V

vacancy
vaccination
valiant
valuable
vegetable
vehicle
vengeance
venture
victim
violence
visitor
voucher
vulnerable

W

waiter
wardrobe
water
weak
weapon
weather (climate)
wedding
whale (animal)
wilful
wolves
worry
would
wreck
writer

X

X-ray

Y

yacht
yawn
year
yesterday
yoghurt
young
yours

Z

zealous
zero
zone

Writing letters and C.V.s

When you write a letter you should make sure that you:

- **Format** your letter correctly.
- **Plan** what you want the letter to say.
- Use a suitable **tone**. Make sure that the *words* you choose and the *way* you use them are suitable for the occasion.
- Use the best possible **presentation** for your letter, and make sure that you check it.

Format

Most formal letters follow the pattern used in the example below.

41 Rawlinson Road
Sutton Park
West Midlands
B98 5ZU

1 Your address
Notice how it is lined up
No punctuation is used

Mr T Bertram
Customer Services Department
ShopWorks
Birmingham
West Midlands
B33 4KL

2 The name and address of the person you are writing to

17 July 1997

3 The date in full

Dear Mr Bertram

4 The greeting
There is more about this opposite

'Sunny Barbecue' sets

5 Heading
This makes it clear what the letter about, but you do not *have* to use

I am writing to enquire whether you are likely to stock any more 'Sunny Barbecue' sets, model number 09876JX.

   I bought one in your shop two years ago and would now like to purchase one as a present, but cannot find one for sale. I particularly wish to get this exact model as my friend was very impressed with its appearance and performance.

6 Introduction
Why you are writing

7 Body of the letter
Giving background information an explaining what you want in detail

   If it is no longer produced, I should be most grateful if you would let me know whether something similar is available and at what price.

   Thank you very much for your help, and I look forward to hearing from you.

8 Conclusion
Saying what you would like to happen

   Yours sincerely

9 Ending
There is more about this opposite

   C T Evans

Greetings and endings

It is important that the greeting and ending of your letter tie up, as follows.

♦ If you know the name of the person you are writing to, use their name to greet them. For a formal letter you would usually use 'Dear' followed by 'Mrs/Ms/Miss/Mr', as appropriate, then the surname.
Correct ending for this greeting: 'Yours sincerely'.

♦ If you do not know the name of the person you are writing to, you should greet them using 'Dear Sir or Madam'.
Correct ending for this greeting: 'Yours faithfully'.

Plan

When you are preparing to write a letter, list all the points you wish to include, then put them in a logical order. As you can see in the example, most letters include:

♦ an **introduction** explaining why you are writing

♦ the **body of the letter** giving background information and explaining what you want in detail

♦ a **conclusion** which 'winds up' the letter and makes it clear what its purpose is. If you wish to reader to **do** anything, make sure they know what you would like.

Tone

Make sure that the *words* you choose and the *way* you use them are suitable for the occasion. It is important that you make the best impression in your letter. In most formal letters:

♦ do not use slang or dialect phrases or words

♦ do not use short forms like *you've* or *haven't*

♦ do not write in a very personal way which may be inappropriate.

Presentation

Letters can be handwritten or word-processed. In an examination you have no choice, as your handwriting and presentation are being assessed. Likewise, some job advertisements ask you to handwrite a letter of application. However, if you have untidy handwriting, it might be worth word-processing an important letter.

♦ Check your letter for spelling and punctuation errors. The final letter should be perfect.

♦ Keep the letter neat and tidy, protect it in a plastic sleeve if necessary. Tatty letters will be rejected.

♦ Write in the same colour ink throughout.

♦ If you have to handwrite a letter but know your writing is poor, space your writing out. This space around your writing helps to make it easier to read.

♦ Use good quality paper and envelopes that match. This creates a good first impression and can help to take attention away from your handwriting if necessary.

♦ Use a decent pen that does not smudge. Black is a good colour as it highlights the letters and makes them easier to read. Try to avoid bright colours like turquoise or light colours that strain the eyes when you read them.

♦ Do not be afraid to ask for advice.

PRACTICE 1

1 Write a letter of complaint, making sure that you plan your letter and use the correct format and tone.

♦ You have bought a 200gm jar of Three Bean Aroma coffee granules from Adams Stores in Swindon on 19th June 1997.

♦ When you opened the jar, you found that most of the coffee was powdered, with just a few granules in it. It smelt very bitter and was impossible to drink. The seal had not been tampered with. You are enclosing a sample for inspection.

♦ You are seeking an apology and a refund at the least.

♦ The whole experience was difficult for you as you had bought the coffee for a dinner party, and it caused you embarrassment.

♦ The *Best before* date was June 2000 and the *quality code* number was 597SRD.

Write your letter to a named person or 'Sir or Madam', at the following address: Consumer Services Department, Aroma Coffee, Swindon, Wiltshire, SN3 7UV.

Letters applying for jobs

One of the most important letters anyone ever writes is a job application. It is therefore surprising to hear employers criticising the poor standard of letter they receive from many would-be applicants. Read the advertisement below, then the letter from the successful applicant which follows.

TRAINEE CHEF REQUIRED
for a busy hotel and restaurant.
Day release scheme available
for the right applicant.
Please write with a C.V. and letter to:
The Personnel Manager, The Cawdor Hotel, Royal
Leamington Spa.

16 Beech Road
Royal Leamington Spa
SA3 1LN

The Personnel Manager
The Cawdor Hotel
Royal Leamington Spa
SA8 2LN

21 July 1997

Dear Sir

I wish to apply for the post of trainee chef as advertised in the June 25th edition of the Leamington Crier. I am seventeen years of age and have just completed a GNVQ Business course at Intermediate Level successfully. In addition to this I gained a *A in my Home Economics GCSE and have completed one year of the Advanced Home Economics course.

I realize that it might seem strange to apply for a post half way through an Advanced Studies course. However, I always intended to leave school after I had obtained the GNVQ qualification. I have always wanted to be a chef and have thoroughly enjoyed the first year of the Advanced Level course but now I cannot wait to start work. I enclose my most recent report from my Home Economics Teacher.

For the last four years I have helped my grandmother in her cafe. It is called 'Grades' and is in the High Street. It is quite popular and recently won a national award for its home-baked cakes and innovative menu. Last year I got to the final of our area Masterchef competition and won.

I realize that hotel work requires a lot of commitment on my part and that it will involve me working long and unsociable hours but I am quite prepared for this. Helping in my gran's cafe has also shown me that working with the public can be trying at times! However, I am not afraid of hard work and have always enjoyed working with people.

I hope that you will think me suitable for the job as I would really like to be a fully trained chef. I am available for interview at any time.

Yours faithfully

Nicholas Stein

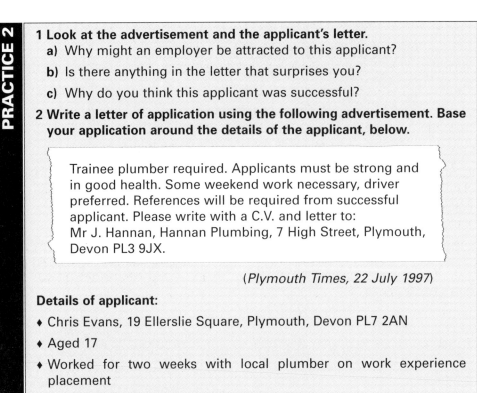

1 Look at the advertisement and the applicant's letter.

  a) Why might an employer be attracted to this applicant?

  b) Is there anything in the letter that surprises you?

  c) Why do you think this applicant was successful?

2 Write a letter of application using the following advertisement. Base your application around the details of the applicant, below.

> Trainee plumber required. Applicants must be strong and in good health. Some weekend work necessary, driver preferred. References will be required from successful applicant. Please write with a C.V. and letter to:
> Mr J. Hannan, Hannan Plumbing, 7 High Street, Plymouth, Devon PL3 9JX.

(*Plymouth Times, 22 July 1997*)

Details of applicant:

♦ Chris Evans, 19 Ellerslie Square, Plymouth, Devon PL7 2AN

♦ Aged 17

♦ Worked for two weeks with local plumber on work experience placement

♦ Soon to take driving test

Writing a Curriculum Vitae

What is a C.V.? The letters C.V. in full stand for Curriculum Vitae. This is a Latin term. Roughly translated it means 'course of life' – in other words, a summary of your academic and employment history. This is a form that you design yourself and it gives your academic and employment details in an easy-to-read form which can be sent to a potential employer, college or university. It is worth word-processing your C.V. (or getting someone else to do it for you) and printing out a lot of copies that can be sent with applications for jobs. It is important to update it regularly. It should contain the following information.

♦ Name, address, date of birth.

♦ Marital status (this is optional).

♦ Schools attended with dates and qualifications obtained, including the levels and the dates you undertook the examinations.

♦ Other qualifications obtained outside school.

♦ Employment information if you have been employed, starting with present occupation and working backwards.

♦ Hobbies and interests, listed towards the end, giving interest. Remember that you might be asked about hobbies and therefore it is wise to be honest.

◆ Names and addresses of two referees. These are people who can speak for your character and ability. If you are employed, it is usual to include your employer as a referee when applying for another post.

The most important thing to remember about a C.V. is that there is no set rule about what you have to include. If your academic record isn't as good as you would like it to be, then there is no reason why you can't leave some of the worst results off the form. Although you have to tell the truth on the C.V., it doesn't state that you have to tell the whole truth! If you haven't yet had a job, miss out the employment section. Your C.V. is supposed to improve your chances of gaining a job or place on a course, so be sensible about what you include and what you leave out.

PRACTICE 3

Look at the C.V. that Nicholas Stein included with his letter for the job as a chef, then write your C.V. Check that you have included all the important details and presented it in the best way.

CURRICULUM VITAE

Name	Nicholas Stein
Address	16 Beech Road Royal Leamington Spa SA3 1LN
Date of Birth	23 May 1980
Schools	Hellcott Primary School, Leamington Spa Leamington Comprehensive School

Qualifications	1996 GCSE in English B, Geography C,
	              Maths C, Science C, Home Economics A*,
	              History D, Physical Education B
	
	1996 GNVQ Business: Merit
	              (equivalent of 4 C grade GCSEs)

Other information	Completed one year of an Advanced Course in Home Economics
Other qualifications	Grade 5 Saxophone
Hobbies/interests	Bronze Medallion lifesaving Play football for Leamington Under 18 team Playing in a local band called 'Ginger Fission'

Persuasive letters

It is important to be able to recognize and write persuasive letters. Read through the letter below. You may have seen one like it before.

THE ROYAL SOCIETY FOR THE PROTECTION OF BIRDS AND WOODLAND ANIMALS,
Woodland Road, London

An amazing offer when you join the RSPBWA
- A garden bird table or bird book absolutely free
- Free entry to 75 RSPBWA nature reserves
- Free monthly newsletter and 4 quarterly magazines packed with information.
  (Family memberships **Bertie Bird Cartoon News**)

Dear Friend

It is a while now since you enjoyed membership of the **Royal Society for the Protection of Birds and Woodland Animals**. We very much regretted losing your valuable support. For the success of our schemes, and in order to protect Great Britain's rich and varied wildlife population and their habitat, we depend on the support of people like yourselves. We were sorry to lose you as members and that is why I am writing now. <u>I am writing to appeal to you to rejoin and once more help us with our important and vital work.</u>

Because we value your help and support we are offering you a free gift. Since your last membership we have also started printing **Bertie Bird Cartoon News**. This is a magazine especially written for those younger members of the family who want to know about the countryside and the rich variety of animal life that is abundant there. This is provided free and you will also notice that the membership fees have remained the same. This makes this offer even more outstanding and beneficial to you.

The RSPBWA desperately needs your help – we need the support of those who are committed to looking after wildlife and the environment. By rejoining you will be helping us to protect our countryside, making it a place where everyone can still enjoy the sight of many different species of bird flying freely in the natural beauty of their surroundings.

The RSPBWA is a charity and as such we receive no state aid – what we do for wildlife and the environment costs a great deal of money. With your help we can do more. Remember, that once a species of bird or animal or flower has died out, no amount of money will replace it.

Help now by filling in the form attached to this letter. We will return your membership pack, free gift and the current newsletter.

Help us to make the world around us a better place.

Yours sincerely

Robert T Bridge
Chief Executive

1 See if you can identify *how* this letter persuades you.

♦ Why was this letter written?

♦ How does the writer of this letter persuade the reader to rejoin?

♦ Look at the language used. How does the writer try to make the receiver of the letter feel about not rejoining?

♦ What do you think of this letter? Has its persuasion been successful?

2 Write a persuasive letter similar to the one you have just read, asking someone either to rejoin an organization like this, or to support a charity by sending a cash donation.

♦ Decide first on whether you are going to sell a membership or try to get a cash donation.

♦ If you are going to sell a membership, would you offer a free gift? What is the advantage of doing this? Are there any disadvantages?

♦ What type of organization are you representing? Think about whether it is one that is likely to gain support. Are some organizations more difficult to gain support for? If so, which ones?

♦ Plan and write your letter carefully, checking back to pages 226–227 if you need to.

Writing a report

Reports are used to convey information in an easy-to-read and logical format. They may be used for many purposes, such as:

♦ to convey information about research carried out for a project or an assignment

♦ to convey an account of an event such as an accident report, a report on a visit, work experience, or a job carried out.

As reports are made for a variety of reasons, it is difficult to say exactly how one should look. The task and type of information to be presented, as well as the intended audience, will obviously affect this.

Organizing a report

Whatever your report is for, you can organize it in a way that helps to present the work in a more readable fashion.

♦ **Sub-headings** help to break up the information and highlight it, concentrating the reader's attention.

♦ **Numbered points** help the reader find their way about the text. These are sometimes subdivided.

♦ **Formal and condensed language** gives the information in as brief a manner as possible.

♦ **Only important information** is given in a report.

Read the following report. It was written by a student following a GNVQ Intermediate Business course.

REPORT ON THE BUSINESS ENTERPRISE SCHEME

Candid Cambria Newspaper.

Background

Candid Cambria is a newspaper published by our school twice yearly. It comes out as a supplement of the *Carmarthen Journal*. This is a weekly paper with a circulation figure of 22,000 and a readership of approximately 49,000.

We publish in February and July. Revenue of £1, 800 is required to publish and this is raised through the selling of advertising. The production of the newspaper relies on the setting up of two teams: an editorial team and a business team. The editorial team is in charge of the journalistic side of the paper, they collect articles from school and go outside and interview local/national celebrities. The paper provides a way of broadcasting school

---

successes and ventures. It also allows those who want to pursue a career in journalism a chance to work on a real newspaper alongside experienced journalists in the *Carmarthen Journal* Office. The business team is in charge of selling the advertising space, designing advertisements, booking the advertisements into the spaces provided in the newspaper and invoicing and collecting payments.

Selling the space

The team first met with a Mr Paul Rees, he is in charge of advertising for the *Carmarthen Journal*. He told us that it was important to try to make the advertisements look good in the newspaper and showed us how best to lay these into the pages to create the best effect. We decided on an advertising rate per cms. A list was drawn up of potential advertisers:

1   those who already had advertised
2   those who dealt with the school and who might wish to advertise
3   those who members of the business team felt could be approached – either relatives, friends with businesses, people who the business team had part-time jobs with, or that year 12 and 13 might use; driving schools were top of the list.

Advertisers who wanted adverts on the front, back or middle pages or wanted adverts in colour were to be charged more.

Mr Paul Rees suggested that before approaching those in category A, we should re-design their advertisements. The aim was to:

a)   increase the size slightly, thus encouraging them to buy larger advertisements
b)   improve the design by introducing more sophisticated artwork.

Most of the potential clients were approached personally by one of the team. Where this was a problem then they were approached by telephone. It was important that the phone conversation was planned beforehand so that the team sounded as professional as possible.

Filling the space

The business team managed to sell the required amount of advertising. Once this was done and on a date convenient with the Journal the business team met with the staff who book in the advertisements. The team had to fill in a form for each advertisement and give detailed information about how the advertisement was to look on the page. This was because all advertisements are now scanned in centrally.

This was time consuming and for the next production due in July the business team have already decided to do this as the advertisements are obtained.

Booking the advertisements and invoicing

The business team spent one day working on the invoices to be generated from this enterprise. Some of the advertisers already had accounts with the Journal and this made the job much easier. We had to log into the computer the following important information.

Name of client, address, tel no, no of advertisement, placement in paper, cost per cm and overall costing.

The business team found that some accounts had to be prepaid before the Journal would publish this meant that invoices had to be sent out promptly.

The finished product

The newspaper was published last week. 2,239 more copies were sold. This was accounted for in two ways.

1   600 were ordered by the school to be given free to each pupil
2   the rest were bought by parents, etc. of children who were featured in the supplement.

The Journal had published 2,000 extra copies to take account of increased demand.

It was decided that if the same business team is involved in the summer we would plan and carry out the work differently.

a   We will, as stated earlier, book the advertisements as they arrive. This will avoid a rush at the end to get this done by the advertising deadline.

b   We will also check all advertisers with the sales team at the Journal, as invoicing for prepayment left the team unsure till the last minute whether advertisements could run. Or we will invoice the school who could follow up payments; we felt this was a risky option but could be worth taking.

c   It was important for the editorial team to know how much space on each page would be taken up by advertising. Initially, a plan had been made and grids drawn of how each page would look. By the end this had to be changed and this meant a lot of unnecessary work for the editorial team at the last minute. In future each advertisement will be listed on two stickers as per example:
ABC computers page 8 column 4 5x2cms Bus
ABC computers page 8 column 4 5x2cms Edit

Two copies of the grids will be kept one by editorial chief and one by Business chief. As advertisements are sold then an appropriate sticker will be placed on grids.

This will avoid confusion at the end.

The business enterprise was successful and at the end £38.00 more advertising was sold than was needed to pay for the production. The team worked well and each shared the workload equally. The business team spent approximately 10 working days on this venture.

PRACTICE 1

1 **Do you think this report provides information in a clear and understandable manner?**
   ♦ Could you improve the layout or the use of sub-headings?
   ♦ Can you improve the use of verb tenses and punctuation?
   ♦ What parts of the report did you like?
   ♦ What parts did you not like?
   ♦ What subjects do you have to write reports for?
   ♦ If it would be useful, prepare a standard report layout using the best features of report writing.

2 **Write a report based on the following request and using all the features of a report that you have identified.**

   A business from another part of the country is thinking of relocating to your area. You have been asked to write a report on your area that gives information about the following: transport, housing, education, leisure, health facilities. The firm have also asked you to include any other information that you think will be helpful and relevant.

Drafting and editing

Step 1: Starting out

Before you begin any piece of writing, make sure you are clear about:
- *what* kind of writing you are setting out to complete
- *who* your writing is aimed at – who are your readers?
- *why* you are writing – what is the purpose of your writing?

Step 2: Planning your writing

You are now ready to plan your writing. Make sure that you:
- think carefully about your ideas, and jot them down
- do any research required, making notes under headings
- decide the key points you wish to make, and in which order
- organize your notes into the right order.

Step 3: First draft and edit
- write the first draft of your text
- read your draft through, and note any changes. If possible, work with a partner or in a small group and read and comment on each other's draft. Ask yourself:
  - if someone read this for the first time, would they know who it was written for and would it make sense to them?
  - is the text organized so that it flows logically from one idea to the next?
  - is there a clear beginning and end?

Step 4: Further drafts and edits

When planning further drafts, ask:
- have you included the points that were noticed on the previous draft?
- is it in the best order?
- have you got across your ideas as clearly as you can?

The amount of time you spend drafting and editing will vary depending upon the circumstances in which you are writing and how soon you feel you have reached a good result.

Step 5: Your final version

When you are satisfied with *what* you have written, check *how* you have written it. Proof read your text for the following:
- correct grammar – have you written in complete sentences, breaking up your text into paragraphs?
- correct punctuation – have you used commas and full stops in the right places?
- correct spelling – is your spelling accurate?
- presentation – have you presented your work in the best possible way, with a clear layout and good use of headings?

Answers

In the 'Get it right!' section which starts on page 192, there are practice questions. Where it is appropriate, the answers to these questions are given below.

Sentences

Page 194: practice 2

1 The subjects of the sentences are in bold.
  a) **John** seemed to be enjoying himself this evening.
  b) Why don't **you** pay for the tickets for a change?
  c) **I** really don't want anyone to get hurt.
  d) **My doctor** says there is nothing to worry about.
  e) **The train driver** arrived just in time to leave on schedule.

2 The main verbs in these sentences are in bold.
  a) We really **wanted** our team to win the match.
  b) **Isn't** the weather horrible today!
  c) Why can't you **be** more like your sister?
  d) I **put** the kettle on to make a mug of coffee.

3 The complete sentences are:
  1 My cousin is about eighteen.
  2 I often see him out and about enjoying himself.
  4 Last week I met him at about 10.30 in the evening.
  5 It was a cool evening.

4 Check your punctuation by looking at lines 77–81 on page 50.

Page 196: Practice 3

The auxiliary verb to be inserted should have been: a) **is** or **was**; b) **were**.

Page 196: Practice 4

The full stops should be inserted as follows:

Dear Janice

I'm writing this in a hurry before I go out tonight. I was hoping you'd be home next weekend. It's my birthday and I'm going to go out with Lisa and Jane. We were hoping you would be able to come too. I have just heard that you aren't coming home until Monday. I hope you can make it earlier, we'd really love to see you.

Page 199: Practice 7

1 The words *was* or *were* should be inserted as follows:

Yesterday, I **was** hoping to go to the fair. I asked Jane if she wanted to go. We **were** deciding what time to go when Jane's brother arrived. He and his friend **were** planning to go to the fair as well. We **were** pleased that they wanted to come as they had a car and could give us a lift.

2 With the correct agreement of number and tense, the passage should read as follows:

The small party of men came to a halt at the top of the hill at a signal from **their** leader. Everyone in the party, especially the youngest of the soldiers, **was** very tired because they **had** been marching all day. All the men except the leader dropped wearily to the ground and lay there without moving. The leader **was** a tall, bearded man who **wore** a cap with a peak which **shaded** his face and eyes from the sun. As he was standing there, he was scanning the countryside from left to right through binoculars which **were** slung from a leather strap round his neck. He **was** hoping he **would** see some sign of movement.

Page 200: Practice 8

The words *have* or *of* should be inserted as follows.

I could **have** caught the bus but I put too many eggs in the cake and I couldn't take it out **of** the oven in time. I should **have** 'phoned you but my 'phone was out **of** order. I could **have** phoned you from the corner kiosk but I didn't have any money with me.

Punctuation

Page 201: Practice 1

Check your question marks by looking at lines 21–31 on pages 111– 112.

Page 202: Practice 3

The extract should be punctuated as follows:

We arrived at Longleat about lunch-time. Hannah was so excited that she hadn't been able to sleep the night before. She had read about Longleat in the local library in a book called, 'Places to Visit in England' by A. N. Explorer. Rachael and Alys wanted to see the hippos on the lake so we booked a ride on the boat which was grandly named S. S. Titanic. I wasn't sure about the boat's name and I was glad there were no icebergs around. On the boat we were so careful watching the children didn't fall out that we didn't see Gran going greener and greener in colour. We had forgotten that she gets sea sick on any patch of water bigger than a paddling pool. Oh, the man in the boat was happy to see us get off! I'm just glad they didn't make us clean up the mess.

Page 203: Practice 4

The commas should be inserted as follows:

When we got back to the river, John, a friend of Dave's, asked us to get into the boat. Although I can swim I really didn't feel like going out on the river, especially as the weather was getting worse. However, everyone else wanted to join John, so we clambered into the boat. As soon as we got into the middle of the river, Dave, who was rowing alongside John, began to warn us about rapids ahead. Excited and nervous, the others began to laugh.

Page 205: Practice 5

1 The sentences should be punctuated as follows. In some instances it is a matter of personal taste whether or not to use the exclamation mark.

   a) I need to buy the children new shoes, trainers, and shorts. However, before that I need to find myself a new, understanding bank manager.

   b) Yes, you were right. I didn't win the lottery, but I will one day!

   c) He is a caring, kind and considerate father.

   d) I think that restaurant is in such a bad area, that success will depend on how efficient the bouncer employed is, not how good the chef is.

   e) I have got six tickets for the Cup Final. The problem is that I have six good friends. I can't take them all, so someone is bound to be upset.

   f) He turned up for his wedding one-and-a-half hours late! He had overslept, and then the taxi driver took him to the wrong church.

   g) Luckily, he also got the time of the wedding wrong, so all ended well as he was really half-an-hour early!

   h) I wouldn't marry Harry if I were her. He can't remember anything.

   i) Only last week Harry forgot which train to catch home from work. He tried to ring Sally to find out, but had forgotten her number as well.

2 The passage should be punctuated as follows:

The bead-bangled Big Chief Wingle-Wangle had three lovely redskin squaws who slept in his wigwam: one on a hide of moose, one on a hide of reindeer and the third, his favourite, on a hide of hippopotamus. Eventually his wives presented him with lovely redskin babies. A son from the squaw who slept on the reindeer hide, a son from the one who slept on the moose hide, but twin sons from the squaw who slept on the hippopotamus hide. This all goes to show that the squaw on the hippopotamus hide of the bead-bangled Wingle-Wangle was equal to the sons of the squaws on the other two hides.

Page 206: Practice 7

The use of the apostrophes are incorrect because whenever you use an apostrophe the word that follows it should be owned, and in these cases they are not.

Page 207: Practice 8

1 The apostrophes should be inserted as follows:

a) The children's coats were soaked when the cloakroom flooded.

b) The horses' saddles needed cleaning.

c) The ladies' bags were on sale in that shop.

d) The man's car radio was stolen.

e) The dogs' leads are kept behind the door in the utility room.

f) The kestrels are building their nests early this year.

g) The members' badges have not yet arrived and the members are very annoyed.

h) The Christmas Day's festivities start whenever the children get up.

i) Holiday bookings for 1997 are already looking promising.

j) Scottish Homes' holiday cottages are very good value.

2 The apostrophes should be inserted as follows:

Bob, Sharon and I were in the middle of a planning meeting when Mr Price-Edwards called.

'You have done it,' he exclaimed.

'Done it?' I asked.

'Last week's edition sold 10.2 K.'

'Your mam's parlour must be floor to ceiling with newspapers,' Sharon said to me.

We returned to the office after a small celebratory lunch and Bob had to attend to some negatives in the dark room.

'Our lord and master is rightly pleased with us,' I said.

'We've almost doubled the sales in six weeks and we are having to beat off advertisers with a pointy stick.'

'Can we forget the snow then?' Sharon asked me.

'I've had it up to here.' She held her hand to her throat.

'That's funny,' I said. 'Because in 1947 there was a snowdrift exactly that deep just outside this very . . .'

I ducked as she threw a pencil at me. Then we laughed, then smiled at each other. We held each other's gaze for just a little longer than usual.

Page 209: Practice 9

The punctuation should be inserted as follows:

A man was sitting in his kitchen, admiring a newly painted white wall.

'Have you finished the mural?' his wife shouted from the hallway.

'Yes,' he said.

She entered the room and looked at the blank wall, thinking she had missed something. She asked him what he had decided to call it.

' "Men drinking beer," ' he said.

'But there's no beer in the picture,' she said.

'Well, that's because they drank it all,' he said.

'But there are no men in it, either.'

'Well, that's because they've gone to the off-licence to buy some more!' he exclaimed.

Page 211: Practice 10

The punctuation should be inserted as follows:

It was a warm, sunny day in late June. He walked the dog in the nearby park every day at this time. Suddenly, his peace was shattered.

'Oh, oh! What a wonderful dog!' an angelic voice exclaimed.

'Is she?' said the man, questioningly.

The woman halted and was suddenly embarrassed as she realised that she was looking at a guide dog.

'Well, yes; actually, she is quite beautiful.'

'Would you describe her to me?' said the man.

'Of course,' said the young woman as she looked into the depths of his unseeing deep blue eyes.

'What is the best pick-up line you have ever used?'

'Well, I was most impressed with: "I bet you like bacon and eggs for breakfast!" '

'Did it work?'

'No, he was a vegetarian! What about yours?'

'Well, I don't bother with the line; I just pick them up.'

'Does it work?'

'No; so far I've had my nose broken twice and have two permanent black eyes.'

'Oh, I wondered how you got those!'

Page 212: Practice 11

The punctuation should be inserted as follows:

1 Jeanie had been working non-stop all day. Her friends wanted her to go and see a film with them but she was too tired – she just wasn't up to it.

2 After ten minutes at the pre-school visit, four-year-old Ben dissolved in tears. 'I want to go home –' he broke off abruptly as the paints were brought out.

3 When David arrived at the hospital he was only semi-conscious. He looked bad – really awful – and we were very worried.

The extract should be paragraphed as follows:

She remembered as a girl at the cottage combing her hair in spring sunshine each day taking the dark hairs from the comb and dropping them out of the window with the same fidget of her fingers. A winter gale blew down a thrushes' nest into the garden and it was lined and snug with the black sheen of her own hair. For ages she kept it but it fell apart eventually, what with drying out and all the handling it got as she showed it to the children in class.

She lifted her raffia basket and put into it the magnesia, the pack of cards and a handful of teabags. In the hall she put on her heavy overcoat. The driveway to the house had not been made up, even though the house had been occupied for more than three years. It was rutted with tracks which had frozen over. She stopped to try one with the pressure of her toe, to see how heavy the frost had been. The slow ovals of bubbles separated and moved away from her toe. They returned again when she removed her weight but the ice did not break. She shuffled, afraid of falling, the ice crisping beneath her feet. Above her she saw the moon in its last phase shining at midday. The air was bitterly cold.

She had a pain in her throat which she experienced as a lump every time she swallowed. She had to chew what little she ate thoroughly or she felt it would not go past the lump. Everyone accused her of eating like a bird. Everyone said that she must see a doctor. But she knew without a doctor telling her that she would not see another winter. In September her son Brian had offered to buy her a heavy coat but she had refused, saying that she wouldn't get the wear out of it.

Spelling

Page 220: Practice 3

The 'ing' and 'ed' forms of the words are as follows:

scrape	scraping	scraped
mop	mopping	mopped
till	tilling	tilled
tile	tiling	tiled
file	filing	filed
wire	wiring	wired
fake	faking	faked
walk	walking	walked
fill	filling	filled
mope	moping	moped
jog	jogging	jogged
operate	operating	operated
legislate	legislating	legislated
judge	judging	judged
fine	fining	fined

Page 222: Practice 4

The plurals of the words are as follows:

apple	apples	man	men
box	boxes	ocean	oceans
quiz	quizzes	people	peoples
tomato	tomatoes	branch	branches
land	lands	city	cities
island	islands	estate	estates
leaf	leaves	scarf	scarves
individual	individuals	snake	snakes
bath	baths		

Coursework checklist: Speaking and Listening

Throughout your course you will have a number of opportunities to be assessed for Speaking and Listening coursework. The following checklist shows specific oral assignments you will find in this book, and your tutor or teacher may also find further opportunities for oral work and for oral assessment.

You may find it useful to keep track of when you have been assessed for oral coursework by filling in this checklist.

Page	Assignment title	Skills	Date assessed
14	Breaking the ice	explain, describe, narrate	. . . .
14	Guess the famous person	explain, describe, narrate discuss, argue, persuade	. . . .
27	Telling stories	explain, describe, narrate	. . . .
38	Writing to persuade	discuss, argue, persuade	. . . .
42	Arguing a point of view	discuss, argue, persuade	. . . .
62	The Village that lost its Children	explore, analyse, imagine	. . . .
66	The National Lottery	discuss, argue, persuade	. . . .
74	Homelessness	discuss, argue, persuade	. . . .
103	St Agnes' Stand	explore, analyse, imagine explain, describe, narrate	. . . .
114	An Imaginative Experience	explore, analyse, imagine	. . . .
148	Growing Up	explore, analyse, imagine explain, describe, narrate	. . . .
154, 156, 158	Sheenagh Pugh	explore, analyse, imagine explain, describe, narrate	. . . .
162, 165, 166	William Blake	explore, analyse, imagine explain, describe, narrate	. . . .
170, 171	Comparing poems	explore, analyse, imagine explain, describe, narrate	. . . .

Other